AMMACHI

*The Life of the
Holy Mother Amritanandamayi*

by
SWAMI AMRITASWARUPANANDA

MATA AMRITANANDAMAYI CENTER
San Ramon, California

AMMACHI
The Life Of The Holy Mother Amritanandamayi

PUBLISHED BY:
Mata Amritanandamayi Center
P.O. Box 613
San Ramon, CA
U.S.A. 94583-0613
Tel: (510) 537-9417

Printed in the United States of America

FIRST PRINTING, December 1994

ALSO AVAILABLE FROM:
Mata Amritanandamayi Mission Trust
Amritapuri P.O., Kollam Dt., Kerala 690525
INDIA
Tel: 91-4756-21279

ISBN 1-879410-60-5

ACKNOWLEDGEMENTS

Many incidents which are narrated in this book were taken from the biography of the Holy Mother written in Malayalam by Prof. M. Ramakrishnan Nair to whom our heartfelt gratitude is due. Many thanks also to my spiritual brothers and sisters who put so much effort into editing, typing and proofreading the book.

PREFACE

Pradīpajvālabhirdivasakaranīrājanavidhih
Sudhāsūtēshcandrōpalajalalavairardhyyarachanā

Svakīyairambhōbhih
    salilanidhisauhityakaranam
Tvadīyābhirvāgbhistava
    janani vāchām stutiriyam

Oh, Mother! This praise of words in your honour com-
posed with Your own words is like the worship of lights
in honour of the sun done with its own rays, the obla-
tion in honour of the moon with the water emanating
from the moonstone, and the pleasing of the ocean with
its own waters.

SAUNDARYALAHARI
VERSE 100

Here is a mystic accessible to anyone and everyone, with whom you can converse and in whose presence you can feel God. She is humble but firm as the Earth. She is simple yet beautiful like the full moon. She is Love, She is Truth, She is the embodiment of Renunciation and self-sacrifice. She not only teaches but does. She is a giver of everything and a receiver of nothing. She is soft like a flower but hard like a diamond. She is a Great Master and a Great Mother. Such is Mata Amritanandamayi.

She was born in full Awareness. Having undergone or displayed (we know not which) rigorous sadhana (spiritual discipline), She then embraced the entire world with love and compassion of indescribable dimensions, the love and compassion that is Her very fibre and being.

From Her tender childhood She sought out the Divine Mother and Father even without the guidance of a Guru. She withstood the attacks of Her kith and kin, of rationalists and miscreants all of whom tried to destroy Her. All alone in the midst of this battlefield, She confronted everything unperturbed and with steadfast courage. At the age of twenty-one, She outwardly manifested Her state of God-Realization and at twenty-two, began to initiate seekers of Truth into spiritual life. By the age of twenty-seven, the Holy Mother had established the spiritual headquarters of Her international Mission in the house of Her birth. Five years later there were nearly twenty branch ashrams throughout India and abroad. At the age of thirty-three, in response to the invitation of Her devotees in America and Europe, the Holy Mother made Her first world tour inspiring and uplifting many people around the world.

Above all She has counselled, wiped the tears and removed the burdens of thousands and thousands of people from all walks of life and from every corner of the Earth. It is left to you, dear reader, to decide who and what She is through the intuition of your heart....

Swami Amritaswarupananda

CONTENTS

PART ONE

Life

CHAPTER ONE

FROM BIRTH ITSELF

From birth itself I had an intense liking for the Divine Name. I would repeat the Lord's Name incessantly with every breath, and a constant flow of divine thoughts was kept up in my mind irrespective of the place where I was or the work I was attending to. This unbroken recollection of God with love and devotion would be of immense help to any aspirant in attaining Divine Realization.

— MATA AMRITANANDAMAYI —

Thīrthikurvanti tīrthāni sukarmikurvanti
Karmāni saccāstri kurvanti śāstrāni
Mōdante pitarō nrityanti dēvatāha
Sanātha cēyan bhūrbhavati

The Great Saints impart sanctity to places of
pilgrimage, render actions righteous and good, and
give spiritual authority to the scriptures. When such
a Saint is born, the Fathers rejoice, the Gods dance
in joy, and this Earth gets a savior.

NARADA BHAKTI SUTRAS
VERSES 69-71

THE LEGEND

In the Alappad Panchayat, district of Quilon, Kerala state, South India, there is a small village named Parayakadavu. This village lies amidst an endless expanse of coconut palms stretching along a narrow peninsula separated from the mainland to the east by an intercoastal waterway, while the western shore of the village is buffeted by the sparkling blue-green Arabian Sea.

The people of the village belong to a humble clan of fishermen who proudly trace their ancestry as far back as the sage Parasara. It is sage Parasara who married the fishermaid Satyavati, mother of Sri Veda Vyasa, the renowned codifier of the *Vedas*. There are many legends told about the sanctity and greatness of this village where daily life and social custom are still closely associated with divine myths, stories which the villagers strongly believe took place thousands of years ago. One such legend is as follows:

Once Lord Subramanya, son of Lord Siva and God-dess Parvati, committed a serious error. Infuriated by the transgression of His son, Lord Siva cursed Subramanya, causing him to be born as a fish. De-jected by the fate of Her son, Parvati requested the Lord to forgive Subramanya's fault. Instead of consol-ing Her, Siva became more angry and condemned Parvati as well to be born as a fisherwoman. Later when Lord Siva's anger had subsided, He told Subramanya that He Himself would come and liberate both of them at the appropriate time and thus blessed them.

In accordance with Lord Siva's curse, Lord Subramanya assumed the form of a fish, rather, of a huge whale. Appearing in the sea of Alappad, the whale caused the fishermen terrible harm. Accustomed to fishing both during the day and night, the fishermen could now no longer venture into the seas. Sometimes the whale tore the cast nets of the fishermen to shreds, and at others it overturned their boats, endangering their very lives. The villagers were doomed to poverty and starvation.

The king of the fishermen failed to find a solution. His treasury was becoming bankrupt, as he was feed-ing the starving people. Finally, in an attempt to solve the problem, he made a proclamation: the person who could catch the troublesome whale would be richly rewarded, and would also be given the hand of the king's beautiful daughter in marriage. Yet the huge whale was so fearsome that nobody came forth to ac-cept the challenge. The king and his subjects were completely disheartened, when an old man mysteriously appeared from the north. Nobody knew who he was.

Approaching the king, his back bowed with age, he
boldly declared that he could catch the huge whale
and save the people from complete devastation. Accompanied by the astonished king and his subjects,
the old man walked confidently toward the sea.

Making a long rope by twisting long strands of vines,
the old man threw one end into the sea while holding
the other end tightly in his hand. The rope of vines
encircled the place where the huge whale was lying
submerged. Passing the rope to the fishermen, he instructed them to pull with all their strength while chanting a particular mantra. As instructed by the old man,
the fishermen started pulling the rope while chanting
the mantra. After hours of tremendous effort, the giant
fish, entrapped in the vine rope, was dragged to the
shore. Suddenly, to everyone's amazement, the whale
vanished, and in its place stood Lord Subramanya,
released by Lord Siva from the curse. A temple for
Lord Subramanya was built on the spot where the giant
fish had been beached. That temple stands today as a
living monument to remind us of the old story.

The legend does not end there. Now Lord Siva, in
the guise of the old man, stepped forward and stood
before the king, demanding the reward of the hand of
the princess in marriage. The king, who had promised
his only daughter to the champion who saved his people,
was now trapped in a dilemma. He and his subjects
were completely distraught. How could a father, especially as king, give his exquisite young daughter in
marriage to an old man? The king begged him to ask
for anything in the entire kingdom but his daughter.
The old man calmly replied that a king must keep his
promise and be truthful to his word.

Now the king was in a real quandary. Truth was the strength of the fishermen; they firmly believed that truth was their protector. If one were not truthful, they said, one who went fishing was jumping into the wide open, fierce mouth of death. The king was paralyzed; he could neither break his vow nor give his beloved princess in marriage to the old man. At this point, the princess, who was in fact Goddess Parvati Herself, stepped forward and spoke without hesitation: "Father and most noble king, it is everyone's duty to protect and preserve righteousness (*dharma*). Nothing should stand against it." Despondent, the king had no choice but to allow her to depart with the old man. No one suspected that the humble fishing kingdom had become the stage for a divine drama in which Lord Siva and Goddess Parvati had been reunited. With heavy hearts, the people followed the divine couple for some distance asking, "Where are you going? We would like to come with you." They replied, "We don't have any particular dwelling place (*uru*); the spot we reach will be our dwelling place (*chellunna uru*)."

Lord Siva and Goddess Parvati continued on their way, followed by the fisherfolk, finally reaching a spot where they stopped. As Lord Siva stood facing east and Goddess Parvati faced west, the two became transformed into stone images. *Chellunna uru* (the place reached) later became Chenganoor of the present day.

In time a temple was constructed and daily worship was begun, when something very strange occurred. Whenever water was brought to the sanctum sanctorum to perform the worship, the priests found a fish in it. This made the performance of the daily worship impossible.

In order to find a solution, the temple authorities made an astrological calculation and discovered the whole story of Lord Siva, Goddess Parvati, and the curse of Lord Subramanya. The astrological forecast further revealed that the marriage ceremonies of the old man and the princess had never been conducted. According to the custom, the people of the Alappad coast, where Goddess Parvati had been born as a fishermaid, should come with dowry and other marriage presentations to Chenganoor in order to conduct the marriage. Subsequently the necessary preparations were made in Chenganoor and Alappad. The villagers of Alappad duly assembled the paraphernalia and traveled to Chenganoor to conduct the divine marriage ceremony. To this day, every year during the festival season, this custom is followed in memory of the ancient legend. The temple still remains a center of attraction to thousands of devotees.

A few decades ago an interesting incident took place in connection with this story. One year the people from the Alappad coast did not participate in the festival by observing the customary rules and preparation, thinking it meaningless and wasteful to spend a lot of money to travel all the way to Chenganoor. They thought, "Why should we cooperate in a festival which is conducted in a distant place?" Mysterious happenings immediately took place in the Chenganoor temple. The decorated elephant which was to carry the Lord's idol in the procession stood still, refusing to take even a step. All efforts to make it move failed. Word was immediately sent to Alappad of this inauspicious occurrence, but too late. Smallpox had already broken out there.

Realizing their foolish mistake and with deep remorse, the villagers made their way to Chenganoor without delay, bringing all the preparations for contributing to the festival according to the custom.

Such is the ancient lore which is intimately inter-woven with this coastal landscape and its people. Is it a wonder then that this sacred place has again become center stage for a divine drama?

ANCESTRY

The Idamannel family was an ancient family whose land in Parayakadavu village formed a small part of Alappad Panchayat. Though their hereditary work was fishing, they did other work as well. A vital part of their daily life was to perform religious practices and to observe various vows. The fishermen of the family were also known for their generosity. On returning from the sea with their day's catch, the first thing they did was to give some fish to all the villagers who had gathered, without accepting any money. After selling their day's catch, they would distribute a handful of coins among all the children.

Many pious souls had been born in the Idamannel family. Sri Velayudhan was such a man. He was a very compassionate, truthful and generous person, who firmly held the ideal of *ahimsa* (non-violence). He would not allow even a little rat to be killed. Velayudhan was married to Srimati Madhavi, a chaste and pious woman, whose habit was to get up early in the morning before dawn in order to make flower garlands for all the deities in the family shrine room. As she worked, she always chanted the Divine Names of God. Even today, now in her eighties, she sits daily before the temple stringing garlands with the same devoted spirit.

Sugunanandan was their eldest son of five children. Inspired by the devotional atmosphere of his family, he became an ardent devotee of Lord Krishna. When he was nine or ten years old, he began studying *Kathakali*, a classical dance drama of Kerala, which depicts the games and playful diversions of the gods and goddesses. While the actors present the story through dance and *mudras* (divine gestures), singers narrate the story through their songs. The character Sugunanandan most loved to portray was Sri Krishna. Once during a *Kathakali* performance he became so identified with his role of Krishna that he fell unconscious on the stage.

The atmosphere around the Idamannel compound was very peaceful and calm. On three sides it was skirted by the backwaters, which were alive with wildlife and surrounded by lush vegetation consisting of coconut, fruit and cashew trees. There were very few houses nearby in those days. Coming home from school when he was a young boy of thirteen or fourteen, Sugunanandan and his cousin engaged in their favorite pastime of climbing cashew trees and eating the delicious cashew fruit. One day the two boys were busily plucking cashews, when they noticed a *sannyasin* (wandering monk) with long hair and beard approaching Idamannel. They had never seen him before, and were intrigued by his radiant appearance. After roaming about the property a while, the *sannyasin* suddenly burst into blissful laughter and proclaimed loudly: "I can see many a cetics sitting immersed in deep meditation in this place. Previously this was the abode of many great souls whose tombs lie under this spot. Many *sannyasins* will attain liberation here. This will become a holy place." The *sannyasin* again burst into rapturous laughter and continued on his way. Puzzled by the mendicant's statement, the boys resumed their play. Many years would pass before Sugunanandan and his cousin would shake their heads in wonder, recalling the prophetic words of the wandering monk.

Before long Sugunanandan became busy with his work of marketing fish. When he was twenty-one, he married Damayanti, a twenty year-old girl from the neighboring village, Bhandaraturuttu. Damayanti came from a devout family, which performed religious practices daily without fail. Her family even had its own temple. From childhood, Damayanti had led a virtuous life. Her father, Punyan, and mother, Karutta Kunya, were exemplary devotees of God. The whole family atmosphere supported her in leading a religious life.

Damayanti was so pious that she was reverently called by the villagers 'Pattathi Amma', or the '*brahmana* lady'. As devotion to God was her focus in life, she would observe various religious vows almost every day of the week. She frequently undertook fasting and would break her fast by drinking the water of tender coconuts which mysteriously fell from the trees.

Thirteen children were born to Damayanti and Sugunanandan, though four died at birth and another after fifty-three days. The remaining children, four daughters and four sons, are named as follows in chro-ological order from eldest to youngest: Kasturbai[1], Sunil

Kumar[2], Sudhamani, Sugunamma, Sajani, Suresh Kumar, Satheesh Kumar, and Sudhir Kumar. Of these children, it was Sudhamani who was destined to become known throughout the world as Mata Amritanandamayi, the Mother of Immortal Bliss.

During her fourth pregnancy, Damayanti began having strange visions. Sometimes she had wonderful dreams of Lord Krishna; at others she beheld the divine play of Lord Siva and Devi, the Divine Mother. One night Damayanti dreamt that a mysterious figure came to entrust her with an idol of Sri Krishna which was cast in pure gold. Around the same time, Sugunanandan had a dream of the Divine Mother. As he was a devotee of Lord Krishna, he was unable to understand why Devi should suddenly appear to him. Upon relating his story to Damayanti, he found that she had recently had many strange visions also. They both wondered what the significance was, and whether some great good fortune would soon befall them.

At this time Sugunanandan and Damayanti were living in a small hut right on the seaside, as this was more convenient for their fishing business than staying at their other hut on the Idamannel family property some five minutes walk inland. During her three previous pregnancies, Damayanti had always experienced a swelling of her whole body a few weeks before her delivery date. This was the signal for her to relax her daily routine and return to her own family house in Bhandaraturuttu, where she would be cared for during the delivery. Damayanti was still waiting for the swelling to occur before making ready for the birth of her fourth child.

One night Damayanti had a wonderful dream that she had given birth to Krishna, and that He was lying on her lap drinking her breast milk. The next morning she was working at the seaside, when suddenly she had the feeling that she was going to deliver. Damayanti discounted the sensation, however, since the telltale swelling had not yet appeared. The strange feeling persisted though, and Damayanti put her work aside. For some reason she felt an inexplicable urge to go to Idamannel, and, crossing the backwaters alone, she headed inland. Entering the little hut, she began collecting a few items. A moment later, she felt a familiar sensation and realized that she was about to deliver. By the time she had spread a mat and lain down, the child had been born! Damayanti was shocked. She noticed that the baby was a girl. The atmosphere that enveloped the child's birth was completely silent and peaceful. Other than the initial sensation which had alerted her, Damayanti had not felt any discomfort. Now that she was coming to her senses, she was filled with concern. Was the child alive? She heard no cries of a newborn. Anxiously she examined the child. Now Damayanti was even more amazed. The babe had a beaming smile on her tiny face! The gaze of the child penetrated Damayanti's innermost heart and was never forgotten.

At this moment a woman from a neighboring house appeared in the doorway of the hut. Quickly realizing what had happened, she scurried around making the mother and the baby comfortable. Thus it was that on the morning of the twenty-seventh of September, 1953, a tiny girl child was born in a humble hut of woven palm leaves to the sound of the ocean waves echoing on the nearby shore.

The parents were puzzled by the babe's dark blue complexion and the fact that the child lay in *padmasana*[3], holding her fingers in *chinmudra*[4] with the tip of her thumb and forefinger touching to form a circle. They feared that this dark blue shade might be the symptom of some strange disease and that the peculiar posture might be due to abnormal bone structure or dislocation. Various doctors were consulted. The fear of bone abnormality was allayed when the doctors confirmed that there was no such handicap. As for the skin color, it could not be attributed to heredity, since both Damayanti and Sugunanandan were light tan in skin tone. Hence, the parents were advised not to bathe the child for six months in the hope that the mysterious ailment would disappear.

Six months passed, and still the baby girl retained the dark blue hue reminiscent of Lord Krishna and Divine Mother Kali. Eventually, over the course of time, dark-blue changed into dark brown. Yet, when the little girl's desire intensified to behold the vision of Lord Krishna, her skin color once again assumed its blue hue. Even today, especially during the Divine Moods of Krishna and Devi, one can observe a dark blue skin tone.

Ironically, it was because of her blue-black complexion, that Damayanti and the other family members would look upon the child with great disdain. Their aversion for the dark child eventually led them to treat her as the thankless servant of the family and relatives. In fact, only a few close relatives were ev informed of the birth, as not much importance was given to this newborn child. It was a girl, and Damayanti had already given birth to three other children.

Who could imagine that this strangely blue-colored child, born smiling benignly in a small hut along the shores of the Arabian Sea was, in truth, a spiritual giant come to this world to shower peace and godly love upon suffering humankind? Who could foresee this little one's spiritual destiny of helping thousands and thousands of seekers to cross the Ocean of Transmigration?[5]

From the moment of the tiny girl's birth, the family began noticing unusual signs which would be understood only years later. Typically, before walking, a child progresses through various stages of development. First it lies on its back, then rolls over, then lies on its belly and pushes itself up with the forearms. Eventually, the child begins crawling and, after some months, it gets up on two legs by holding onto something. All this culminates in the toddling stage around one year of age. This little girl's case was entirely different, as none of these stages occurred. One day, after turning six months old, the little girl suddenly stood up and walked straight across the verandah. Not long after that, she started running, which filled everyone's heart with wonder and joy.

AMBROSIAL JEWEL

The parents gave the name Sudhamani, "Ambrosial Jewel", to their remarkable baby daughter. Unlike most of her children her age, Sudhamani started speaking her

mother tongue, Malayalam, when she was barely six
months old. Her passion to sing the Divine Names
manifested as soon as she began to speak fairly well.
By the age of two, without instruction from anyone, she
began saying prayers and singing short songs in praise
of Sri Krishna. Needless to say, the family was stunned,
when they happened to overhear her. Over the course
of the next year, Sudhamani established the habit of
melodiously chanting the Divine Names aloud. To this
day, her custom has continued without interruption.
By age four, she sang with devotional fervor her one or
two line compositions, seated before her favorite small
picture of the Lord.

From infancy, Sudhamani was full of life and vigor.
She was an obedient child, and everyone in the village
loved her. Even strangers felt an inexplicable attraction and affection for little Sudhamani. Love for God,
concern for others, and other admirable traits manifested themselves in her from early childhood. Because
of her virtuous qualities, everyone in the village called
her by the pet name, "Kunju", which means "the little
one". Strangely enough, these same qualities later became the excuse for severe abuse and maltreatment
meted out to her by her own family and relatives.

By the time Sudhamani turned five, a visible stream
of inborn devotion to Lord Sri Krishna flowed from her
heart, and before long this love took the form of full-
fledged devotional songs. The songs were filled with
poignant longing for her beloved Krishna, and her enchanting, soulful singing of these simple, yet deeply
mystical songs became well-known throughout the vil
lage. While chanting or singing, she would focus he

eyes on a little picture of Krishna, which she always
kept tucked inside her shirt. Then she would sit un-
moving for a long time. This extraordinary behavior
and intense devotion amazed everyone and attracted
the attention of all the devout villagers. They would
rise early in the morning just to hear Sudhamani's angelic
singing greeting the new day.

> O Lord Who has protected Gokulam as the Dear
> Child of Ampati, O Lord of the Ocean of Milk,
> Who art the color of clouds, O Thou with the
> lotus eyes, I adore Thee with joined palms...
>
> Please give relief from sin to the sinners, O Thou
> Who art the color of dark clouds. Please show com-
> passion to the poor ones in this village...
>
> O Lord of the flute Who wears yellow raiment,
> Who wears the garland of jasmine, please come
> play the flute. O Destroyer of Putana, please pro-
> tect me! O One Who reclines on a huge serpent,
> O Lord of Gokulam Who has prevented the tor-
> rential rain, please make me one with Thy Lotus
> Feet, thereby ridding me of the pain in my soul...

Even at this age, certain visible traits of divinity
were appearing in Sudhamani. While engaged in childhood games or other activities, she would suddenly
become indrawn. On these occasions, her parents or
other family members would find her sitting motionless in some lonely, isolated place. At other times,
they would find her sitting near the backwaters, looking intently into the water or silently gazing at the
blue sky as if transported to another world. It was not
uncommon to find her sitting in solitude with closed

eyes. When she was aroused, her mood seemed abstracted.

Unable to understand the import of their daughter's
unusual states of consciousness, the parents would scold
Sudhamani for not being playful like the other children. This marked the beginning of a long period of
maligning their daughter and misinterpreting her flights
to the realm of the Divine. For their part, the parents
were worried that her peculiar behavior might indicate
a psychological disorder.

When Sudhamani turned five, she was enrolled as
a student of the first grade at Srayicadu School in the
nearby village. Even at this age, she exhibited brilliant intelligence and memory. Having heard a lesson
once, she never forgot even part of it. She could effortlessly recite any of the lessons which had been taught
in the class or which she had read. When Sudhamani
was studying in the second grade, she would easily
recite the lessons of the advanced grades, simply by
overhearing the text when it was read aloud. Her older
classmates, including her brother and sister, sometimes
received harsh punishment from the teacher for being
unable to learn verses of poetry by heart. Meanwhile,
little Sudhamani, who was studying in the lower grade,
would melodiously sing the poems and dance to the
melody like a delicate butterfly. All the teachers ad-
mired her and were amazed by Kunju's astonishing
memory. She scored full marks in all subjects and was
ranked first in the class, despite the fact that she was
often absent because of household responsibilities.

Another incident which illustrates Sudhamani's remarkable memory occurred five months after Damayanti

had given birth. That day she left the house and the child in the care of Sugunanandan. For some unknown reason the babe became restless and began crying. Unaccustomed to such behavior, Sugunanandan tried hard but could not console the child. When her crying continued, Sugunanandan eventually became exasperated, lost his patience and flung her on the cot.

Many years later, Sudhamani remarked to her father, "Oh, the way you threw me away that day! You were about to kill me!" At first, Sugunanandan did not understand the import of Sudhamani's words, then, after a few moments, the old incident flashed through his mind and he was once again astounded by his daughter's memory.

Whatever free time she had in school, Sudhamani spent in completing her homework with the thought that, after reaching home, she could use that much time in the remembrance of God. Returning home, the little girl would first help her mother with the household chores. Otherwise, she would forget herself singing devotional songs.

Even from childhood Sudhamani was very careful about the proper use of time. She never wasted even a moment sitting idle. While attending to her steadily mounting household duties, Sudhamani constantly chanted the Divine Name of Lord Krishna. Visualizing her beloved Krishna's beautiful form within her heart while repeating His Divine Name, Kunju spent her days and nights in her own world.

The house where Sudhamani spent her childhood consisted merely of two tiny rooms and a kitchen. To alleviate the inconvenience caused by such tight living quarters, Sugunanandan built a small room alongside the cowshed.[6] This was used as a study room for the children, but it was also where little Sudhamani spent her childhood days meditating and singing devotional songs. There were two other refugees in the cowshed, an abandoned woman named Potichi, who was a barber, and her child. Taking pity on their helpless condition, Sugunanandan had allowed them to stay there. Potichi, the barber woman, loved Sudhamani very much. She would always carry the little one on her hip, and in those days it was Potichi who looked after Sudhamani much more than Damayanti.

Thus we find gentle Sudhamani living in the cowshed, while focusing her heart and soul upon the enchanting form of Lord Krishna. Just as cows were very dear to Sri Krishna, the little girl also adored them. Whatever free moments she had she spent sitting with them in solitude, lost in a divine reverie, reveling in the bliss of longing to behold the resplendent vision of Krishna.

Because of Sudhamani's loving nature, she was always surrounded by children. Whenever they could, they came to Idamannel to play with her. Together they would go to gather grass for the cows. Though Sudhamani's little friends were not interested in doing strenuous tasks, they would happily join her in order to enjoy her cheerful company. All of them had a mysterious attraction and strong bond of love for her. Having completed the work, Sudhamani would involve the children in various games and draw other children into her play, by her enactment of Krishna Leela, the pranks of Sri Krishna as a child. Without difficulty, she would encourage the whole group to sing in loud

chorus the devotional songs which were always flowing
through her mind.

Nobody could understand Sudhamani's devotional
moods, which were becoming more and more intense.
As weeks and months passed, she became increasingly
absorbed in her devotional activities, singing with deep
longing to see the divine beauty of her Lord. Her ecstatic moods became more and more frequent and were
not always confined to the cowshed. Oblivious to the
world around her, Sudhamani would sometimes dance
in ecstasy while moving in a circle and singing devotional songs. The following is a song composed by Kunju
when she was seven:

> Protect me, O Supreme Lord who resides
> In the city of Guruvayoor...
> O Child Krishna, who acted as a cowherd boy,
> O Lord of the Universe, Consort of Goddess
> Lakshmi,
> Protect me, O Krishna, the Beloved of Radha,
> O Krishna, the Beloved of the Gopis,
> O Krishna, the son of Nanda,
> O Krishna who is worshipped and adored by
> everyone...

The family and neighbors were totally ignorant of
the exalted moods of little Sudhamani and took them
to be mere childish games. Who could imagine that
this seven year-old girl, having received no spiritual
instruction, was swimming in the Ocean of Pure Love
and Bliss? Lost to this world, Kunju would sometimes
lock herself in a room to sing and dance ecstatically.
Once Damayanti peeped through the door and exclaimed,
"See how our daughter dances! We should give her
dancing lessons!" Poor parents! They were acquainted
only with worldly dance. Never had they heard about

someone dancing in God-intoxicated bliss. Had there been somebody present who had studied the lives of Great Souls, perhaps he would have recognized Sudhamani's spiritual states. Even then, who would expect to find such a rapturous state in a child so young? As it was, the family concluded that they were witnessing merely the antics of their slightly eccentric and overly imaginative daughter.

Sudhamani's longing to behold her Supreme Lord and merge in Him continued to deepen. Ceaselessly she gazed at the little picture of Krishna which she kept safely tucked in her shirt. Pouring out her heart to Him in song and prayer, the little girl would cry out, "O my darling Krishna, I am seeing troubles and suffering all around me! O Krishna! Please do not forget to look after this tiny child. I am always calling You; won't You come play with me?"

The following song was composed by Sudhamani at the age of eight and gives a glimpse of the depth of her spiritual intensity:

> O Essence of Mercy, O Compassionate One,
> O Krishna, give me refuge!
>
> O Krishna, is the story of these burning
> Tears that flow unknown to Thee?
>
> Offering flowers at Thy Feet that have
> Crushed the serpent Kaliya, I will worship
> Thee, O Krishna...
> Thou didst come as the charioteer of Arjuna
> At Kurukshetra to protect Truth and Righteousness.
> O Lord Who preserves Dharma
> Show a bit of compassion to us!

O Lord of the Gita, Lover of Divine Music,
Give the capacity to sing Thy song...
O Lover of devotional singing,
Do You not hear Thy sacred Names
Uttered from the innermost heart?

The little one's despondent face and her sorrowful songs captured the sympathetic hearts of the villagers. But the great mystery of Sudhamani's inner life still remained unknown to all. Who could imagine the ecstatic rapture of her childhood devotion? Who could understand it but the Wise?

CHAPTER TWO
THE DIVINE SERVANT

Mother is the servant of servants. She has no special place to dwell. She dwells in your heart.

- MATA AMRITANANDAMAYI -

Kāminīriti hi yāminishu khalu kāmanīyaka
        nidhē bhavān
Pūrnasammada rasārnavam
        kamapi yōgigamya manubhāvayan
Brahmaśankara mukhānpīha
        pashupanganāsu bahumānayan
Bhaktalōka gamanīyarūa
        kamanīya drishna paripāhi mām

*O Treasure-house of Beauty! Thou who thus didst
during nights confer on the lovelorn gopikas that
same immense and intense joy of the Spirit which
only yogis attain, and thereby didst make them
worthy of respect even for Brahma and Shiva. May
Thou, O Krishna of lovely form, accessible only
to men endowed with devotion, be pleased to protect me!*

SRIMAD NARAYANEEYAM
CANTO 69, VERSE 11

At the age of nine, Sudhamani reached the fourth grade.
By this time she was performing most of the household duties, as her mother was chronically ill. Getting
up before dawn, she attended to her many duties, and
only after finishing her work she hurried off to school.
Returning home in the evening, she spent in prayer
and meditation whatever time was left after her chores.
Always carrying her precious picture everywhere, she
wept embracing and kissing it.

Sometimes Damayanti went to fetch water in a distant place, leaving behind little Sudhamani, who would
follow her unobserved, thinking that she might be able
to help her mother. When Damayanti tried to prevent
her from coming, Sudhamani protested loudly. Exas-

perated by her daughter's stubbornness, sometimes Damayanti even locked her in a room. She would try to frighten the little girl saying, "Here comes a ghost! It is coming to get you!" But nobody could frighten Sudhamani. Though only a small child, she was fearless. This fact also commanded the respect of the local villagers who already had great affection for the extraordinary child.

There was a woman in the village well known for frightening small children. When children became too mischievous, the parents would call her to frighten them into obedience. Her name was Appisil Amma, and sometimes she was called to Idamannel to frighten little Sudhamani. The notorious woman would sneak up to the window where Sudhamani was sitting. Covering her head with a sack, she jumped and shrieked, making frightening gestures. Peering through the window Kunju would boldly retort, "Go away, I know who you are. You are that Appisil Amma. Don't try to frighten me!"

Like a forlorn, forsaken child Sudhamani would call on her beloved Krishna. The villagers now considered her to be one who dwelt in another world. Unable to understand the reason for the little one's agony, they used to sympathize with her saying, "What a pity! Poor child! What has happened to her? Tears are always streaming down her cheeks. What a deplorable condition! Was she born only to cry? Is the family abusing her? What has she done to undergo such hardships?" Everyone took pity on Sudhamani and some even tried to console her. Yet who but the Beloved of the *Gopis* could appease her unquenchable thirst for spiritual Union?

By this time Sudhamani's equal vision, noble character, compassion toward all living creatures, and enchanting singing had endeared her to all the villagers. Those who had the good fortune to know her soon found themselves opening their hearts to her. Fate was not so kind when it came to her own family. Sudhamani's mother and elder brother were particularly antagonistic toward her because of her unusual behavior.

Eventually, following the birth of five more children, Damayanti's health completely deteriorated and she was no longer capable of tending to any household chores. These tasks, already shared by Sudhamani, now fell entirely on her shoulders. Kasturi, the eldest daughter, was studying in a local college, and Subhagan, the eldest son, was also attending school. Her tribulations increasing, Sudhamani toiled from three o'clock in the morning, as she set to work cleaning the house, sweeping the compound, fetching water, cooking the food, tending the cows, milking them, washing the clothes and scrubbing the cooking vessels.

Such a hard routine was extremely arduous for the child. Even to look after the family livestock and poultry was enough work for one person. Yet Sudhamani patiently and devotedly did all the work without complaint. By this point her education had nearly come to an end. Overburdened with work, the little one could not reach school in time. Sometimes when she managed to discharge her duties and run to class, the class had already begun, and, as a punishment for her tardiness, the teacher made the child stand outside the classroom. Even though forced to remain outside, Sudhamani focused keenly on the lesson, and, in this way, she managed to complete the fourth grade.

However, by the time she reached the fifth grade,
Sudhamani could no longer keep up with her studies
as well as perform her endless stream of household
chores. At ten, Sudhamani was forced to abandon her
schooling. From early morning before dawn until late
at night she labored. Yet even while engaged in bur-
densome work, the little one always sang or chanted
the Divine Names of her beloved Krishna. Sometimes
in the middle of a task she became so absorbed in her
devotional mood that she completely lost touch with
her external surroundings.

As noted earlier, Sudhamani's day began well before dawn. If she overslept a bit from exhaustion,
Damayanti did not hesitate to pour a pitcher of cold
water over her. Soon after waking, her first chore was
to beat coconut husks with a pestle to turn them into
soft fiber, later to be used to manufacture coir, a local
product. Then she began a round of tidying the house
and yard, fetching water from the village water tap some
distance away, washing the utensils, cooking the meals
and getting her younger brothers and sisters ready for
school. The next round involved bathing the cows, feeding
them fodder, again washing the cooking vessels after
serving lunch, washing all the family's clothing and
gathering grass for the cows. By now it was four o'clock
in the afternoon and time for her brothers and sisters
to return from school. Sudhamani prepared a snack and
tea for them, then somehow found time to visit neighboring houses to collect vegetable scraps or rice gruel
for the cows. Furthermore, Damayanti had instructed
the child to discharge any duties in the houses she
visited which had not been properly done. Again the

child would prepare the evening meal for the family and wash the vessels without assistance from anyone.

Sudhamani was considered to be the family's servant, and all domestic chores were hers alone. In addition, Damayanti scrutinized her every action. When she detected any error, however slight, she hastened to mete out swift punishment. Sudhamani's only friend was Krishna; her sole inspiration was His Name. As she performed her many tasks, the intense thought of her beloved Lord would bring tears to her eyes, and she would cry for hours, contemplating His beautiful form.

Finally Sudhamani's day would come to an end at around eleven at night. The innocent girl now had a little time for rest. Still she had no desire to lie on the bed or to sleep, rather she sought only to rest in herself, that is, to be with her Lord. When everyone else was at last asleep, she would sit in the small family shrine room pouring her heart out to Lord Krishna in devotional songs. In the darkness of the night, Sudhamani would cry with longing and sing until she finally fell asleep.

> *O Krishna, please show compassion to me!*
> *O Lord Vishnu, I adore You with joined palms!*
> *Please rid me of the burden of speech,*
> *Mind and body!*
> *Please protect me with affection!*
>
> *O Krishna, do You, Who are the friend of the*
> *miserable, not have even a bit of compassion?*
> *Are You dwelling only in the golden temple?*
> *Have Your shining eyes become dim?*

O Ocean of Compassion,
You are affectionate towards the devotees!
Your Feet are the Eternal Support!

Even in those days, Sudhamani's mind was so enraptured that it instantly soared to the heights of divinity when moved by any heart-capturing sight or song.
One day while returning home after making some purchases at the market, she heard the melody of a devotional song coming from far off. Attracted by the song
and in a semiconscious mood, Sudhamani turned and
walked in the direction of the singing. The lament was
rising from the house of a Christian family where someone
had died that day. The relatives were sitting around
the body, singing hymns in a tone full of sorrow. The
child's heart was immediately moved, and she became
lost to the world, standing motionless in a God-intoxicated mood. Her eyes were closed, and tears rolled
down her cheeks. The purchased goods fell from her
hands, and the people gathered there did not know
what to make of the unknown girl's sudden transformation, mistakenly thinking that she, too, was moved by
the death of their relative.

A half hour passed before Sudhamani partially regained her normal consciousness. Picking up the fallen
packages, she hurriedly continued on her way home,
but too late. Damayanti was waiting for her angrily,
and, in a fit of fury, chastised Sudhamani and beat her
severely. The little one was still in an indrawn state
and received Damayanti's harsh treatment silently and
untouched. What external force can distract a mind
which is absorbed in God?

Besides her exceptional brilliance, undaunted cheerfulness, exemplary devotion and poignant singing, Sudhamani was known most of all for her loving compassion for the poor and needy. Although she did her best to serve and please her mother, Damayanti, hot-tempered by nature, never hesitated to punish her harshly for any imagined fault. The particular justification for Damayanti's aversion to little Sudhamani was her dark complexion. Moreover, Damayanti would sometimes catch the little one sneaking off with butter, milk and curd, just like the notorious butter thief, Sri Krishna. What Damayanti didn't discover for some time was that the food was being offered to starving families which Sudhamani had befriended.

Unnoticed by others, the child would surreptitiously slip out with milk and curds, after replacing the pilfered quantity with water. When discovered, she invariably received a painful beating. Often her compassionate tendency was exploited by her brothers and sisters who would also steal food, but for themselves, and then accuse Sudhamani. Though she knew who the real thief was, she never uttered a word, but silently endured the harsh blows rained on her by her mother.

When Sudhamani came to know of any family which was starving, she would pilfer money from her mother's little collection box, so that the necessary purchases could be made. If this were not possible, she would obstinately pester her father until he gave her a bit of money. When these two means failed, then she would take raw foodstuffs from her own family's meager storeroom and give them to the family in need.

Except for certain childhood pranks and lighter moods, all Sudhamani's mischief was based on a selfless intention. Her actions were the fruit of her natural compassion for anyone who was suffering. However, such charitable acts only inflamed Damayanti, who was quick to inflict harsh doses of corporal punishment. Regardless of her own suffering, Sudhamani found immense satisfaction and bliss in giving peace and help to others. She was not at all deterred from these benevolent practices by continuous punishments. She never let others know what she had to endure in order to render her services to poor villagers.

Most of the time Sugunanandan was absent from Idamannel for days at a time, attending to his fishing business, returning only late at night when all the children were fast asleep. Immediately on his return, Damayanti hastened to enumerate her accusations against her servant child. On one such occasion, Sudhamani, who was pretending to be asleep, suddenly shouted out, "I am not your daughter! I must be your daughter-in-law!" Damayanti was stunned to hear Sudhamani's outburst. The little one's implication was clear; she was reminding Damayanti that a real mother would patiently forgive the faults of her daughter, whereas only a mother-in-law would report so meticulously the mistakes of a daughter-in-law exaggerated ten times over.

Who could imagine that the virtuous little Sudhamani's insatiable appetite for relieving sorrow and suffering would soon bring thousands of people from around the world to the distant shores of the Arabian Sea, just as those dying of thirst seek out an oasis? How can one grasp the fact that Sudhamani, barely ten years old, was creating a wave of compassion in this remote fishing village which was destined to be felt throughout the world?

Though she discharged her duties with utmost sincerity, her mother often warned her saying, "Hey girl, don't be lazy! If you sit idle God won't give you any work, and you will die of starvation. Always pray to God, 'O God, please give me work.' That is how everyone prays." Hearing these words, Sudhamani then adopted the prayer, "O Krishna, please do give me work, please give me Your work!"

The patience, forbearance and sacrifice which Sudhamani showed were incredible. Her capacity to take persecution in stride, while incessantly remembering her Beloved, foreshadowed the advent of one more Great Soul in India's continuous legacy of God-Realized Saviors. Although she underwent countless ordeals and was tortured cruelly, she took everything as the benevolence of Divine Providence. All her sorrow was kept in her heart and confided only to the Divine Flute Player, Lord Krishna.

In the dark of the night behind the closed doors of the family shrine room, she would pray to Krishna with tear-filled eyes, "O my Beloved Krishna, nobody but You can understand my heart. This world is full of sorrow and suffering. Selfishness reigns supreme. People seek only their own happiness and pleasure. My darling Kanna[7], I desire nothing else but complete oneness with You. O Lord, didn't You see my suffering today? O Lord, please come! Let me see Your Divine Form! These miseries are nothing for me, but the separation from You is agony." The following song was composed by Sudhamani during this period:

O Embodiment of Compassion
Who art of black color,
Deign to open Thy eyes.
Art Thou not the Destroyer of Sorrow?
This being so, do remove my sufferings!

In this world Thou art the shelter,
O bright-colored One with eyes like the petals
Of a red lotus, I worship Thee forever
With the flowers of my tears, O Krishna...

O Gopala, Enchanter of the mind,
I am groping in the darkness.
O Thou Who fillest the fourteen worlds,
O Sridhara, open Thy eyes and rid me of sorrow...

Thus, three years of intense yearning and painful ordeals passed. Sudhamani, now thirteen, still worked arduously. As she grew older, her responsibilities also grew. Without uttering a complaint, she continued her struggle as before. At the same time, her spiritual practices also became increasingly intense. One could see the little one's lips always moving, chanting the Divine Name. Internally and externally the Sacred Name flowed in a constant stream from her heart.

LIFE WITH THE RELATIVES

Servants were not available in the coastal area for kitchen work and other domestic chores, as there was much more profitable work such as sewing fishing nets and manufacturing coir. Not only that, the people of the fishing clan considered any work other than fishing disgraceful. Therefore, any girls who had discontinued their studies were forced to work ceaselessly

doing domestic chores. Moreover, they were often sent
to their relatives' houses to render service. It was the
custom for the relatives to ask the parents of such girls
for their services.

And so it was with Sudhamani. Her relatives insisted that she be given in service to their households.
Finally, giving in to their persistent pressure,
Sudhamani's parents were forced to send her to the
home of her maternal grandmother. Thus Sudhamani
spent the next four years playing the role of domestic
servant in various relatives' homes.

Sudhamani's grandmother lived six kilometers to
the south of Parayakadavu at Bhandaraturuttu. One could
reach her village either by traveling by boat down the
backwaters or by walking along the shore of the Arabian Sea. As one might imagine, either route had an
intoxicating effect on little Sudhamani. Riding in the
ferry boat, she would gaze at the blue sky, softly weeping with joy, thinking of blue-colored Krishna and
chanting 'OM' in harmony with the humming engine.
She would focus her attention on the tiny ripples dancing on the water, while visualizing the form of her Beloved
there and imagining His divine play. Entering into a
state of devotional fervor, her soft 'OM' would blossom
into devotional singing. Her fellow passengers greatly
enjoyed the little one's charming singing, and were not
at all surprised by her conduct, as they had always
considered her to be one from another world. Losing
herself in these practices, Sudhamani never felt the
distance or boredom of the trip.

The joy of the boat journey was short-lived. One
day when she asked her mother for boat fare, Damayanti

quickly scolded, "Who are you to travel in a boat? Are you a college girl? For you walking is good enough." It was during this time that Kasturi had begun her college studies, a rare privilege for a girl from the coast. Damayanti was very proud of this fact and always gave her enough money for all her daily expenses. For a parent's child to become a college student was a great thing among families far too poor to send their children for advanced studies. Even if the parents could afford to send their children, they often quickly abandoned the idea when the children showed a lack of interest or initiative. Damayanti was thus showing a bit of understandable vanity.

Sudhamani, being black and a mere servant, was unnoticed, uncared for and completely misunderstood by her own family. Nevertheless, she peacefully accepted prejudice and poverty, as she was full of the presence of Krishna. She was not at all displeased by the crude words of her mother. Quite the contrary! She was happy to walk along the seashore to her grandmother's house. Singing and dancing joyously in solitude, she thought only of the blessing! The six kilometer walk became an exalting experience for Sudhamani who considered the ocean to be her own mother.

One can easily imagine her walking along the shore loudly singing, accompanied by the surging of the ocean waves. As she forgot the outer world, her steps became slower and slower. The sight of the dark blue ocean and the blue-gray storm clouds overhead ravished her mind. The roaring sound of the ocean resembled 'OM' and invariably had a divinely intoxicating effect on Sudhamani. Seeing Krishna in the waves, she would sometimes run to embrace them! The ocean breeze was for her the soft caress of Sri Krishna Himself. Sometimes she would cry aloud, "Krishna! Krishna!" Deeply absorbed in a state of supreme devotion, she would move along the shore with faltering steps. Eventually she would lose all external consciousness and fall to the sand.

Partially regaining her normal consciousness, Sudhamani would burst into tears praying, "Kanna, my dear Krishna, come running! Where have You gone leaving me here? Why did You abandon me on this unknown shore? Where am I? O Beloved Krishna, come running before the waves of this Ocean of Transmigration swallow me up! O Krishna, lift up this destitute from the sand of pleasures. Are You not the Savior of Your devotees? Do You not know my heart's pain? What mistake have I committed for You to allow me to suffer like this? O Lord of all worlds, won't You show a little compassion to this humble servant of Yours? Daily I am waiting to hear the magical sound of Your divine flute playing. O Krishna, please come...please come!"

After some time, she would return to a manageable state of mind and continue her way along the shore, still singing ecstatically. Again the little one would fall several more times on the sand, oblivious to the world around her.

> *O Krishna, Ocean of Compassion,*
> *Life's miseries are ever increasing.*
> *There is no peace for the mind...*
> *Alas, confusion is so great ... Forgiving all wrongs,*
> *Wipe the sweat from my brow.*
> *O Kanna, now I have no support other than*

Thy worshipful Lotus Feet...
O Krishna, the throat is drying up,
The eyes are failing,
The feet are tired,
I am falling to the ground, O Krishna...

In this way, drinking the nectar of supreme love
and devotion, Sudhamani would somehow reach her
grandmother's house only to have to confront a back-
breaking workload. Yet the young girl would contentedly chant the Names of Lord Krishna and carry on
with her labors. As far as she was concerned, every
moment of life was an opportunity given by the Supreme Lord to serve and remember Him.

Occasionally, Sudhamani was sent to a grain mill
some distance from her grandmother's house in order
to husk rice paddy. Cheerfully she made the journey,
singing her favorite devotional songs as she walked.
On the way to the granary, she had to pass through a
section of the village where many families lived in
appalling poverty. Sudhamani, whose very nature was
compassion, would feel very disheartened seeing their
plight. While returning home after husking the paddy
she used to give some rice away to those families who
had been starving for days. Sometimes her grandmother
would detect the missing portion of rice, and thinking
that Sudhamani had sold it in exchange for a snack,
scolded and beat her. No matter how much Sudhamani
was pressed, she never divulged the name of the family to whom she had given the rice. She thought that if
she revealed it, her grandmother would surely go quarrel with them.

While staying at Bhandaraturuttu, Sudhamani was
also sometimes sent to guard the newly sown paddy

fields from crows and chickens. As the field was in a
distant place, this duty offered her a chance to be away
from all family members and to spend time in solitude
remembering and praying to the Lord. Her every breath
sounded with the Name of Krishna. Each step was taken
remembering His Divine Form. So intense were her
love and devotion, that she often collapsed near the
field, weeping.

One great solace for Sudhamani was that her grandmother was a devotee of Lord Krishna, and a portrait
of Krishna hung on her wall. Sudhamani used to stand
in front of it to sing songs to her Lord. At these times,
her uncle, Ratnadasan, who loved the little one very
much, used to bring a stool for her to sit on while
praying, so that she did not have to stand for such a
long time. Then Sudhamani would refuse saying, "Oh,
how can I sit when Krishna is standing!" The portrait
of the Lord was not a piece of painted paper for her;
it was Krishna standing there in flesh and blood. For
a true devotee there is no such thing as inert matter;
every object manifests the glory of the Lord.

Attracted by the heartfelt songs of Sudhamani, the
neighbors often used to come to listen to her. The child's
exalted singing always filled their minds with love and
devotion. Gradually, they too learned Sudhamani's compositions and would sing them in their own shrine rooms.
To prevent the cast of the evil eye[8], Sudhamani's uncle
would smear sacred ash imbued with special prayers
on the forehead of his niece.

Autumn, winter, spring and summer passed. Sudhamani, now fourteen, was sent to the house of Damayanti's
elder sister. As usual, she was forced to bear a heavy

load alone. First she would boil unhusked rice paddy, then dry it in the sun. The duties of cooking, cleaning and washing all the clothes were hers as well. All the children of the family were in college and considered housework shameful. They had no faith in God, teased Sudhamani mercilessly for her devotional attitude, and tried to prevent her from singing. What could the loving child do, surrounded by these insensitive people? Hiding her face in her hands, she would burst into tears when they temporarily succeeded in preventing her from singing. Though she was externally silenced, no one could check the incessant flow of her heart toward her Beloved.

As the house lay close to the ocean, all the water from the nearby taps was salty. To fetch drinking water, Sudhamani had to row a small boat across the backwaters to a distant fresh water tap. Sometimes she even acted as boatman and ferried her relatives' children across the backwaters to school. With great pleasure she ferried other people's children as well.

Sitting in the canoe on the return trip, the little one took great delight in the beauty of the natural scenery. Crying freely to her Lord, her longing heart's desire to see Krishna would become tremendously intense. She would question the ripples rising on the surface of the river saying, "O little waves, did any of you see my Krishna Who is the color of a dark blue storm cloud? Have you ever heard the sweet music of His enchanting flute?" Seeing the waves still rising on the water, Sudhamani imagined they were giving a negative reply. Sobbing, she thought, "Oh, like me these little waves are in deep agony without seeing Krishna."

Everywhere she perceived the reflection of her own excruciating pain of separation. Imploringly she cried aloud, "O dark blue clouds of the infinite sky, where did you hide my beloved Krishna? O white cranes swiftly flying across the sky, are you going to Vrindavan?[9] If you happen to meet Krishna, please tell Him of this poor child who is always weeping thinking of Him!" Soon Sudhamani would lose all external consciousness and sit in the boat as motionless as a statue. Slowly regaining her normal state of awareness, she would find herself still sitting in the boat which was drifting with the current. Because these exalted spiritual moods occurred spontaneously, there were times when Sudhamani had to face dangerous situations which could have taken her life.

One day little Sudhamani had finished the job of husking paddy and had begun rowing her tiny canoe back to the house. While rowing, gazing at the sky, she saw storm clouds moving across the horizon. The sight filled her innocent heart with the thought of her beloved blue-colored Krishna. The next instant she lost all outward awareness and merged in *samadhi*.[10] The oar fell from her hands. Her eyes were fixed on the sky and, oblivious to her surroundings, she remained transfixed in complete stillness. Now and then calling out, "Krishna, Krishna!", she was entirely lost to the world. The canoe moved into the current, carried on a haphazard course. Suddenly the roar of a loud engine announced the approach of a large boat which was heading directly toward Sudhamani's tiny canoe! The passengers in the boat shouted in alarm, making a vain effort to arouse the little girl. People standing on the banks of the river shouted, and some threw stones in the water around her. At the last possible moment the child partially regained external consciousness and somehow managed to steer her boat clear of danger.

Another year had passed when Sudhamani was sent next to the house of Damayanti's eldest brother, Anandan, in the town of Karunagappally, about ten kilometers inland from Parayakadavu. With utmost sincerity and enthusiasm Sudhamani discharged her daily chores to the delight of Anandan and his wife, who even rewarded her with a pair of earrings for wholeheartedly performing her duties.

Compassion for the poor was one of the outstanding features of little Sudhamani's character. Whether she was in her uncle's house, her aunt's, or her own family home, nothing could stop her from extending help to those in need. Many Muslim families lived around her uncle's house, and most were very poor. The little one would carefully pocket various articles from her uncle's and secretly pass them on to the needy families. Though at first nobody noticed, after some time her pilfering was discovered. On several occasions Sudhamani received a beating from her auntie, yet she never felt offended by her aunt's actions. She thought, "Why should I feel offended? Aversion comes only when I take myself to be different from them. I never consider them to be separate. Even at home my parents beat me. Why should I not receive such treatment here as well?"

Although severely beaten several times, Sudhamani was not discouraged from showing mercy to the afflicted. Her habit of giving things to others continued. Such incidents show the immense patience, compassion and forbearance which were her very nature. Taking every event in her life as a lesson, she offered her life as a unique sacrifice as she prepared her future message of love.

Sudhamani's sharp intellect easily penetrated every situation to extract the essential spiritual principles. She would later describe all the trials which she endured as rare blessings bestowed by the Lord to make her understand the ephemeral nature of the world and its relations. As she explained, "From all these experiences I clearly understood that the world is full of sorrow. We have no true relations, for all our relatives love us only to fulfill their own selfish needs. Human beings love each other out of desire. Nobody loves us selflessly. Only God loves us with selfless love."

Sudhamani clearly understood that to continue a close association with her uncle and aunt would be an obstacle to her goal in life. Finally she created circumstances which would free her from that bondage. One morning she quarreled heatedly with the family in order to break the agreement and left the house. The callous relatives even took back all the gifts which they had given her previously, including the earrings, and sent her home empty-handed. On leaving, Sudhamani exclaimed, "One day you will have to come to me begging. Until then I will never enter this house."

Eleven years later, financial troubles arose to plague her uncle's family, and they did come to Idamannel to plead for assistance from Sudhamani. Only then did she return to their house to perform worship and thereby bestow her blessing. That day Sudhamani's aunt bemoaned her past actions saying, "Oh, I never imagined

that the little one would become so great! How ruth-
lessly I scolded and beat her!"

The Supreme Lord never fails to fulfill His promise
to His true devotee. In the great epics of India many
such incidents exemplify the truth that God is the servant of His devotees.

CHAPTER THREE
TEARS FOR KRISHNA

Having no butter and milk to offer to Thee, I will offer Thee a little of my pain. O Kanna, at Thy feet I will offer the pearl drops of my tears.

- MATA AMRITANANDAMAYI -

Śrī Bhagavan Uvāca:
Mayyāveshya mano ye mām
    nitya yuktā upāsate
Śraddha parayopetās te me
    yuktatamā matāha

Mayyeva mana ādhatsva mayi
    buddim niveshaya
Nivasishyasi mayy eva ata
    ūrdhvam na samshayaha

The Blessed Lord said:

*Those who, fixing their mind on Me, worship Me,
ever steadfast and endowed with supreme faith,
they, in My opinion, are the best versed in Yoga.*

*Fix thy mind on Me only, place thy intellect in
Me; (then) thou shalt no doubt live in Me hereafter.*

SRIMAD BHAGAVAD GITA
CHAPTER 12, VERSES 2 & 8

RETURN TO IDAMANNEL

Returning to Idamannel from her uncle's house, Sudhamani, now about sixteen, became fully immersed in her spiritual practices while simultaneously shouldering the mountainous burden of household chores. Even in this land of saints, her tremendous passion for spiritual austerity while facing great opposition, stands unique and unparalleled.

As always her work was continuous worship of the Supreme. Anyone seeing Sudhamani in those days would have gasped with wonder. How could her little body

withstand such a heavy load? Damayanti had become
even more hot-tempered and cruel, since she now suffered from chronic rheumatism which had been aggravated by doing the housework during Sudhamani's
absence. Moreover, Sudhamani's compassionate nature,
which had led her to steal things from the relatives'
houses, had brought her a bad name. This redoubled
Damayanti's animosity toward her daughter. Even when
she faultlessly discharged her household duties,
Damayanti constantly scolded and beat her.

Despite such harsh treatment from her own mother,
Sudhamani held no grudge against her. In fact, years
later she would refer to Damayanti reverently as her
spiritual Guru. In her own words:

"Damayanti Amma was, in a way, my Guru. She
inculcated diligence, devotion and discipline in me.
She observed all of my actions meticulously. If there
were even a little scrap left in the courtyard after
sweeping, she would hit me. When all the vessels were
washed, she scrutinized them, and if there were even
a tiny trace of dirt, she would scold me. If even a
single twig of the broom happened to fall on the ground
as I swept, she would not spare me. If a speck of dust
or ash fell into the cooking pot, punishment would follow. Mother expected her daughters to say their prayers
early in the morning; she would not hesitate to pour a
pot of water on our faces, particularly on mine, if we
were late to rise because of exhaustion. When I plucked
grass for the cows, she would watch me from a distance to see if I indulged in gossip with others. She
even hit me with a wooden pestle used for pounding
rice. Witnessing my mother's actions, the local people

would often implore her, 'Please do not punish her like this! She will have to be given in marriage some day!' But all the while I realized that such experiences were only for my own good."

Readers may feel shocked by Damayanti's heartless treatment of her own daughter, especially since she was known as a pious woman. Actually, this is not hard to understand when we consider that her devotion was not based on knowledge. Many devotees have reverence for the gods and goddesses and regularly perform religious rites, but their concept of God is very limited. God is not perceived as dwelling in all beings, but rather He is contained within the four walls of the temple. Such devotees perform religious rites with an aim to fulfill their desires or to satisfy God. Their view of religion and worship has nothing to do with character building nor eradication of their own negative tendencies. These devotees have no desire to realize God or Self as their Supreme Goal. They worship because their fathers did so, or out of fear of incurring sin. However, devotees with understanding perceive God as all-pervasive and serve Him in all beings. They renounce all worldly desires and surrender their whole being at the Lotus Feet of the Lord. Their ultimate goal in life is to realize and become one with the Supreme Reality. Damayanti had a very limited vision of God and of spirituality, which was reflected in her harsh actions toward her unusual daughter.

Sometimes when Damayanti was about to thrash Sudhamani, the child would catch hold of her hand. Though small, Sudhamani was very strong. Unable to release her hand from Sudhamani's grip, she would

then try to kick her. The little one would then catch
hold of Damayanti's leg as well. Finding no other way
to punish her daughter, the mother resorted to biting
her. On occasion Damayanti even struck Sudhamani
with a machete used to open coconuts. The mother
regularly piled vulgar abuse upon the innocent child
without restraint.

Sudhamani could be very bold and impertinent at
times when dealing with her mother. When Damayanti
commanded, "Don't speak!" she would immediately
retort, "I will speak!" When Damayanti said, "Don't
do it!" Sudhamani would unhesitatingly insist, "I will
do it!" But the more she retaliated, the harsher the
punishment became. Damayanti would even curse her
daughter saying, "Let this defiant girl be damned! If
she grows up like this, she will surely bring a bad
reputation to the family. O God, why are You not put-
ting an end to her life?"

For her part, Sudhamani was not at all bothered by
her mother's cruel ways. In her eyes all people were
equal. Even from childhood, she would call elderly men
"father" and all elderly women "mother". This further
irritated her parents, who considered her peculiar way
of addressing others a disgrace to the family. They would
scold her saying, "Is it proper for you to call all these
dirty people your father and mother?" Sudhamani would
reply, "I have never seen my real Father and Mother.
Therefore, all are my father and mother."

The little one was prohibited from applying sacred
ash to her forehead. The family members would taunt
her saying, "Hey girl, are you going to become a *sannyasin*?" Sudhamani was not even permitted to dress

like ordinary girls. If she applied vermilion[11] to her forehead or wore a checkered blouse or clean jacket, she was mocked. "Why do you wear these colored clothes and apply vermilion? Who are you making a show for?" Girls should live with utmost modesty."

More amazing than the deplorable abuse of her family, was Sudhamani's unwavering tolerance for whatever befell her. Though at times she was saucy, she never harbored an iota of hatred for her tormentors. Later she would simply say, "Damayanti was not punishing me. She treated me poorly only because of her limited vision. All those trials led me along the correct path, so I have no hatred toward her."

One elder brother, Subhagan, was a veritable terror, not only to Sudhamani, but to the family and villagers as well. He was an arrogant atheist who insisted that women should be absolutely quiet and reserved. His hot temper was well known and Sudhamani became his frequent victim. He would not allow her to make friends with any girls her own age, as he was convinced that companions would ruin her character. When Sudhamani went to fetch drinking water for the family, she always went alone. If she happened to talk to some other girls, she could count on receiving a severe beating from Subhagan. This rule did not dismay Sudhamani; she much preferred to be alone remembering God without distraction.

In those days there was only one water tap for the whole village, and it ran on wind power. There was always a long queue for getting water from the pipe, and each person had to wait in turn. Sudhamani and the village women would gather with their clay pots, sometimes standing for hours waiting for the wind to blow. If there were a long queue, Sudhamani would have to leave her pots in the queue in order to gather grass for the cows. The other ladies, knowing her piety and hard-working nature, would lovingly fill her pot and keep it aside for her.

As mentioned earlier, Sudhamani often visited neighboring houses to collect vegetable scraps and rice gruel for the cows. If there were any delay, she would enter the family shrine room to sing a few devotional songs or meditate. Then she would spend some time with the elderly ladies of the house, lovingly inquiring about their well-being and listening intently to their sad tales. Even their own children maltreated and neglected them, just because they were old and infirm. Thus Sudhamani witnessed early in life the transience and selfishness of human relationships. Whenever possible she would take these old women home with her and give them a good hot water bath, a nourishing meal, and dress them in her family members' clothes.

If she came to know of anyone who was going without food, she would give them at least some raw foodstuffs from her own house. Sometimes she would bring home small children whom she would find wandering around, not properly attended or nourished by their own parents. Sudhamani would extend the necessary care before returning them to their homes.

One day Sudhamani was caught in the act of taking some food to give to a poor man. Though severely beaten, she refused to desist from her compassionate activities. She continued in the same way whenever she saw that help was needed. On another occasion Sudhamani saw a family starving for want of food. Finding nothing else, she gave them a gold bangle belonging to her mother which they could sell for enough money to buy the desperately needed food. When her father discovered the theft, he tied her to the trunk of a tree in a fit of fury and mercilessly beat her until her tender body bled. Despite such treatment, Sudhamani remained courageous and forgiving. She was overheard praying for God to pardon the terrible actions committed out of ignorance by her misguided relatives. While sitting in solitude, she prayed,

"O Krishna, what kind of world is this? Even the mother who gives birth treats the child with no kindness. Even she has no pure love for her own family. Where can I find selfless and pure love in this world? Is any love that I see truly genuine? Is it not a mere delusion?" Sometimes sitting in the family shrine room she would burst into tears thinking of all this and would cry aloud, "Krishna, Krishna! I have none in this world but You! My mind is always running after You, yearning to see Your Divine Form. Will You not take me with You? O Krishna, please come running!"

During this period an elderly man, who was a distant relative of the family, came to live at Idamannel. He no longer had any family or relatives and was in very poor health, unable even to walk. Completely bedridden, he was incontinent, and the bed was constantly soiled. Without being asked, Sudhamani immediately began attending to the old man and took complete responsibility for serving him. The other family members would barely look at him, let alone take on any of his care. Thus, in addition to her domestic chores,

Sudhamani sincerely and patiently attended to his needs. She would wash his clothes, give him a hot bath each day, remove his excreta and urine, and administer the prescribed medicines at the proper time. Though Sudhamani manifested an extraordinary abundance of noble virtues, no one in the family took any notice, much less understood or appreciated her all-embracing attitude toward life. It can only be divine paradox that the little one received only heaps of abuse for all that she did.

While she was doing her work, Sudhamani's habit was to remember Krishna by pretending that she herself was Krishna, Radha, the *Gopis*, or some other personality associated with Krishna's life.

Sometimes as she did the cooking, her heart would be filled with the form of Krishna's mother, Yashoda, who would churn the milk, nursing her babe Krishna. While Sudhamani readied her brothers and sisters for school, she imagined that she was adorning Krishna, Balarama and the *Gopas*[12] before they went out to graze the cows. Perceiving all this with her inner eye, she wept tears of joy. When she went to the market to purchase household goods, she recalled the *Gopis* who used to walk along the streets of Vrindavan selling milk and butter. Instead of calling out, "Milk, butter...," they would call out "Krishna, Madhava, Govinda, Achyuta...!" So intense was their devotion!

The *Gopis*' pure love and devotion for Sri Krishna was always a source of great inspiration for Sudhamani. At times she would imagine herself to be Radha, the beloved of Sri Krishna. The mere thought of Radha was enough to steal her mind and soon her awareness

of the outer world ebbed away. She would become totally absorbed in a divine mood and would sing, dance
and shed tears in ecstasy.

> *O dark-colored One,*
> *My eyes are pitifully burning for the sight of*
> *Thy Feet. O lotus-eyed One, come running*
> *With the cows and the music of the flute.*
>
> *For how many days have I been calling Thee?*
> *Hast Thou not even a little compassion?*
> *What great error have I committed?*
> *Art Thou not the Lover of devotees?*
>
> *Before I fall down crying,*
> *Deign to come with Thy flute,*
> *Unable to live as I am without seeing Thee*
> *Who art the sole Reality, come, come...*
>
> *Fulfiller of desires, Cause of all,*
> *O dark-colored One, come, come...*
> *Without wasting time and increasing my sorrow.*
> *O Embodiment of Compassion, come, come...*

While going to fetch water, Sudhamani would remember the *Gopis* who would go to the river Yamuna
carrying pots on their heads. As she washed her family's
clothes, she would imagine that she was washing the
silken robes of Krishna and the *Gopis*. After hanging
the clothes to dry, Sudhamani watched them fluttering
in the wind and thought, "O, see how beautifully
Krishna's golden yellow silk robes are dancing in the
breeze!" While collecting grass for the cows and feeding them, she would think intensely of Krishna who
daily acted as shepherd boy to the cows in the mead-

ows and forests of Vrindavan. Sudhamani would revel in the thought of the games of the divine Cowherd Boy and the *Gopis*.

Sudhamani's favorite time of day was dusk, when she would wade through the backwaters looking for the domestic animals, the ducks, goats and cows which had gone astray during the day. While doing so she would remember Krishna, who used to search for the cows and calves which had wandered away from the herd. If she heard any devotional singing, which is common in India during the twilight hour, she would stand motionless, transported to another realm. This would happen often, and an irritated family member would have to go out searching for the child.

Though Sudhamani was ceaselessly engaged in some sort of work, her mind was not at all in the work. Her mind was filled with longing, always chasing after Krishna. His Sacred Names were always on her lips and the very word "Krishna" would bring tears to her eyes. Because she was constantly carrying water, washing the family's clothes or wading through the backwaters, her simple garment would remain drenched day and night. In her own words, "I wanted so badly to see my clothes dry! Even though I had so much work, I would pray to God for more, so that I could always be busy dedicating my actions to Him. Carrying water for cooking and steaming pots of rice gruel on my head caused the hair on top of my head to fall out."

Whatever Sudhamani was doing, her lips kept moving. Nobody understood that she was incessantly repeating the Lord's Name. One day her younger brother, Satheesh, who had picked up the family members' habit of verbally abusing Sudhamani, cuttingly remarked, "Always moving one's lips is a symptom of madness!" Though she overheard Satheesh's comment, Sudhamani was unperturbed. Nevertheless, whenever Satheesh had a severe asthma attack, Sudhamani would carry him on her hip all the way to the hospital, even though there were others in the family who could have done it more easily. Nobody cared about his asthmatic condition but the innocent girl who was always waiting for a chance to serve and help others.

It was very late at night when Sudhamani finished her chores. Not a single light remained burning in her own house or in the neighborhood. Then Sudhamani would loudly sing to her Lord in the family shrine room. Damayanti and Subhagan would tongue lash her for singing in the darkness and disturbing their sleep. Her elder brother, Subhagan, would remark, "Why do you shout and howl like this? Is it so God can hear it in the heavens? Is your God deaf?" Though she had to suffer punishment and scolding, Sudhamani was not deterred from singing to God in the silent hours of the night. Once Subhagan came angrily into the shrine room and criticized her for singing in the darkness. Quick came the reply, "You behold only the external lamp, but within me burns a lamp which is never extinguished!" Needless to say, the inner significance of her remark was lost on the callous Subhagan.

Sudhamani had a fear that God would punish her mother, father, and brother for beating her while she chanted devotional songs. Therefore, she would often sing softly to prevent them from doing such evil actions. Deeply dejected by the obstacles created by her

family, Sudhamani would weep as she sat in the shrine
room. They then insisted that it was a sin for her to
weep while singing devotional songs, and that this would
cause them great danger. It made no difference what
Sudhamani did, they would find fault. Poor little Sudhamani! She silently endured everything and dissolved
all her miseries in the sweet memory of Sri Krishna.

Even from her childhood Sudhamani never confided
her sorrows to any human being. The only one to whom
she unburdened herself was Lord Krishna. Sudhamani
also had the habit of talking to animals and to Nature,
imagining that Krishna was listening attentively to her
words. Perceiving everything as Krishna, she conversed
with all creatures. If a cow happened to be lying down
resting, she would also lie down, leaning against its
body contentedly, thinking that she was lying on
Krishna's lap.

Looking at the stars, the moon and the flowering trees,
Sudhamani would ask, "O my friends, have you seen
my Krishna? O gentle breeze, have you ever caressed
His enchanting form? O glittering stars and silent moon,
are you also in search of Him? If you find Him, please
tell Him that this poor Sudhamani is also waiting to
see Him."

> Did anyone of you see my darling Kanna?
> You can see Him, but He never appears
> before my eyes...
>
> The mark of sandlepaste on the forehead,
> The beauty of the yellow silk robes,
> The waving locks of hair with the peacock
> feather...
> Oh, when will I behold all this?

Of what use is this body and this life of mine?
All my good fortune has ended...
For how much longer will these sufferings persist?

'Mother Sea' was also one of Sudhamani's friends, and she considered the ocean to be her own mother. Whenever she had a free moment, the child would slip off to the seaside and pour out her heart's miseries while gazing at the vast expanse of water. The dark blue color would remind her of her blue Beloved, and before long her external awareness slipped away.

Sudhamani had observed some of the neighbors earning their living by doing tailoring jobs. Prompted by the idea to help others with the money which she might earn from tailoring, she now cherished a desire to learn sewing. In this way, she could avoid the unpleasantness of having to take things from her house in order to help others. Full of hope, Sudhamani expressed her wish to her parents. Damayanti's reply was discouraging, "You are not going to be sent to learn sewing, but will soon be given in marriage to a coconut tree climber!" The coconut tree climbers were a low class of people in Kerala whose sole source of income was gained by plucking coconuts. Sudhamani had often been caught stealing coconuts, which Damayanti thought she ate, but which she had always given to the needy.

Sudhamani persisted, nevertheless, until her parents allowed her to learn sewing for one hour a day, with the condition that she complete all the domestic chores before leaving the house. On those days Sudhamani's routine was astounding. Somehow she would manage to complete the chores which had to be done before noontime, and then race off to her sewing class.

On some days other girls from the class, knowing Sudhamani's situation, would come help her finish her chores. In the scorching heat of the midday sun, Sudhamani would walk two or three kilometers to the sewing class. After one hour she would dash home in time to serve the noon meal.

The rest of the day continued as usual with her grueling schedule. The only moments she had for her most important duty, prayer and meditation, were in the silent hours of the night. Sobbing with longing, the little one would merge in a God-intoxicated state. Returning eventually to a semiconscious mood, she would drift off to sleep.

Sudhamani's patience, endurance and seemingly inexhaustible energy, which continue today, were miraculous. Whatever work was heaped on her she did happily, without murmuring a complaint. Sudhamani felt that her birthright and *dharma* were to extend help to everyone without being asked. Later she explained, "My joy lay in seeing others' happiness. I never thought of my own comfort and workload. Whenever I had the opportunity to serve others, I tried my best to assist them with utmost sincerity and love."

Initially Sudhamani studied sewing in two separate places. After some time she chose to attend the classes which were given in a parochial workshop in a nearby chapel. Quickly learning the mechanics of sewing, she began doing small tailoring jobs for the poor ladies in the neighborhood. At first she refused to accept money for her services, as this was not her way of doing things. Yet when her parents refused to pay the course fee for her classes, she was compelled to accept wages for her labor. Thus she managed to pay the class fee and used what remained to help the destitute villagers. She was also able to buy a few essential items for doing her sewing tasks. Sudhamani was adept at tailoring and earned a good wage. Without giving even a *paise*[13] to her house, she used her earnings only to help the poor.

While sewing in the chapel workshop, Sudhamani became immersed in devotional singing and shed tears which would fall on the sewing machine. The priest of the church was a pious, elderly man who took quick notice of Sudhamani's remarkable character. While the other girls gossiped, Sudhamani was absorbed in her devotion. The priest was deeply touched by this, and Sudhamani became very dear to him. This created jealousy among the other girls, yet the little one would show affection to them just as before, without a trace of animosity.

Satheesh always accompanied his sister to class, waiting for her in the church grounds or sitting in a corner. One day during prayer time Sudhamani asked, "Why are you not participating in the prayer?" He replied, "Are we not Hindus?" Sudhamani told him, "You ask the priest if you can also participate in the prayer." The priest happily agreed. From then on Satheesh always attended the prayers.

When her sewing was completed, Sudhamani would go to the church graveyard to do her embroidery. She loved the solitude there. Sitting in the graveyard she questioned the departed souls: "How is your life? Where are you living? Are you happy there? Do you have any feelings?" She clearly felt their company and sought to console them. A friend of Sudhamani's elder sister,

Kasturi, was buried in that cemetery. The girl had shown boundless love for Sudhamani even when her family was terribly abusing her. Perhaps this was another reason that Sudhamani liked visiting the graveyard. She would talk to the souls drifting along in their subtle bodies and would sing a sorrowful melody for their peaceful rest. Sometimes while sitting in meditation, Sudhamani entered into *samadhi* in the silence and stillness of the Christian graveyard.

If there were any time remaining after completing her embroidery work, Sudhamani would return to the chapel, which had an inner apartment like a cave. In the dim light, she would gaze upon the crucified form of Jesus Christ. Seeing Jesus on the cross, she felt Him to be her beloved Krishna. Immediately, she would become enraptured. Returning to the plane of normal consciousness, she would weep, thinking of the love and sacrifice of Jesus Christ and Krishna. She would think, "O, how They have sacrificed everything for the world! People turned against Them, but still They loved them. If They have done it, then why can't I? There is nothing new in it."

Sudhamani was acutely aware of the extreme poverty of the villagers. Seeing their sorrows and sufferings, the little one would weep in the silent hours she spent in the shrine room. She would pray, "O God, is this life? People are toiling day in and day out just for a bit of food to satisfy their hunger. O Krishna, why do you allow them to starve? Why do they become afflicted with diseases? Everywhere I turn I come face to face with selfishness and people's sufferings caused by it. Youngsters pray for a long life and children pray for an early death for their aged father and mother. Nobody is at all interested to care for the elderly. O Lord, what kind of a world is this? What is the purpose of creating such a world? O Krishna, what is the solution for all this?" Such were the prayers of the innocent girl.

Three years had passed when Sudhamani decided to discontinue her tailoring classes, considering them to be a distraction from her spiritual practices which she wanted to intensify. At that time the priest was also transferred to another parish. Before he left, he sent a few of the girls from the class to Idamannel to express his wish to bid farewell to Sudhamani. Accompanied by Satheesh, she went to visit the priest for the last time. Gazing at the child, the priest burst into tears and wept. Sudhamani stood with subdued emotions. The priest said, "Daughter, I am going to give up this job now. I have decided to lead the life of a *sannyasin.*" As Sudhamani and Satheesh were about to leave, the priest said to Satheesh, "You will see, Sudhamani will become great in the future." Perhaps the perceptive priest had already become aware of the shining divinity within the little one.

Having now mastered stitching, Sudhamani expressed her wish to have a machine of her own. Damayanti scolded her for being ambitious, but Sugunanandan promised several times that he would get a machine for her. However, the sewing machine never materialized. Sudhamani decided, "I won't ask for a machine again. Only if God gives one I will use it." After several years, when devotees began flocking to Idamannel, one of her Dutch devotees named Peter purchased a sewing machine for her, and she was reminded of her vow. God cares for every need of His true devotee.

All the children except Sudhamani were studying either in secondary school or college. They all were light in complexion and fair looking. Sudhamani's dark blue complexion and hard working nature made them all look down on her as a mere servant. She was not even given enough clothing. Seeing all these hardships of young Sudhamani and the antagonism of her parents and elder brother, the villagers would say, "Sudhamani was purchased in Quilon[14] in exchange for some paddy husk." Her parents would take all the children to the temples for festivals and other ceremonies, but always ignored Sudhamani and left her behind.

One day, Sudhamani received a checkered blouse and happily put it on. Her elder brother ordered her to remove it instantly. Snatching it from her hand, he set it on fire right in front of her shouting, "Only to attract the attention of others you wear these colored clothes!" Another time, Damayanti abused her for wearing a yellow silk jacket which belonged to one of her sisters. From then on, she decided that she would wear only clothes provided by the Lord, only old, worn out ones discarded by others. Sudhamani would cut these clothes up to make a blouse and skirt from them. She used the loose threads from an old clothesline to stitch the scraps of cloth together and felt happy not to be a burden to anyone. About those days she later said, "Without having proper thread, scissors or a sewing machine I would somehow manage to stitch my own clothes!"

CHAPTER FOUR

THE REAL FLUTE

The Real Flute is within. Try to enjoy playing It. Once that Sound is heard, one can be without death and birth.

- MATA AMRITANANDAMAYI -

Vaggadgadā dravatē yasya cittam
Rudatyabhīshnam hasati kvacicca
Vilajja udgāyati nrityatē ca
Madbhaktiyuktō bhuvanam punāti

The devotee whose voice is choked with emotion,
whose heart melts out of Love, who sobs again
and again, and at times begins to laugh, and shak-
ing off bashfulness begins to sing loudly and dance,
sanctifies the whole world.
                                    SRIMAD BHAGAVATAM
                      SKANDA X, CANTO XIV, VERSE 24

Spiritual glory and the strange behavior of a God-
Realized Soul are far beyond the understanding of
the consciousness of an ordinary human being. Some
people consider the thirst for God as madness, others
call it psychological repression, and still others refuse
to accept its reality altogether. The Great Souls remain
unperturbed. They never heed the senseless remarks
of skeptics and critics who cannot be blamed for their
limited perception of the subtle realms of consciousness. Is the physicist concerned because the man on
the street scorns the existence of sub-atomic particles?
Is he vexed by their baseless criticism?

No scoffing, no mockery, no derision had any effect
on the saintly Sudhamani. As she reached her late teens,
she was immersed in an unbroken stream of spiritual
awareness. Her devotion to Sri Krishna was indescrib-
ably intense. Sudhamani would ascend naturally and
spontaneously from one plane of consciousness to the
next. Wholly untouched by physical ordeal and mounting ridicule, she yearned incessantly for her Beloved,

pouring out her heart in melancholy love songs which she sang continually throughout the day and night.

> *A rainbow without colors, a flower without fragrance, when such is my heart, why cry for compassion?*

> *Life has become full of coldness, without even a trace of warmth, like a veena which has no sweet melody, but sorrowful silence alone...*

> *Can the lotus flowers in a small rivulet deep within the forest blossom where the rays of the sun cannot reach?*

> *Seeing the clouds in the sky, the peacock spreads its wings to dance, but in vain, and a chataka bird[15] waits for drops of water...*

Unable to grasp the significance of her rapturous devotional moods, Sudhamani's parents and elder brother would chastise and torture her mercilessly. They were convinced that all her godly activities were symptoms of some mental weakness or depression.

Sudhamani now spent her days and nights meditating, singing, and repeating the Divine Name. Often she would lock herself in the family shrine room and dance in ecstasy to the great disgust of her elder brother. At other times she would cry, overwhelmed by the pain of separation, and later be found unconscious in the sand. One can only wonder how her love for Krishna could continue to increase, for this love of hers knew no bounds. Her heart's gate stood wide open, and Sudhamani eagerly awaited the appearance of her Lord. How can one possibly describe the intensity of her dedication and self-surrender?

Sudhamani had an unquenchable thirst to hear the tales of Sri Krishna; whenever she overheard someone narrating His stories, her attention was immediately absorbed in Him, and she would enter into *samadhi*. Long after the story had ended, Sudhamani would sit motionless. By now the villagers found nothing strange or surprising in her otherworldly behavior. Sometimes Sudhamani would call small children aside and encourage them to enact the stories of Krishna. She would watch their plays with tears in her eyes, and during their story-telling would imagine that Krishna was sitting by her side narrating the tales. Forgetting the circumstances, she would hug the small children, thinking they were really Krishna Himself. Unaccustomed to such behavior and unfamiliar with Sudhamani's unusual moods, the youngsters would occasionally become frightened. It became the innocent girl's habit to worship small children by offering them *naivedyam*[16] and delicacies while singing prayers, genuinely seeing them as Sri Krishna.

If anyone happened to be awake in the silent hours of the night, he could hear the pitiful entreaties of the little one appealing to her Lord,

"Krishna, Krishna! My life's goal! When will I behold Your beautiful Form? Will my life and all my effort to see You end in vain? Are my prayers to become united with You unheard? O Krishna, You are said to be full of compassion for Your devotees. Have I displeased your merciful heart? Am I undeserving of being Your servant? For how many days will these prayers go unanswered? Do you feel no compassion for this lowly, forsaken child? O Kanna, have You also abandoned me? Where are You?...Where are You?..."

Finally she would collapse on the ground, but her nights remained sleepless. She waited and waited without closing her eyes, expecting that the Lord would come at any moment.

Sometimes Sudhamani would sculpt an image of Krishna out of clay and offer worship to it. She would mentally confide to her Beloved, "See, nobody has taught me how to serve You and how to worship You. Please forgive my errors!" Then, for lack of flowers, she would offer sand at the feet of the image. When the worship was over she would feel that Krishna Himself had arrived and was standing right in front of her. With trembling body and tear-filled eyes, Sudhamani would become overwhelmed with devotion and prostrate again and again before the clay image. The next moment she would feel that Krishna was about to run away, and in haste she would jump forward to catch hold of Him. Then she would realize that the whole play was only her imagination and that the clay idol was still only clay. Dissolving in tears and sobbing in dismay, she continued imploring Him, "Krishna, Krishna! Please come and bless this one who is being torn to pieces with longing for Your vision! Is this all to test my love for You? Why do You hesitate? O Kanna, I can endure any torment except this separation from You. O Krishna, has Your heart lost all its compassion?"

Sudhamani was not to be discouraged. Full of eager anticipation, the humble girl confidently waited for the arrival of her Lord. Sometimes she considered herself to be the beloved of Krishna, while at other times she was His servant. This unlettered child, who hadn't studied past the fourth grade and had never read the *Vedas* or *Upanishads*, became the embodiment of supreme devotion to Lord Krishna. Different aspects of supreme devotion spontaneously manifested in young Sudhamani.

At this point, the financial affairs of the family took a sharp turn for the worse, as Sugunanandan suffered a great loss in his fish marketing business. Damayanti and the family became very desperate. One day Damayanti told Sudhamani, "Why is God giving us sorrow? Daughter, pray for your father. All his businesses have ended in failure. Sudhamani thought, "O Krishna, how does sorrow begin? What is the root cause of it? Mother is dejected because she desires happiness from her husband and wishes to live comfortably. Is it not desire which brings unhappiness? O darling Krishna, let me not get entangled in it! If I depend on human beings who are immersed in desire and ignorance, then surely I too will become sorrowful. O Krishna, let my mind always cling to Your Lotus Feet!"

During this time, despite their financial trouble, Sudhamani's parents decided to get her married somehow. Damayanti had always been very particular about the raising of her four daughters and her conceit on this point was no secret among the villagers. Her daughters should be perceived as upstanding and virtuous by the community. If their reputations were damaged, then everything was lost in Damayanti's eyes. Toward this end, Damayanti brought up her daughters with extremely strict discipline. They were not permitted to talk to any men, especially young men.

In those days all four sides of Idamannel were surrounded by water, yet Damayanti had a fence built around the house for further protection from intruders. Even then she was not satisfied, so she kept a dog in the house in order to give warning if anyone came near. When the dog barked, she would call Subhagan to see who it was. If it were a stranger or a young man, the brother refused to open the door. Damayanti was always worried about her grown-up daughters. Hence she was eager to be rid of Sudhamani, a big part of her burden.

Sugunanandan and Subhagan finally found a suitable bridegroom for Sudhamani, and a day was arranged for the first meeting to take place. In this way the parents could make sure that the young people liked each other before the marriage was performed. The arrangements were made without Sudhamani's knowledge or consent. Not only that, the meeting was to take place in another house, far away from Idamannel. On the chosen day, a lady came to Sudhamani's home on the pretext of employing her to do a tailoring job. She asked Sudhamani to accompany her to her house in order to take all the measurements for her daughters' skirts and blouses.

When Sudhamani arrived at the house, she understood that their intention was entirely different. Offering her a glass of tea, the lady said, "Look here, Sudhamani, there is someone sitting in the next room. Give this tea to him." This is the customary way of introducing a bride to her groom. Clearly knowing their secret intent, Sudhamani replied in a serious tone, "I cannot. I have come to take measurements, not to serve tea." Walking out of the house, she returned home and told Damayanti about the incident. Only then did she understand that all the arrangements had, in fact, been made by her own parents and elder brother.

Another marriage proposal came for Sudhamani. This time the bridegroom and his party were to come to Idamannel. When the prospective husband arrived, Damayanti sweetly asked Sudhamani to bring some bananas for him. In the guests' presence the unwilling bride retorted, "I won't do it! If you want, you can go buy bananas for him!" That was the end of that proposal!

But the parents refused to give up their idea. Still another proposal came for Sudhamani, and it was arranged again for the groom to visit Idamannel. Beforehand, Damayanti approached Sudhamani pleading and crying, "Daughter, please don't bring a bad reputation upon us. Please act politely to your future husband." When the expectant youth arrived to meet Sudhamani, he sat quietly in the living room. Sudhamani was busy in the kitchen pounding dried red chilies with a wooden pestle. She had already decided to face the situation in a more crude way than before. Holding the pestle with both hands like a soldier ready to attack his enemy with a bayonet, Sudhamani stood screaming, threatening him by waving the pestle, and making ridiculous gestures. Damayanti nearly fainted from shame, but the little one was not ready to give up so easily. She continued her drama until the bridegroom's party fled the house, thinking that she was insane. Sudhamani, of course, promptly received her punishment of harsh kicks and blows.

After this incident, Sudhamani decided that if her

parents again disturbed her with marriage proposals, she would quit the house and continue her devotional practices in a cave or some other lonely place. In this matter of marriage she was determined, but she felt certain that her parents would not make another attempt for a long time.

The family's ill treatment continued to worsen. Unwilling to endure the situation any longer, Sudhamani decided to run away from home. On the same day, a scrap of newspaper, blown by the wind, fell on the ground right in front of her. She picked it up and, to her astonishment, found that it was a clipping which reported the terrible fate of a girl who had run away from home. Taking this as an obvious communication from God, Sudhamani gave up the idea of leaving the house.

On another occasion, the fierce harassment by her family members led her to decide to put an end to her life by jumping into the sea. Considering this idea, she thought, "Who is dying? Who is taking birth? Who can harass a true devotee of the Lord?" This strong conviction chased the thought of dying from her mind.

During those days of intense *sadhana*, Sudhamani could not sleep in any other house or eat food prepared in a worldly person's kitchen. If she happened to eat such food, she became extremely restless or vomited. For this reason, most days Sudhamani would fast. If she tried to stay in some other house, where worldly people had slept, she could not get a moment of rest. Yet, she was not bothered about sleep, as she preferred to stay awake to meditate and call on her Beloved. She even had a fear of falling asleep, lest

Krishna come at that moment and she miss the long-awaited Vision of His Divine Form.

Even at this stage, Sudhamani somehow managed to discharge her household duties without fail. Because of her continuous toilsome work, the villagers nick-named her "Kaveri". Kaveri was an ideal character endowed with all virtues. Even if she were ill, she would go from house to house selling milk. Seeing her terrible hardships and her noble qualities, the villagers had immense respect and love for Sudhamani.

The bitter experiences of life which she had to face and the brutal environment in which she grew up convinced Sudhamani of the fleeting and selfish nature of worldly life. Only deep contemplation of life and its goal occupied her mind. Contemplating the mystery of life, she would think, "O God, do You not see all these sorrows and sufferings? Am I alone in this world? Who is my real relative? Who is my Father and who is my Mother? Where is the Truth in all of this? If one takes a human body, is one destined to suffer?" Sudhamani always had sympathy for ordinary people who craved the momentary pleasures of worldly life. She would pray for them, "O Lord, please save those who suffer from ignorance, mistaking the ephemeral world for something great. Please give them right knowledge."

Cows were very dear to Damayanti. Even if the family members had to suffer, she would not allow the cows to undergo any hardship. In her eyes, cows were equal to God. During the season of the southwest monsoons, the Kerala backwaters would overflow the riverbanks and become one with the Arabian Sea, causing flooding all along the coast. At Idamannel, the family cowshed would succumb to the rising floodwaters, and during those times Damayanti would herd the cows inside the house! The living room would become filled with cow dung and urine. All the family members would protest, cursing Damayanti, except Sudhamani of course, who loved the cows even more than her mother did because of the affectionate role they played in the life of Sri Krishna.

To her all seasons were equally inspiring, for her everything was the Divine Play. She was not at all worried about the scorching heat of summer, the heavy downpour of the monsoon season, nor the chilling ocean breezes of winter. She could see nothing in Nature but her Beloved. She had nothing to gain from this world; her sole aim was to merge in the Lotus Feet of Sri Krishna. Even the sound of the rain falling would fill Sudhamani's heart with love. For her, all sounds resembled the sacred syllable, 'OM', especially that of the falling rain. She would sing the praises of her Lord in consonance with that sound. Happily she would watch the rain, visualizing Krishna standing in each raindrop.

As Sudhamani's spiritual practices intensified, her abstracted moods became more and more noticeable. Sometimes she would enter the bathroom for a shower, but would be discovered there hours later, oblivious to the surroundings. These states of Sudhamani were a mystery to the family who was convinced that she was suffering from some kind of mental aberration. The little one was a lonely traveler in her own world. How can we imagine the spiritual depth of this innocent girl whose love knew no bounds? What force but God Himself was leading her deeper and deeper toward Self-Realization?

Often, while collecting leaves to feed the goats, Sudhamani was accompanied by small companions who always followed her wherever she went. They loved her company; Sudhamani was their leader. Sitting on a branch of a tree plucking leaves, Sudhamani would become overpowered with the distinct feeling that she herself was Krishna. She later recalled, "All the boys and girls standing below me seemed to be the *Gopas* and *Gopis*."

She had many divine visions. Krishna would come late at night and appear before her. The Divine Flute Player would catch hold of her hands and dance with her. At other times, He would play with her and make her laugh. In those blissful moments, she would dance like never before in divine ecstasy, the dance of Radha and Krishna. At these times, she would hear the enchanting sound of Krishna's flute. At first, she thought that Krishna was playing His heavenly flute standing somewhere nearby, but then realized with astonishment that the sound was coming from within her! Immediately she would burst into tears and collapse in front of Sri Krishna's portrait. If she happened to sleep, within no time Krishna would appear to wake her. Sudhamani later remarked, "His complexion was a combination of dark blue and light red." Sometimes she saw a cot spread with different kinds of fragrant flowers. Catching hold of the little one's hands, Krishna would dance on it with her. He would take her up above the clouds and show her different worlds and beautiful scenery. But Sudhamani thought, "What attraction do these things have if He is not there? He is the Essence; the external appearance of these worlds will go on changing!" Her conviction held firm. Her inner flight to her Beloved was a frequent occurrence. The little one's surrender had become complete.

Sometimes Sudhamani saw Krishna walking along beside her. At other times, when she herself became inwardly identified with Krishna, she would feel like tearing all the pictures of gods and goddesses, including that of Krishna, off the wall. "These portraits are just paper and paint; they are not Krishna! I myself am Krishna!" The next moment her attitude would change, "No, I should not tear down these pictures; it was this portrait which helped me to attain Krishna. Everything is pervaded by Krishna, the Supreme Consciousness. Therefore, this portrait is also That!"

Beholding and realizing everything as Krishna marked the culmination of years of sacrifice and yearning. Now Sudhamani was seen embracing trees, kissing plants and small children as, wherever she turned, she saw the enchanting form of Lord Krishna. There was not even an infinitesimal point where He was absent.

Later, she said about this period,

"I used to look at Nature and see everything as Krishna. I could not even pluck a single flower, because I knew that it was also Krishna. When the breeze touched my body, I felt that it was Krishna caressing me. I was afraid to walk because I thought, 'Oh, I am stepping on Krishna!' Every particle of sand was Krishna for me. Now and then I strongly perceived myself to be Krishna. Gradually this became a natural state. I could no longer find any difference between myself and Krishna who dwelled in Vrindavan."

Thus Sudhamani became established in the Ocean of Pure Existence and Bliss and attained perfect peace of mind. However, her identity with the Supreme still remained unknown to the family and villagers. Though externally she looked like the same ordinary village girl, internally she was one with the Lord Krishna, the natural state of abiding as the One Reality.

CHAPTER FIVE

FOR THE GOOD
OF THE WORLD

All the Deities of the Hindu Pantheon, who repre-sent the infinite aspects of the One Supreme Being, exist within us as well. A Divine Incarnation can manifest any one of them for the good of the world by mere will. The Divine Mood of Krishna (Krishna Bhava) is the manifestation of the Purusha or Pure Consciousness aspect of the Absolute.

- MATA AMRITANANDAMAYI -

Vamsī vibhūshita karāt navanīra dabhāt
Pitāmbarāt aruna bimba phalā taroshtāt
Purnēntu sundara mukhāt aravinda nētrāt
Krishnāt param kimapi tatva maham na
jāne

*I know no Reality other than Sri Krishna Whose
hands hold the flute, Who is beautiful like a fresh
raincloud, Who wears yellow robes, Whose lips
are red like an aruna bimba fruit, Whose face is
charming like the full moon and Whose eyes are
elongated like lotus petals.*

MADHUSUDANA SARASWATI

ADVENT OF KRISHNA BHAVA

Young Sudhamani, whose entire being had found eternal rest in the Supreme, now struggled to carry on
with the household chores as before. She tried hard to
discharge her duties, but, as we shall see, this was not
what the Divine had in store for her.

On a Wednesday evening in the month of September, 1975, certain events occurred which would later
mark the beginning of a new chapter in the annals of
India's spiritual history. Sudhamani had just finished
collecting grass for the cows, and was returning home
about five in the afternoon, accompanied by her younger
brother, Satheesh. Carrying a big bundle of grass on
her head, she was in her usual sublime mood and the
melody of a devotional song was on her lips. As the
two passed the entrance gate of the neighboring house
on the northern side of Idamannel, Sudhamani came to

an abrupt halt. She had overheard the final verses of the *Srimad Bhagavatam* being read aloud in the courtyard.[17] The reading had come to an end and the devotional singing was just beginning.

Sudhamani stood motionless, captured by the moment, and appeared to be intently listening to the singing. Suddenly her mood changed dramatically. The bundle of grass fell from her head as she ran to the spot and stood in the midst of the devotees gathered there. Overwhelmed with divine bliss, her inner identification with the Lord overflowed into her external being, transforming her features and movements into those of Sri Krishna Himself!

Stunned, the devotees believed that Sri Krishna had indeed come to them suddenly in the form of this village girl in order to bless them. Sudhamani asked one of the devotees to bring some water, which she then sprinkled on everyone as sacred water. News of Sudhamani's Divine Manifestation spread quickly, and soon a large crowd gathered. Some skeptics raised objections to the little one's sudden Divine Mood saying, "If you are really Lord Krishna, then you must show us proof through a miracle. Otherwise, how can we believe?" Instantly came the reply,

"An object which does not already exist cannot be brought into existence. All things are really only the projection of the mind. Having the Real Gem within you, why do you crave an imitation? Even though Pure Being is within you, ignorance is veiling it!"

Unable to grasp this sublime truth uttered by one established in Pure Being, they pressed her again and again to show a miracle. Sudhamani responded,

"I am not interested in making someone a believer by showing a miracle. My intention is not to show miracles. My goal is to inspire people with the desire for liberation through realization of their Eternal Self. Miracles are illusory. They are not the essence of spirituality. Not only that, once a miracle is shown, you will demand to see one again and again. I am here not to create desire, but to remove it."

The skeptics insisted, "No, we won't ask again; show us a miracle once, we won't insist again!" At last Sudhamani conceded, "In order to inculcate faith in you, I will do it once, but never again approach me with such desires. Those who doubt, let them come to this same place on the day of the next *Srimad Bhagavatam* discourse."

When the next *Bhagavatam* discourse was held, a huge crowd had gathered inside and outside the house. The nonbelievers even climbed trees and perched on rooftops, hoping to expose a fraud. Revealing her oneness with Krishna, Sudhamani told one of the doubters to bring a pitcher of water, which, as before, she sprinkled on the devotees as sacred water. Then she asked the same man to dip his fingers in the remaining water. To everyone's amazement the water had become pure milk! This was then distributed among the crowd as a holy offering from God. Then Sudhamani called another skeptic, asking him to dip his fingers in the pitcher. The milk in the pot had now turned into a sweet and fragrant pudding (*panchamritam*) made of milk, bananas, raw sugar, raisins, and rock sugar. All present raised a cry, "O God! O God!" and believed themselves to be truly in the Divine Presence of Lord

Krishna. The *panchamritam* was distributed among more than a thousand people who had gathered, yet the pot remained full to the brim. Some people who were sitting at a distance near a small banyan tree at the seaside also received the sweet pudding, but still the vessel's contents did not diminish. A few skeptics, still not satisfied, declared the whole incident a feat of mesmerism, insisting that the *panchamritam* would vanish within a few seconds. Much to their disappointment, it did not vanish, and the sweet scent remained on everyones' hands for several days. This event greatly increased the faith of the villagers, who now all firmly believed in Sudhamani's divinity.

Referring to the advent of *Krishna Bhava*, Sudhamani subsequently explained,

"In the early days, I used to dance in bliss and move about alone, persisting in *Krishna Bhava*, but no one knew. One day I strongly felt the urge to be absorbed in the Supreme Being without returning. Then I heard a voice from within saying, 'Thousands and thousands of people in the world are steeped in misery. I have much for you to do, you who are one with Me.'"

It was after hearing this voice that Sudhamani manifested her inner identity with Lord Krishna to the villagers. Sudhamani continued,

"I was able to know everything concerning everyone. I was fully conscious that I, myself, was Krishna, not only during that particular time of manifestation, but at all other times as well. I did not feel, 'I am great'. When I saw people and knew their sufferings, I felt immense pity for them. I was conscious of devotees offering salutations to me and addressing me as 'Lord'. I could understand the sorrows of the devotees, even without being told."

From that time on, Sudhamani regularly revealed *Krishna Bhava* near a small banyan tree growing on the western side of Idamannel near the seashore path. Around the tree there were lovely flowering plants as well. A few years earlier the villagers had planned to construct a temple there. To inaugurate the temple site, some of the village youth had planted another banyan tree and lighted a sacred oil lamp.

Sugunanandan had encouraged the youths and had actively participated in their efforts. His elderly mother, Madhavi, often accompanied by Sudhamani, would come each evening, light the oil lamp and sing some sacred songs. A tiny hut, thatched with woven coconut leaves, had been built in front of the banyan tree, and portraits of Lord Krishna and Mother Kali had been installed inside.[18]

Now several years later, this became the spot where Sudhamani revealed her identity with Lord Krishna. As the piece of land was public property, it was a convenient location for people to gather to participate in the auspicious *Krishna Bhava*. Lying horizontally on a slender branch of the banyan tree, Sudhamani would assume the posture of *Anantasayana*, Lord Vishnu reclining on the thousand-headed serpent, Ananta. By self-will her body would become as light as air at this time. This was a wonderful sight for the devotees.

This sacred spot became a veritable Vrindavan, the Abode of Sri Krishna, and the atmosphere was pervaded with devotional songs in praise of the Lord. Devotees began to flock to the place, not only for the auspicious darshan of Sri Krishna, but also to obtain relief from their problems. The devotees' distress would mysteriously vanish after they had unburdened their troubles to Sudhamani during the *Krishna Bhava*.

In those days, when people prayed for a solution to their problems, Sudhamani, as Krishna, would instruct them to light a piece of camphor and place the burning camphor on her protruding tongue. She would then swallow it along with the fire! After the *Bhava* had ended, nobody could find a trace of a burn on her tongue. This practice also increased the faith of the people.

News of *Krishna Bhava* quickly spread, and people from Kerala and other parts of India began flocking to Parayakadavu. This marked the beginning of a pilgrimage to this holy place which has continued with ever increasing numbers of seekers to this day. Some people came asking for relief from disease, some sought freedom from material difficulties, others came out of curiosity, and some came out of devotion. But one thing they all discovered was that after coming to Sudhamani, they found a solution for their problems.

One group of local skeptics began coming with the hope of exposing a fraud, which was how they perceived Sudhamani's Divine Mood. But the little one remained equipoised under all circumstances. She would later explain,

"During the *Bhava*, different kinds of people come to see me, some out of devotion, others for a solution to their worldly problems, and others for relief from diseases. I discard none. Can I reject them? Are they different from me? Are we not all beads strung on the one life thread? According to each one's level of thinking

they see me. Both those who love me and those who
hate me are the same to me."

During the first two Krishna *Bhavas*, Sugunanandan
had been out of town on business. When he came to
hear of the mysterious transformation of his daughter,
he suspected it to be some undiagnosed disease. However, he decided to see the *Krishna Bhava* for himself
before making a decision. Therefore, he arranged a
Bhagavatam reading at Idamannel, and, on that day,
Sudhamani again revealed her oneness with Sri Krishna.
Having seen the Divine Mood of his daughter, who since
birth had been full of surprises, Sugunanandan was
wonderstruck and could not utter a word. From then
on, Sugunanandan, who had always been an ardent
devotee of Lord Krishna, participated in all the *Bhava
Darshans*, which had become a regular event in this
sacred coastal fishing area.

At this point, the parents still believed that
Sudhamani's Divine Moods were only possessions of
Lord Krishna and that her devotional practices were
temporary aberrations that would stop one day. They
waited for that day to come, so that they could give her
in marriage. They cannot be blamed for their misconception, as they were not at all aware of Great Souls
and their behavior. Theirs was a simple view of God:
His manifestations on earth were, in their mind, limited strictly to the idols of the gods and goddesses in
the shrine rooms and temples. God was not to be found
elsewhere, least of all in their eccentric daughter!

Notwithstanding their previous experiences, the parents again made arrangements for Sudhamani's marriage, and again Sudhamani fiercely threatened any

prospective groom who was unfortunate enough to arrive at Idamannel. Finally, Sudhamani angrily warned her parents, "If you succeed in giving me in marriage, I will kill the man, and then come back to Idamannel!"

The parents, having bitterly failed to marry off Sudhamani, decided to seek the advice of a well-known astrologer,[19] who lived in a distant place, and had never heard of Idamannel, Sudhamani or her Divine Mood. The parents were full of hope that at last they would circumvent her stubbornness. After consulting Sudhamani's horoscope, the astrologer turned to Sugunanandan, and said in a solemn tone, "This girl is a *Mahatma* (Great Soul or Saint)! If the marriage is not yet arranged, please do not make any further effort to do so. If the marriage has already taken place, call her back immediately. Otherwise you will have to face a great calamity; it will be the cause of great sorrow for you." The dejected father returned home with a heavy heart, and all plans for Sudhamani's marriage were dropped.

When people understood that Sudhamani's manifestation of *Krishna Bhava* was genuine, more and more of them came to receive her blessings. At the same time, some people came hoping to take advantage of Sudhamani's divine benevolence to further their selfish motives and to make money. One night, some people approached Sudhamani to see if she could be tempted by money. They offered her a large sum if she would show them some miracles. Sudhamani laughed out loud and affectionately told them,

"I have nothing to gain by showing miracles. My goal is not to gain fame and material prosperity by exhibiting miracles. There is an immense and inexhaustible wealth of divinity within us. Discarding that, why should one chase after the perishable and trivial wealth of the world? Selfless service to God and suffering humanity is my life's goal. I am here not to earn anything, but to renounce everything for the happiness of others."

Every day the number of devotees increased, as the wonderful experiences of those who had come to Sudhamani in *Krishna Bhava* inspired others also to take refuge in her. The seashore around the banyan tree came alive with devotional singing, and the villagers, forgetting their differences, gathered together to receive her blessings.

On one occasion, a huge crowd of devotees had gathered at the sacred banyan shrine during *Krishna Bhava*. Suddenly, dark menacing storm clouds gathered overhead, and a downpour quickly followed. As there was no shelter available nearby, the devotees simply stood waiting for the inevitable drenching. But to the amazement of all, no rain fell on the place where the devotees were standing, although it fell in torrents all around them!

During this period, a poisonous cobra often frightened people walking in the village, particularly at night. People frequently saw the cobra moving freely about, and everyone became afraid to walk along the seashore at night. Some of the villagers approached Sudhamani during *Krishna Bhava* to pray for a solution. Then one evening during the Divine Mood the dreaded serpent made an appearance. The crowd scattered, cowering at a distance. Sudhamani fearlessly caught hold of the cobra and touched its flicking tongue to her own! Then she released it. Never again were the villagers troubled by the venomous snake, and once more they were able to walk freely along the shore.

Once the 'Children of Mother Sea,' as the fisherfolk were known, were starving, because they had been unable to catch any fish for many days. They approached Sudhamani during *Krishna Bhava* and confided their misery to her. Giving them a *tulasi* leaf,[20] she instructed them to have a young boy drop it into the sea at a particular spot and then to fish there. In order to test her, the fishermen did not act on her advice but approached her again during the next *Darshan* (audience). Before they could say a word, Sudhamani pointed out their mischief and once again offered them a *tulasi* leaf. Surprised and remorseful, they accepted the leaf and proceeded to the sea, but somehow they failed to drop it in the designated spot. Taking pity on them during the next *Darshan*, Sudhamani blissfully danced on the seashore and, in that way, bestowed her blessing. To the fishermen's great joy and relief, the next day a vast school of fish swam right up to the shore. Never before in the history of the village had there been such a bountiful catch. On two other occasions Sudhamani performed similar wonders in response to the sincere prayers of the fishermen. But this self-centered and desire-prompted devotion of the villagers did not win much favor or encouragement from Sudhamani.

Though *Krishna Bhava* was the external manifestation of Sudhamani's infinite spiritual power, which she expressed through the form of Krishna, her parents and most of the villagers believed that she was merely being possessed temporarily by Lord Krishna during the time of the *Bhava*. Her elder brother and parents also had the idea that she was suffering from schizophrenia or some other mental delusion. For her part, Sudhamani was willing to let them believe that. At this point, apparently she was content that the people were feeling devotion to God and relief from their worldly sufferings as a result of the *Bhava Darshan*. This divine drama was to unfold in its further stages and at the proper moment according to the needs of the people.

Conducting the *Bhava Darshan* near the seaside had its drawbacks, although it was true that the devotees could gather there freely. While some came out of reverence and devotion, a persistent group came to abuse and harass Sudhamani. Not only that, but the rapid increase in the number of devotees had given rise to some odd developments around the banyan tree. One self-motivated group of villagers had even formed an administrative board which promptly decided to install a locked box for monetary offerings for themselves. This was the forewarning of the formation of a troublesome alliance.

These occurrences made Sugunanandan very sad. One night he approached Sudhamani during the *Krishna Bhava* and expressed his concern, "It is painful for me to see You performing *Bhava Darshan* on this roadside. Also it is intolerable to hear nonbelievers poking fun at You. Besides, You are my daughter, and it breaks my heart to see You surrounded by all sorts of people in a public place." Saying this, he burst into tears.

Sudhamani replied, "In that case, give Me another place to receive My devotees. If there is no other place, that cowshed will suffice." Sugunanandan readily agreed, and arrangements were made to repair the cowshed. It was cemented, and a half-wall added down the middle to divide it into two sections. One side remained a cowshed, and the other side was prepared for the *Bhava Darshan*. All four sides were covered with woven palm leaves.

Soon the *Bhava Darshan* was shifted from the seaside banyan tree shrine to Idamannel, where it continues to the present day. During *Krishna Bhava*, Sudhamani stood now in the newly built shrine. While leaning on the half-wall, she would now and then reach over to put her hand on one of the cows which were standing on the other side.

One night during *Krishna Bhava*, Sudhamani called her father and told him, "My devotees will come from far and wide. Many of the devotees will settle here permanently. You will have to face many obstacles, but do not be afraid. Endure everything. Do not take revenge against anyone. Do not be envious. Do not seek anything from anyone. Everything you need will come to you unasked. Always give part of what you receive in charity. In time, this place will become a great spiritual center. The little one will travel around the world many times. Though you may have to suffer a lot in the near future, God will always bless you and provide for your needs. Your relatives and even the villagers will hate you and abuse you, but in time they will become your friends. Thousands of My devotees will become like your own children. From this day on, the little one is ever pure."

Once more, Sugunanandan was wonderstruck! His

dark blue daughter, who had suffered countless beatings at his own hands, was going around the world?! Why, she had never been as far as Cape Comorin![21] Thousands of people were coming to Idamannel? Where on earth would they all stay? The house was tiny! And what was the meaning of her saying that the little one was ever pure?[22] Though these words left a deep impression in Sugunanandan's mind, at the time he dismissed them as crazy utterances. Only after years had passed did he realize the absolute truth of what his daughter had said to him that day.

Some of the local people found that their interests had suffered from the relocation of *Krishna Bhava*, and loudly protested saying, "We don't want a God who follows her father's wishes!" The devotees who used to sing at the banyan tree shrine now split into two groups. One group declared its opposition in the form of noncooperation, while the other group came to Idamannel to sing *bhajans* (devotional songs) during the *Bhava Darshan* as before. Exasperated by the loyal group of devotees, a group of villagers began coming to Idamannel with the sole intent to quarrel and cause trouble. They abused the *bhajan* singers openly, as they sang during the *Bhava Darshan*. This antagonistic group, consisting of both men and women, persisted until one day Sugunanandan became completely fed up. He and some other devotees chased them out of Idamannel, but this was only the beginning of the trouble.

THE RATIONALIST MOVEMENT

Some of the truculent group were sons of the village landlords. They banded together to form an organization which they named "The Committee to Remove Blind Beliefs", also known as "The Rationalist Movement." From thirteen coastal villages they managed to round up a thousand youths, who began their campaign to put an end to Sudhamani's Divine Mood.

The villagers had loved the virtuous and noble minded Sudhamani since her childhood, when she used to greet each morning with her enchanting singing to Krishna. Furthermore, they had unwavering devotion and faith in her Divine Mood, but Sugunanandan's unyielding nature aggravated the latent feelings of envy or enmity that some had. From the outset of *Krishna Bhava*, Sudhamani had warned her father during one *Darshan* not to quarrel with anyone or take revenge on anyone who opposed her. Not heeding her divine advice, Sugunanandan took some steps against the committee, which only intensified the enmity of the so-called rationalists.

They began by inventing slogans mocking Sudhamani. They then published notices filled with baseless and irrational criticism of her. Their vindictive campaign did not end there; their effort to defame Sudhamani and bring an end to *Krishna Bhava* had just begun. Their next step was to lodge a false petition with the police against her, stating that she was cheating people in the name of devotion! As a result of the petition, some police officers came to Idamannel to interrogate her. Wholly unperturbed, Sudhamani told the officers, "Please arrest me if you like, and take me to jail. Here, the family and villagers do not allow me to meditate. At least in jail I shall have solitude to

meditate on God. If it is God's Will, let it be done."
Having spoken, she stretched out her hands. The police officers were very much impressed to see her bold
yet innocent way of addressing them and facing the
situation. A few thought she must be crazy, but the
others were charmed by her personality and felt sorry
that such a Great Soul was being rudely scandalized
and persecuted for nothing. These officers paid their
homage and left Idamannel. The following song was
composed by Sudhamani during the time of the false
petition and police inquiry:

> Thou art compassionate to the devotees...
> O Pure Consciousness!
> Destroyer of all transgressions!
> Are there only sinners in this world?
>
> O Bhagavan! O Bhagavan![23]
> Who is there to instruct in the righteous path?
> The Essential Principles[24] are only found
> Printed on the pages of books...
>
> O Bhagavan! O Bhagavan!
> What one sees is just
> False costume and trumpery.
> O Kanna, please protect and
> Restore righteousness!

One evening at twilight while the devotional singing was going on, another police officer, who was not
satisfied with the first investigation, came to Idamannel
on the basis of some new complaint. To his surprise
the atmosphere had a soothing effect on him and, unable to find anything offensive or amiss, he also left
the place without uttering a word.

The miscreants still continued their efforts to put
an end to Sudhamani's Divine Mood. They now turned
to much more direct and aggressive tactics to achieve
their end. Their next plan was to go to Idamannel in
small groups during the *Bhava Darshan* and seize Sudhamani during the Divine Mood, thus dishonoring her
and at the same time making a sham of the *Darshan*.
After catching hold of her, they intended to rough her
up. These hooligans were convinced that their straight-
forward plan would succeed, as they prided themselves
on their courage and strength. However, before the night
was over they left Idamannel full of shame, as, for
some inexplicable reason, not one among them dared
to approach Sudhamani during the Divine Mood.

Undeterred, they now hired a black magician infamous for his deadly sorcery. He himself came to
Idamannel and offered Sudhamani some so-called 'sacred ash', in which he had invoked malevolent forces.
This ash was prepared from the charred body of a cobra
and was known to be so powerful that its evil effects
would cause death to the person to whom it was given.
Even to receive such ash in one's hand was considered
a bad omen which would bring about great disaster.
Fully aware of the supposed consequences, Sudhamani
took the ash and rubbed it on her body in front of the
misguided man. She thought to herself, "If the body is
to perish by this, let it be so. If it is God's Will, can
anyone escape it?" The unscrupulous man waited a
long time to witness the agonizing effects of his sorcery which never materialized. Finally, he had to leave,
admitting utter defeat, as nothing unusual had occurred
even after hours had passed.

Now desperate to finish off Sudhamani and her Divine Mood, the miscreants launched their most treacherous plan. During the *Krishna Bhava* they entered the temple and offered Sudhamani a glass of milk laced with deadly poison. Sudhamani played her role impeccably, and, graciously smiling, drank the whole glass of milk without hesitation. The murderous enemies anxiously waited inside the shrine to see Sudhamani collapse in convulsions and die. To their bitter dismay, after a few moments Sudhamani turned in their direction, vomited the poisonous milk right in front of them, and continued to receive devotees as if nothing had happened. The rationalists fled and temporarily gave up their campaign against her.

The other obstacle which Sudhamani continually faced was the attitude of her own family. Despite the incessant harassment which she received from her relations, Sudhamani's mind never wavered in its equanimity, tolerance and compassionate resolve to assuage the pain of the suffering, whether friend or enemy, family or foreigner.

The formation of the antagonistic organization and its evil intention to harm the innocent Sudhamani created great mental distress for Sugunanandan. During this period, it was Sudhamani's habit to spend her nights outdoors, meditating under the star-filled heavens. Since her childhood she had always held sacred the solitude and silence of the night, when she could commune with the Divine and dance blissfully in a God-intoxicated mood without interference.

Sugunanandan's fear for his daughter increased when he thought that her enemies might stealthily attack her while she sat meditating alone. Hence, one day he commanded, "Daughter, come sleep in the house!" Sudhamani firmly reassured her father, "I have no house of my own. I prefer to sleep outside. God is omnipresent. He is everywhere, outside and inside. So why should I worry? If someone comes to harm me, God will protect me."

As for Damayanti, when the *Krishna Bhava* began, she had faith in Krishna, but once the *Bhava* had ended, her abusive attitude toward her daughter persisted as before. She believed that Sudhamani was possessed by Krishna only during the time of the *Bhava Darshan*, and that otherwise she remained as usual, her lowly servant and eccentric daughter. After the advent of *Krishna Bhava*, Damayanti had no choice but to exempt Sudhamani from her household responsibilities as, at any moment, her mind might soar into *samadhi* regardless of where she was. If she happened to be cooking or wading through the backwaters, this total absorption would put her in real danger.

As previously noted, Damayanti was very orthodox when it came to her daughter's conduct. She prohibited Sudhamani from talking to any devotees after the *Darshan* had ended, particularly to young men. If she did so, Damayanti severely chastised and beat her without hesitation. She still feared that her unusual behavior would bring dishonor to the family name! Although Sudhamani was beyond all attachment and aversion, the parents mistook her for an ordinary girl with all human feelings, attractions, and weaknesses, except during the *Bhava Darshan*. We can only wonder how those who were closest to her were least able to recognize her constant abidance in God-Consciousness.

The most intractable member of the family was Subhagan, Sudhamani's elder brother. He could not accept his sister's manner of receiving devotees and was completely intolerant of her ecstatic devotional singing and dancing. Sudhamani, who was beyond all duality, would receive men and women, children and elders, in the same equal manner. This infuriated Subhagan who, besides being an atheist, fiercely believed that women were inferior to men and should remain silent and unseen. He considered his sister a schizophrenic, and tried his utmost to create obstacles for her.

One day, he intentionally broke the oil lamp which the devotees kept lit in the temple during *Krishna Bhava*. Those who arrived that night for the *Darshan* felt very disheartened to see the broken lamp, as there was no other to replace it. Seeing their unhappy faces, Sudhamani asked some devotees to fetch a few seashells. When they were brought, she asked that wicks be placed in them and lit, although no oil was available. Then the impossible happened. Not only did the wicks light, but they burned throughout the night until the *Krishna Bhava* was over, without even a drop of oil! When asked how this could have happened, Sudhamani simply said, "The lamps burned through the night because of the sankalpa[25] of the devotees." On the next *Bhava Darshan* day, a devotee who was unaware of the broken oil lamp and the subsequent incident, made an offering of oil lamps for the shrine. Responding to the queries of devotees, he explained that he had had a dream in which he was instructed to bring them.

Some of the villagers who arrogantly ridiculed Sudhamani had to face great disasters in life. The following is one such incident.

Sudhamani was returning home one day after visiting a nearby house. By the side of the path stood a group of villagers. As she passed them, Sudhamani overheard one of them teasing her. A wealthy villager was telling another man in a loud voice, "See this girl, she is crazy. She is always singing, dancing and pretending to be Krishna. What nonsense! This is a case of emotional hysteria. If her father would just give her in marriage, her disease would be cured." Hearing his critical remarks, his friends burst into laughter. He continued egotistically, "If her father needs a dowry, I am ready to give him credit for two thousand rupees to marry the girl off. I must tell him today!"

Sudhamani didn't utter a word. Reaching home, she ran to the family shrine room, locking herself inside. Sitting there she began pouring her heart out to Krishna, "O Krishna, don't You hear what they are saying? They call me crazy! They know nothing of Your beauty and instead would bind me to their own self-centered way of life. O Krishna, Protector of those who seek Your refuge, have You too abandoned me? If that is so, then who will worship You, seeing my desperate condition? Is this the reward for the tears I have shed thinking only of You? Is this love and devotion of mine merely the raving of a crazy girl? All these days You have been my only comfort. In the blue sky I see Your smiling face, in the waves I see Your dancing form. The morning doves' song is Your divine flute playing! O Krishna, Krishna..." Thus praying she began sobbing and collapsed on the floor.

Meanwhile, the wealthy man who had teased Sudha-mani, was busy readying his fishing boats and nets for the day's fishing. Gathering his workers, he pushed off into the sea. That day they had an exceptionally good catch and all were rejoicing as they rowed back to shore.

On the way back, some of the workers who loved and worshipped Sudhamani remarked to the boat owner, "You know, it was not right to tease the innocent child the way you did today." The owner sneeringly retorted, "And what if I did? See what happened because I teased her. We got a bigger catch than usual!"

The devotees were tongue-tied and hung their heads. The boat was nearing the shore when suddenly the owner cried, "Hey, why don't we go to Neendakara?[26] There we will get a good price for our catch. In Parayakadavu the prices are very low." Agreeing, they steered the boat to Neendakara. They had almost reached the des-tination when suddenly the sea became rough. In no time huge waves rose up and dashed against the wooden hull. The boat full of fish, nets, and men was hurled about violently by gigantic waves. All efforts of the fishermen to control the craft were useless. The boat began sinking. The next instant, seized by an enor-mous wave, it was dashed on the rocks and broken in pieces. The day's catch was lost, one of the proud owner's best boats was destroyed, and his fishing nets lay torn on the rocks. Only their lives had been spared. With great difficulty, the fishermen managed to swim to shore.

A totally unexpected disaster had befallen the ar-rogant boat owner. Now it was his turn to walk along the shore with his head hanging. Crushed, he collapsed in the sand, unable to bear his great loss. The workers, who were admirers of Sudhamani, whispered to each other, "See the result of God's anger! He was just boasting about his good fortune after teasing the little one. Now see what has happened!" Another worker devotee chimed in, "He left the shores of Parayakadavu after saying that the little one was suffering from hysteria, and even boasted that he would give two thousand rupees to marry her off. Now let us see where he will borrow that money!" Altogether that day he had lost seventy-five thousand rupees. The workers took a bus home, and the news flashed everywhere.

In those days, Sudhamani would sometimes suddenly become playful like a three year old child, and would make playful mischief with the devotees who had come for *Krishna Bhava*. When the *Darshan* was over, she would creep about stealthily and approach sleeping devotees. Sometimes she would tie the end of one woman's sari to the hair of another. At others, Sudhamani would pour a handful of sand on the men who used to sleep with wide open mouths. Harshan, Sudhamani's lame elder cousin, had great respect and love for her. If he happened to be sleeping somewhere after the *Darshan* had finished, Sudhamani would seek him out. Catching hold of him by the legs, she would drag him about, laughing. It was a big joke for him as well, and all the devotees would burst into laughter seeing Sudhamani's childlike sports. Subhagan never liked such actions from his sister and would scold her for her peculiar behavior. How could he, who knew nothing at all of spirituality, understand the exalted state of Sudhamani?

Regarding her strange behavior, Sudhamani said,
"My mind is always shooting up to merge with the
Absolute. I am always trying to bring it down; only
then can I serve the suffering and mingle with the
devotees. That is why I play such games, to keep the
mind engaged in the world of the devotees, though without
attachment."

CHAPTER SIX

AS A CHILD OF
THE DIVINE MOTHER

As noble aspirations clearly manifested themselves in my mind, the Divine Mother, with bright, gentle hands, caressed my head. With bowed head, I told Mother that my life is dedicated to Her.

- MATA AMRITANANDAMAYI -

Śivastvam gurustvanca śaktistvamēva
Tvamēvāsi mātā pitā ca tvamēva

Tvamēvāsi vidyā tvamēvāsi bandhur
Gatirmmē matirddēvi sarvam tvamēva

O Devi, verily You are Siva, You alone are the
Teacher, You alone are the Supreme Energy, You
Alone are the Mother, You alone are the Father.

For me, knowledge, relatives, sustenance and
Intelligence, all are You.

DEVI BHUJANGAM

DEVOTION

The unique charm and beauty of *bhakti* (devotion) are indescribable. A true devotee's sincere desire is to remain a devotee forever. He wishes to attain neither heaven nor liberation. For him, devotion is his life, and the Lord is his All-in-all. The devotee experiences the highest joy in singing the glory of the Lord. That is why the *Bhakti Shastras*[27] declare:

Devotion alone is the fruit of devotion.
In its intrinsic nature this divine love
Is Immortal Bliss.

Even the great saint, Suka, though he was thoroughly established in Supreme Consciousness, experienced ineffable exaltation in singing the glories of the Lord. Such is the bliss derived from pure devotion.

Sudhamani, who was fully established in the consciousness of Krishna, still had an unquenchable thirst to enjoy the bliss of Supreme Devotion, *Para Bhakti*. But her complete identification with Lord Krishna made it impossible for her either to meditate on His Form or to be immersed in His thought. Thus her prayers ceased flowing to Krishna, and her Krishna *sadhana* came to an end.

Then Sudhamani had a vision which brought about a great change in her manifestation of God and her service to the world. This unexpected vision opened the way for Sudhamani's Devi *sadhana*, her passionate quest to realize the Divine as the Mother of the Universe. As she sat alone one day in a room of the house, her eyes open, her mind was turned inwards, absorbed in the Self. Suddenly, right in front of her, appeared a globe of brilliant light, reddish as the setting sun and, at the same time, as soothing as the moon. The globe of light neither rested on the earth nor hung in the sky. It was revolving. Against the background of this radiant, yet cooling disk of light, emerged the enchanting form of Devi, the Divine Mother, with a beautiful crown adorning Her head. Thrilled by this heart-capturing vision of Devi, Sudhamani cried out, "O Krishna, Mother has come! Please take me to Her, I want to embrace Her!" At once, Sudhamani perceived Krishna lifting her. He ascended with her above the clouds, where she beheld strange sights: lofty hills, vast dense forests, blue snakes and terrifying caves. But the little one could not find Devi anywhere. Like a small child, Sudhamani called out, "I want to see my Mother! Where is my Mother?" and began crying.

The exquisite vision of the Great Enchantress had disappeared from her sight, but became firmly fixed in Sudhamani's heart forever. She remained immersed in an enraptured state for a long time. From that moment on, she cherished the desire to behold again the benign smile and compassionate face of the Divine Mother. Sudhamani, who had beheld the Divine Form of Sri Krishna countless times, was ravished by the ineffable radiance of Devi. Her heart rushed after Devi, and her only desire now was to embrace the Divine Mother, sit on the Mother's lap and kiss the Mother's cheek.

Thus Sudhamani, who had never meditated on any form other than that of Sri Krishna, who had strongly believed that there was no Deity higher than Sri Krishna, now dedicated her entire being to realize the Divine as the Universal Mother, *Adi Parashakti*.[28] Except for the time she spent in *Krishna Bhava*, she plunged into deep contemplation of the resplendent form of the Divine Mother. The fire of longing for Her Vision burned in Sudhamani's heart without ceasing. Previously, her household duties had required that she remain functional in the mundane world, but now this fetter had been broken and she became completely lost to this gross plane of existence. It became a struggle for her even to maintain the most minimal care of her body. For months she subsisted only on *tulasi* leaves and water.

Sometimes when Sudhamani came out of deep meditation, she would cry aloud, "Amma! Amma! Where have You gone? Did You come that day only to abandon me? Please have mercy on this child of Yours and again reveal Your exquisitely gracious Form! O Mother,

if I am deserving, make me one with You. I cannot
bear this agony of separation! O Mother of the Universe, why are You indifferent to the heartbroken call
of this child? Please embrace me, do take me on Your
lap!"

> I shall wash Thy Feet with my tears.
> O Katyayani, forsake me not.
> How many days must I wait, my Mother,
> For the Vision of Thy Form?

> Though Thou delayest in giving what I want,
> My mind is satisfied because of Thy Maya.
> Wilt Thou allow me to offer
> A red flower at Thy Feet?

> Through this forlorn path
> I wander in the hope of finding Thee.
> Is there any kindness in Thy hard heart,
> Tell me, O Beloved of Siva?

Just as Sudhamani had perceived everything to be
pervaded by Krishna at the end of her Krishna *sadhana*,
she now felt the Divine Presence of Devi in everything. Even the breeze was the breath of Devi. The
innocent one roamed about talking to plants, trees, birds
and animals. She felt the earth to be her Mother, and
she rolled in the sand calling, "Amma, Amma! Where
are You? Where are You not?"

One day after finishing her meditation, Sudhamani
came out of the tiny shrine room. She was suddenly
overwhelmed with the feeling that she was a small child,
and that Nature was the Divine Mother. In that mood
she crawled like a baby on all fours to the base of a

coconut tree. Sitting there shedding tears, she pleaded, "Mother...my Mother...why are You hiding from my sight? I know that You are hiding in this tree. You are in these plants, You are living in these animals, these birds! The earth is nothing but You. O Mother, how You conceal Yourself in the ocean waves and in the cooling breeze! O Mother, my elusive Mother!..." The next moment she embraced the coconut tree, feeling that it was the Divine Mother.

Sometimes Sudhamani lay down, but not to rest, as she had no fondness for sensuous pleasure. While lying on the bare ground, she would gaze endlessly at the infinite sky, the silvery clouds, the shining sun, the glittering stars, the soothing moon. When dark storm clouds gathered overhead, Sudhamani no longer saw Sri Krishna in them, but imagined the long, cascading, curly hair of the Divine Mother. Each object suspended in the infinite heavens became a sign of the presence of Devi. As she lay under the sky, she never slept, but remained in a state of tear-filled supplication to the Supreme Mother of the Universe.

Referring to those days, Sudhamani later recalled, "While walking I used to repeat the Divine Name with every step. I took each step only after chanting the mantra. Should I forget to chant the mantra while taking a step, immediately I stepped backwards. Having withdrawn the step, I would repeat the mantra. Only then would I proceed. If I happened to be engaged in any external activity, I used to decide beforehand to chant the mantra a certain number of times before finishing the task. While bathing in the river, before plunging into the water, I used to resolve to chant the mantra a certain number of times before coming to the surface. I never had a Guru, nor was I ever initiated by anyone and given a particular mantra. The mantra which I used to chant was 'Amma, Amma'."

There is a scriptural injunction which states, "Actions naturally subside in the state of supreme devotion." This is clearly evident in the case of Sudhamani. In the morning she used to begin to brush her teeth, but the next moment her mind would vanish in the single thought of the Divine Mother. This state of focused concentration would deepen and continue for hours at a time. Her attempts to take a bath usually met with little success. Upon entering the bathroom, she would realize she had forgotten to bring a towel. After fetching the towel, she would notice she had also come without soap. Discouraged, she would exclaim, "O Mother, how much time is wasted just trying to take a bath! Instead, let my mind be fixed on You! To forget You even for a moment creates agonizing pain in my heart..." Abandoning altogether the idea of taking a bath, she would sit in the bathroom merged in *samadhi*. Hours would pass before somebody would discover her sitting there, deeply absorbed in meditation. A bucket of water poured over her head to rouse her sufficed finally for her bath! If she failed to respond, she was shaken violently, or simply carried into the house.

In the area along the coast there were no proper toilets. Each family erected a small scaffold over the backwaters, enclosing the frame with woven palm leaves. As there was no flooring, one had to perch on a board in order to perform one's nature calls. Many times while Sudhamani sat in such a latrine, she would tumble into the backwaters, having lost her external awareness.

Immersed in meditation on the Divine Mother, Sudhamani would sit for long hours. Before beginning, she
used to make an inner resolve: "I must sit for this
much time." Then she would give a command to the
body, "Sit here, body." She would tell Devi, "Don't
play Your tricks on me. Keep them to Yourself. If You
do not allow me to sit and meditate, I won't let You
go!" If any external disturbance impinged on her awareness, she would bite Devi and pull Her hair, until she
realized that she was biting her own body and tearing
out her own hair.

One day, Sudhamani was unable to sit for the chosen length of time, as she felt someone violently shaking her body, and the sensation disturbed her. Thinking, "This is Her trick! Why is She not allowing me to
sit?", she suddenly opened her eyes, ran from the shrine
room, and returned a moment later with a wooden pestle,
intending to threaten Devi. Raising the pestle, the little
one shouted "Today I will...", then the next moment
she realized her senselessness. "What! To beat Devi?
Is it right? Is it possible?" She dropped the pestle and
resumed her meditation.

Sudhamani would not waste even a second without
remembering the Divine Mother. If someone happened
to talk to her, she imagined the person to be Devi. The
person would continue talking until perceiving that the
little one had mysteriously slipped off to another world.
If she realized that a moment had passed without having remembered Devi, Sudhamani would be very distressed and confess, "O Mother, so much time was
wasted!" To make up for the lost time, she would in-

crease the length of her meditation that day. If she happened to miss a meditation, she would pace the ground the entire night, repeating the mantra and sincerely praying, "O Mother, what is the use of this life if I am unable to meditate on You? Without You there is only *Maya* waiting to devour me. O Mother, please give me strength! Grant me Your Vision! Dissolve me in Your Eternal Self!"

Most of all, Sudhamani liked to meditate by the oceanside in the silent hours of the night. For her the crashing waves resounded with the sacred syllable, 'OM'. The vast, deep blue heavens, sparkling with countless stars, reflected the limitless divinity of the Mother. There, in a moment, her mind turned inward to abide spontaneously in the Self.

If Sugunanandan were to search for his daughter on those nights, he would become very agitated when he was unable to find her in the house or yard. Eventually his search took him to the sea, where he would find her absorbed in deep meditation, sitting like an immovable rock. Some of the villagers, mistaking the purpose of Sudhamani's late night visits to the shore, began to spread unkind rumors about her. When these reached the ears of Sugunanandan, he strictly forbade his daughter from going to the sea at night.

These incidents, which characterize the early phase of Sudhamani's Devi *sadhana*, only served to convince her family more fully of her insanity. These high states of pure devotion were far beyond the reach of an ordinary person's imagination. Sometimes Sudhamani would sob like a small child, calling out to an imperceptible Being. At other times she would clap her hands and laugh aloud, then roll on the ground or try to kiss the ripples on the water, calling out "Amma, Amma". It is no wonder that the little one's flight of the alone to the Alone was mistaken for madness. Even the devotees who visited her during *Krishna Bhava* utterly failed to comprehend this passionate quest of Sudhamani's for attaining oneness with the Divine Mother.

It is ironic that although her family considered her to be one gone mad, they never tried to discover the cause or cure. Instead, they persisted in their habit of taunting and tormenting her, especially her elder brother Subhagan. Their treatment finally became so inhumane, that Sudhamani resolved to put an end to her life by jumping into the ocean. She cried, beseeching the Divine Mother, "Am I such a wicked girl? Why do the family members persist in their cruelty? People love only those who are charming. I cannot see pure love anywhere in this world. O darling Mother, I feel everything to be an illusion. O Mother, are You not the Protector of Your devotees? Am I not Your child? Have You also forsaken me? If so, then why should I carry this body? It is a burden for me as well as others. Accept Your child, O Mother Sea!" With a determined mind Sudhamani ran toward the ocean, yet, when about to jump, she saw the vast sea to be Devi Herself. Unable to keep her mind on the physical plane, she entered into *samadhi* and fell unconscious on the sand.

Harshan, Sudhamani's cousin and devotee, had overheard her parting prayer as she ran from Idamannel. He followed her in haste, having understood her intention. Finding her unconscious by the water's edge, he reverently carried her back to Idamannel, thanking God that he had found her still alive.

Many villagers sympathized with Sudhamani, although some of them also considered her mad. They would remark to one another, "See how pitiful her condition is! Poor girl! Nobody looks after her; even her parents have discarded her. When she was healthy and normal she toiled day and night for them, but now they are not even interested in caring for her. Is she not their daughter?"

Some of the women who lived in the neighborhood took pity on Sudhamani and began to serve her lovingly. These women had had deep admiration for her since her childhood. They were now devotees of the *Krishna Bhava* and recognized Sudhamani's spiritual splendor and all-embracing love. Somehow, they had a vague understanding of her sublime spiritual states. Whenever they could, they helped her or rescued her from danger.

Chellamma and her daughter, Vatsala, lived on the plot of land which lay in front of Idamannel. Vatsala considered Sudhamani her close friend and had boundless love for her. Living so close to Idamannel, she and her mother often noticed the little one's unconscious tumbles into the backwaters. Immediately, they would fish her out of the water, dry her off, and dress her in clean clothes.

Pushpavathi and her husband, Bhaskaran, were both ardent devotees. She loved Sudhamani as her own daughter and felt sad to see how the family tormented her. Two sisters, Rema and Rati, who also lived near Idamannel, held the little one very dear to their hearts. Another loyal friend, Aisha, Sudhamani's cousin on her aunt's side, was extremely fond of the kind and affectionate Sudhamani. These ladies were the ones who were blessed to serve Sudhamani during her days of intense *tapas*.[29] Often when Sudhamani became oblivious to the surroundings, one of the ladies would find her lying in muddy water or in a dirty place. If they could not revive her, they would carry her in their arms to their own house. As if she were a small child, they would brush her teeth, give her a hot bath, dress her in fresh clothes and feed her with their own hands.

As before, Subhagan remained always antagonistic to Sudhamani and her Divine Mood. Several times he pressed her to discontinue the *Krishna Bhava*, as he still considered it a shameful display which would bring dishonor to the family name. As his demands were ignored, he decided to take more drastic steps.

One day after the *Bhava Darshan*, Sudhamani was about to enter the house, when she found her way obstructed by Subhagan, who stood menacingly in the doorway. He shouted at her, "Do not enter this house! You will be permitted to come inside only after you stop this shameful singing and dancing!" Taking his words to be Divine Command, Sudhamani walked away without murmuring a word and sat down in the front yard. Loudly Subhagan prohibited her from sitting there either. Upon this, Sudhamani took a handful of sand and gave it to Subhagan saying, "If it is yours, please count this sand!"

Thenceforth, she lived outdoors, which she was happy to do. The sky overhead became her roof, the earth her bed, the moon her lamp, the sea breeze her fan. These austere conditions only served to intensify her renunciation and determination to realize the Divine Mother.

Raising her hands above her head with tears rolling down her cheeks like a small child appealing to its mother, Sudhamani would cry out aloud, "Amma, Amma...have You left me here to die with longing for Your Vision? The days are passing one by one. Still I have no peace of mind without beholding Your enchanting Form. All my hopes lie in You. Will You also forsake me? Do You not see my desperate condition?" During this period, Sudhamani wrote the following songs:

> *O Devi, O Ambika, Beauty Personified,*
> *O Thou Who art affectionate toward devotees,*
> *May Thou dwell here in order to end*
> *The sufferings of the devotees...*
> *Thou art everything, powerful enough to*
> *End my misery, the Tap Root of all...*
>
> *Thou standest as the Empress of all beings,*
> *Thou art the world and its Protector as well...*
>
> *Believing this, I am praising Thee with devotion.*
> *O Goddess of the Universe, I desire to see Thee...*
>
> *For how many days have I been desiring to see*
> *Thee! I am praising Thee without losing even a*
> *moment...*
>
> *Did I commit some error or hast Thou no mind*
> *To end my sorrow?*
>
> *Or perhaps Thou wishest that my inner self be*
> *Burnt to ash. I am getting confused; I know*
> *nothing...*
>
> *Will the truth that I keep in my heart that all*
> *The children are equal to the Mother become false?*

In order to end my misery I will request a
Little of the nectar of Thy Grace pouring
From the glance of Thy holy eyes...

I will fall at Thy Feet in order to see Thy
Gracious face and beg for the boon of
The fulfillment of life...

O Mother, for the satisfaction of my life
Give a drop of Thy Love to my dry, burning heart.
Why O why dost Thou put burning fire
To fertilize this scorched creeper?

Bursting out crying, how many
Hot tears have I offered before Thee?
Dost Thou not hear my heart throbbing
And agony coming out as suppressed sighs?

Let not the fire enter and dance
Through the forest of sandalwood trees.
Let not this fire of sorrow show its strength
And burst forth like shattering tiles...

O Devi, chanting the Name 'Durga, Durga'
My mind has forgotten all other paths.
O my Durga, I want neither heaven nor Liberation.
I want only pure devotion to Thee...

Her *tapas* became so intense that Sudhamani's body
became extremely hot, as if she were standing on burning
coals. The heat became so unbearable that she could
hardly wear clothes. Seeking relief from the burning
sensation, she would roll in the muddy sand of the
backwaters. Sometimes she stood submerged in the
backwaters for hours in deep meditation.

Sincere and ardent devotees of Sudhamani used to invite her to their homes during times of special worship. They believed that her presence would bestow spiritual splendor and power on all who attended. These families used to come to Idamannel to take Sudhamani to their house by bus. Sometimes Sudhamani would become God-intoxicated while waiting at the bus station. Forgetting the external world, she rolled on the ground and burst into blissful peals of laughter. Of course people could not comprehend her state and would gather around her, watching in astonishment. Others would tease and rebuke her, calling her a crazy girl. Children used to stand around her ridiculing her, but such treatment was lost on Sudhamani. What taunting words could reach the world where she was reveling? What harassment could taint the innocent girl's intoxicated mood of Divine Bliss?

In her deep anguish of separation from the Divine Mother Sudhamani would sometimes cry and scream aloud. Small children would gather around her on such occasions begging, "Elder sister, don't cry! Are you suffering from a headache?" Eventually they, too, came to understand that she was crying to see Devi. During these uncontrollable outbursts, one of her younger sisters would stand before her, assuming the pose of Devi, wearing a sari and cascading hair. In great joy, Sudhamani would run to embrace her. If she should notice any beautiful girl when she was in this mood, she would run to her enthralled. Embracing and kissing her, she saw only Devi.

Seeing his daughter's utter neglect of her body and taking pity on her, Sugunanandan tried several times

to build a thatched shelter to protect her from the rain
and sun. As she was lying or sitting merged in meditation, her parents would take the opportunity to construct a shade above her. Coming back to a state of
normal awareness and seeing what her parents were
doing, she would move away from the place saying,
"This also will become a cause for sorrow. For how
many days will you be able to keep it here? If you go
away somewhere, who will maintain it? Unaffected by
anything, let me endure heat, cold and rain, and thereby
transcend them."

In those days of intense yearning for the Divine
Mother, Sudhamani assumed the nature of a two year
old child, the child of the Divine Mother. Her identification with this attitude of child to Mother was so
complete that many of her actions can be understood
only in the light of this fact. One day, coming out of
meditation, Sudhamani felt very hungry and thirsty.
Just then, she saw Pushpavathi of the neighboring house
breast feeding her baby. Sudhamani went to her straight-
away, displaced the suckling baby, and lay in the
woman's lap for nourishment. Instead of feeling awk-
ward about this unexpected act of Sudhamani's,
Pushpavathi overflowed with motherly feelings for her.
Similar incidents occurred several times, until
Pushpavathi realized it was safer to feed her baby out
of sight of the innocent-minded Sudhamani.

One day Sudhamani was lying unconscious in the
mud and sand near the backwaters. Some devotees who
found her felt appalled to see her lying there with her
nostrils, eyes, ears and hair full of dirt and sand. The
incessant stream of tears had left visible streaks on

her dark blue cheeks. The devotees informed Sugunanandan of her pitiful condition, but he ignored their plea. Dismayed by his indifference, they carried her into the house where they were unable to arouse her. They cleaned the dirt from her body, unwittingly laid her on her elder brother's cot, and left her to rest comfortably.

Returning home, Subhagan found Sudhamani lying on his cot. He flew into a rage and began shaking the cot violently. He became like a madman, screaming, "Who put this wretch on my bed? Who put this wretch on my bed?" The bed broke into several pieces, but Sudhamani lay there in the middle of the debris, lost to the world. Later, when she came to know about the incident and her close brush with danger, she simply said, "Whatever happens is God's Will." During the very next *Darshan*, much to everyone's amazement, a devotee who was a carpenter and who was totally unaware of the previous day's incident, presented a cot, a table and chairs to Sudhamani. When he was asked about this, he said that he had had a dream in which Krishna had appeared and told him to bring all those things for the little one.

CHAPTER SEVEN

FAR BETTER THAN MAN

Human beings are not the only ones with the capacity for speech. Animals, birds and plants have this power but we do not have the capability to understand. One who has the Vision of the Self knows all these things.

- MATA AMRITANANDAMAYI -

Ahimsā pratishtāyām tat
sannidhau vairatyāgaha

*On being established in harmlessness, all beings
coming near him (a yogi) cease to be hostile.*

PATANJALI YOGA SUTRAS
SADHANA PADAM, VERSE 35

W hile Sudhamani was living outdoors, dogs, cats,
cows, goats, snakes, squirrels, pigeons, parrots
and eagles all sought her company and became her
intimate friends. This phase of her *sadhana* demon-
strates the power of love, untainted by attraction and
aversion, to bring harmony among animals who are otherwise natural enemies. At a time when her own relations had abandoned her and were vehemently opposed
to her spiritual life, these animals stood by her and
rendered loyal service. Their behavior clearly revealed
that they seemed to understand Sudhamani far better
than human beings.

In those days, Sudhamani could not eat anything
from her own house, as she was extremely sensitive to
food prepared by worldly people. The only food she
could eat was what had been prepared while mantras
were chanted. One day, as she came out of the temple
after meditation, she felt very hungry and thirsty. In
front of the temple was a family cow, which she perceived instantly as a gift from God. Playing the role of
a calf, she drank directly from its udders, thereby
quenching her thirst and hunger, while the cow kept
its legs in a convenient position. From that day on, the

cow lay in front of the temple each day until Sudhamani emerged from her meditation. Before feeding her,
the cow would refuse to graze or to feed its own calf!
Sugunanandan tried several times to force the cow to
move away from the spot where it waited for Sudhamani. He pulled the cow's tail and poured buckets of
water over it, but it would not budge from in front of
the temple.

On some days, someone brought milk from the neighborhood for the little one to drink. However, the milk
was not pure; it had been mixed with water. When
Sudhamani drank it, she vomited, and the one who had
sent the adulterated milk was fated to suffer for the
act. For that reason, Sudhamani decided to eat and
drink only what was provided by God.

Another extraordinary incident occurred about this
time. In the village of Bhandaraturuttu, where
Sudhamani's grandmother lived some six kilometers to
the south, Sudhamani's uncle, Ratnadasan, untied the
cows from the cowshed as usual, to bring them to the
front yard where he fed and bathed them. Suddenly
one of the cows turned abruptly and trotted toward the
ocean, where it took a sharp turn toward the north. The
cow ran rapidly up the beach, as Ratnadasan struggled
to catch up with her. Finally the cow turned into
Sudhamani's village, and ran directly to Idamannel,
where it had never been. Heading straight for the place
where Sudhamani was sitting in meditation, the cow
began gently nuzzling and licking her, as if to express
love to an old friend. As Sudhamani still remained deeply
immersed, the cow lay down nearby, intently watching
her, as if waiting for her to finish her meditation. After

some time Sudhamani opened her eyes and, noticing the vaguely familiar cow, walked over to it. At that moment the cow raised a back leg, inviting her to drink its milk. Sudhamani drank from the udder, as her uncle shook his head in disbelief.

What mysterious power had inspired the cow to visit Sudhamani? Though she had tended that cow during her brief stay at her grandmother's house many years ago, does that explain the animal's unprecedented behavior?

When Sudhamani sat outdoors in meditation, snakes sometimes appeared and coiled around her body, as if to bring her awareness back to the external world. One day, following some harassment from her family, Sudhamani left the grounds of Idamannel. A lady from the neighborhood encountered her as she walked, consoled her, and led the little one to the peace of her own house. Sudhamani promptly entered the family shrine room and began pouring her heart out to the Divine Mother. It was then that she composed the following song:

> Through my mind, speech and actions I am
> Remembering You incessantly.
> Why then are You delaying to show
> Your mercy to me, beloved Mother?
>
> Years have passed but still my mind has no peace.
> O darling Mother, please grant me a little relief...
>
> My mind sways like a boat caught in a storm.
> O Mother, give me a little peace of mind
> Lest I become a lunatic...

I am tired Mother; it is unbearable.
I don't want such a life. I can't stand
Your tests. O Mother, I can't endure it!

I am a miserable destitute.
I have none but You Mother.
Please stop Your tests,
Extend Your hand and pull me up...

Suddenly, her mood changed and she fell into a fit
of divine madness. Crying and rolling on the ground,
she began tearing at her clothes. The next moment she
burst into laughter, still rolling uncontrollably. The family
watched in concerned amazement and had no idea how
to calm her. At this point, a large snake appeared in
the doorway and crawled directly onto Sudhamani's body.
The family stared, horrified, as the snake began licking the unconscious girl's face with its flicking tongue.
This went on for some minutes and immediately had a
soothing effect on Sudhamani. As her mind slowly returned to a normal plane of consciousness, the snake
crawled off her body and disappeared. It seemed to the
family that the snake knew the exact remedy to restore
Sudhamani's external awareness and deftly adminis-
tered to her needs.

Any visitor to Idamannel soon notices that many
kinds of birds live there. Sudhamani used to love the
parrots especially, as they were dear to the Goddess.
Sometimes when she prayed, "O Mother, won't You come
near me?", a flock of parrots would fly to her and settle
on the ground nearby. A devotee once presented her
with a parrot, which always played around Sudhamani,
who never caged it. One day Sudhamani was thinking,

"Oh, what a terrible, cruel world it is! Not even an iota of truth or righteousness exists anywhere. People are deceitful, and the world has become filled with sinners. It seems there is nobody to show the correct path to humanity." As tears flowed down her cheeks, she remained in an introspective mood for a long time. At one point, Sudhamani noticed her parrot was standing in front of her also shedding tears, as if it were suffering from some pain. Her intense agony had moved the bird as well.

Besides the parrot, two pigeons also kept her company. Whenever she sang to the Divine Mother, the three birds would hop before her, dancing joyfully and spreading their wings.

From a big tree on the Idamannel property, an eagle's nest[30] once fell to the ground, and two fledglings tumbled out, dazed and vulnerable. Some mischievous children threw stones at the tiny birds trying to kill them, but Sudhamani quickly rescued them. She carefully nursed them for a few weeks until they were strong enough to fly, and then she set them free. These two *Garudas* always returned at the beginning of each *Krishna Bhava* and would sit on the top of the shrine for a long time. They were a great source of attraction for the devotees, as the Garuda bird was the vehicle of Lord Vishnu. The mysterious connection which the two birds maintained with Sudhamani not only added splendor to the *Darshan*, but also increased the devotees' faith in her divine nature.

During the period of Devi *sadhana*, whenever Sudhamani lost consciousness, weeping to see the Divine Mother, these two birds would appear from the sky to sit beside her as if to protect her. Some of the ladies from the neighborhood watched with wonder as the two birds, gazing at Sudhamani's agonized face, also clearly shed tears with her.

One day soon after meditation, Sudhamani felt terribly hungry. One of the two *Garudas* immediately flew toward the ocean and returned a few minutes later with a fish in its beak. The eagle put the fish on the lap of Sudhamani, who gratefully took it and ate it raw. When Damayanti discovered this, she used to wait for the *Garuda* to come with its daily offering. As soon as the bird dropped the fish, Damayanti swooped in to grab it, so that she could cook it for her daughter. During the *sadhana* period when Sudhamani was intent to realize Krishna, she had stopped eating fish, as even the smell would make her vomit. But now the fish brought by the *Garuda* was food sent by God, so she gladly ate it. The daily practice of the *Garuda* continued for some time.

Another animal which seemed attuned to Sudhamani was a cat. During the *Bhava Darshan* the cat would enter the temple and walk around Sudhamani as if doing *pradakshina*.³¹ It would then sit near her for a long time with its eyes closed and seemed to the devotees to be meditating. Once someone tried to get rid of the cat by taking it across the river, but the next day it returned and stayed by Sudhamani's side.

A unique black and white dog also showed remarkable faithfulness. When Sudhamani cried so much to Devi that she fell unconscious in her prayers, the dog would rub against her and lick her face and limbs in order to revive her. When Sudhamani seemed to be leaving the Idamannel property, the dog tugged at her skirt and barked in protest to prevent her departure. Often he would bring a food packet in his mouth and lay it before her to eat. The dog wouldn't eat even a grain of rice from whatever he had brought as an offering. At night the dog would sleep near Sudhamani, who would use him as a pillow when she lay down to gaze at the sky.

One night the little one was meditating while sitting on the banks of the backwaters. She was steeped in *samadhi* and a thick blanket of mosquitoes covered her body. Sugunanandan called her, but no reply came. When he began roughly shaking her body, he found that she had become as light as a twig. "Her whole body looked lifeless, but as I had found her in that condition many times before, I wasn't worried," Sugunanandan later explained. As he sat by his daughter, the black and white dog appeared, fiercely barking. Within a few minutes, Sudhamani opened her eyes and came back to her normal awareness. Animals seemed to have a greater ability than humans to draw Sudhamani's attention when she became enraptured in another realm.

Sometimes the intense love of the dog made Sudhamani think that it was the Divine Mother Herself. Forgetting everything she would embrace and kiss the dog, calling aloud, "My Mother, my Mother...!"

One day while meditating, Sudhamani felt extremely agitated. Immediately she rose from her seat and walked hastily toward the village. The black and white dog had fallen into the hands of a dog catcher; it was howling and crying piteously, but it was not acting at all

vicious. Unable to escape from the catcher's sling, it
was dragging its paws as its captor struggled to haul it
away. Some of the village girls, who were friends and
admirers of Sudhamani, recognized the dog as her faithful
companion and begged the dog catcher to free it. They
even promised a bribe if he would let the dog go. At
this moment Sudhamani arrived. The dog looked piti-
fully at her and began shedding tears! This was too
much for the dog catcher; he had no choice but to set
the dog free.

Whenever somebody prostrated before Sudhamani,
the black and white dog used to stretch its forelegs
and bow its head down before her. When she danced
in devotional ecstasy, the dog jumped around her as if
joining in the ecstatic dance. When the sacred conch
was blown during the twilight worship each evening,
the dog would howl in a peculiar way, closely imitating
the sound of the conch.

One day Sudhamani had an intense feeling that her
friend, the black and white dog, would die afflicted by
rabies. Shortly thereafter the animal did contract rabies and died as she had foreseen, though without much
suffering. When Sudhamani was asked if she were
dejected to lose her loyal companion, she said, "I am
not at all sad about his death. Even though he died, he
will come to me. Therefore, why should I be sad?"
Later, she commented that the dog's soul had reincar-
nated near Idamannel, but would reveal no further details.

Another dog from the neighborhood also had intense love for Sudhamani. One day during the dog's
pregnancy, it came to the side of the temple and stood
expectantly waiting. When Sudhamani came out of the

shrine after meditation, she found it standing on the temple verandah. It did not step in, but placed its forelegs on the edge of the temple floor and howled in a peculiar way as if it were in pain. Sudhamani embraced and kissed the dog asking, "What happened daughter, what happened?" Thereupon, the creature stepped down from the temple verandah, lay down on the sand, and breathed her last breath.

Sudhamani once remarked regarding a goat which had great love for her, "On account of a disease of her udders, the goat was struggling for life, about to die. I saw her agony and sat down near her, lost in prayer and meditation. When I opened my eyes I beheld the poor animal approaching me, crawling on her knees. Placing her head on my lap, she quietly died, gazing at my face. Her love was pure indeed."

Some years later, recollecting all these incidents she expressed these thoughts: "How blissful were those days! Strangely enough, those animals could understand my feelings and act on them. If I cried, they also would join me in crying. If I sang, they would dance in front of me. When I lost my external consciousness they would crawl over my body. All the traits of various animals can be found in human beings. When one gets rid of all attachment and aversion and attains equal vision, then even hostile animals become friendly in one's presence."

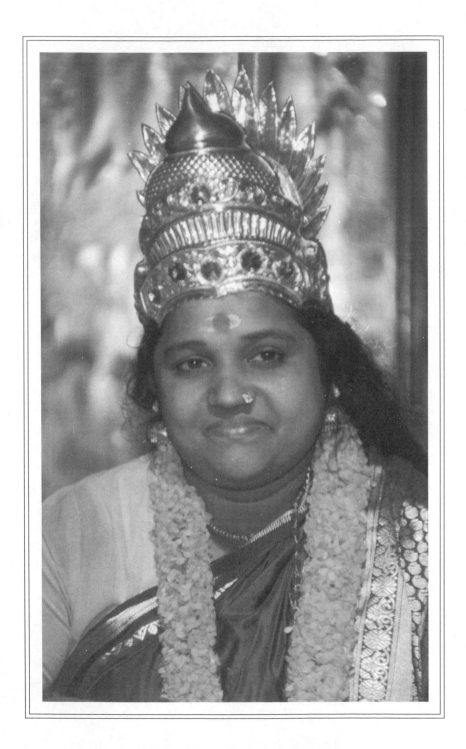

CHAPTER EIGHT

DAZZLING LIKE
A MILLION SUNS

Smiling, She (Devi) became a Divine Effulgence and merged in me. My mind blossomed, bathed in the many-hued Light of Divinity, and the events of millions of years gone by rose up within me. Thenceforth, seeing nothing as separate from my own Self, a single Unity, and merging in the Universal Mother, I renounced all sense of enjoyment.

-MATA AMRITANANDAMAYI-

Drishā drāghīyasyā dara dalita nīlotpala
rucā, davīyamsam dīnam snapaya kripayā
mām api śive

Anenāyam dhanyo bhavati na ca te hānir
iyatāvane vā harmlye vā sama kara nipāto
himakaraha

*O Spouse of Siva! Wilt Thou graciously bathe even
me, who stands helpless at a far off distance, with
Thy far reaching glance, beautiful as the slightly
blossomed blue lily. This mortal will derive the
greatest good of existence from Thy action. By
such action, no loss is, after all, sustained by Thee.
The snow-beamed Moon sheds the same luster on
a forest as on a mansion.*

SAUNDARYA LAHARI
VERSE 57

Placing her absolute faith in the Divine Mother,
Sudhamani swam in the Ocean of Immortal Love.
For her, the whole atmosphere above, below, right and
left, was surcharged with Her Divine Presence. The
breeze was the loving caress of the Mother. The trees,
vines and flowers were all Devi and hence worthy of
Sudhamani's undifferentiated worship. Gazing at the
sky, seeing what we know not, the little one would be
overcome with uncontrollable fits of tears and laughter
which subsided only when she fell unconscious to the
sand. The imploring prayers of this orphaned child to
her vanished Mother echoed in the air of Idamannel
day and night. It was at this level of Realization, seeing all of Nature as being the Divine Mother only, that

she wrote the following song:

> Creation and Creator art Thou,
> Thou art Energy and Truth,
> O Goddess, O Goddess, O Goddess!

> Creator of the Cosmos art Thou,
> And Thou art the beginning and end...
> The Essence of the individual soul art Thou,
> And Thou art the five elements as well.

Attended mostly by the now familiar clan of animals, Sudhamani was neit\her sleeping nor eating. She never made contact with other people unless they first approached her, and even a basic task such as brushing her teeth was ignored by her soaring mind. When she did eat, she sometimes consumed discarded tea leaves, cow dung, glass pieces or human excreta; she was unable to notice any difference between delicious food and all of these. What words are there to describe that state which our mind and intellect are incapable of grasping?

No longer could the little one contain her agony, and her prayers poured forth incessantly to the Divine Mother,

"O Mother, my heart is being torn by this pain of separation! Why does Your heart not melt seeing this endless stream of tears? O Mother, many Great Souls have adored You and thereby attained Your Vision and became eternally one with You. O Darling Mother! Please open the doors of Your compassionate heart to this humble servant of Yours! I am suffocating like one who is drowning. If You are not willing to come to me,

then please put an end to my life. Let that sword with
which You behead the cruel and unrighteous fall on
my head as well. At least, let me be blessed by the
touch of Your sword! What sense is there in keeping
this useless body which is a heavy burden for me?"

Sudhamani's anguish became extreme, her prayers
exhausted. In her own words,

"Each and every pore of my body was wide-open
with yearning, each atom of my body was vibrating
with the sacred mantra, my entire being was rushing
toward the Divine Mother in a torrential stream..."

In unspeakable agony she cried out,

"O Mother...here is Your child about to die, drowning in unfathomable distress...this heart is
breaking...these limbs are faltering...I am convulsing
like a fish thrown on the shore...O Mother...You have
no kindness towards me...I have nothing left to offer
You except the last breath of my life..."

Her voice became choked. Her breathing stopped
completely. Sudhamani fell unconscious. The Will of
the Mother designates the moment. The Divine Enchantress of the Universe, the Omniscient, the Omnipresent,
the Omnipotent Being, the Ancient, Primal Creatrix,
the Divine Mother, appeared before Sudhamani in a
living form dazzling like a thousand suns. Sudhamani's
heart overflowed in a tidal wave of unspeakable love
and bliss. The Divine Mother benignly smiled, and,
becoming a Pure Effulgence, merged in Sudhamani.

The divine event is best described in Sudhamani's
own composition 'Ananda Veethi' or 'The Path of Bliss',
in which she has tried to make intelligible that mystical union which is beyond words :

Once upon a time, my soul was dancing
In delight through the Path of Bliss.
At that time, all the inner foes such as
Attraction and aversion ran away, hiding
Themselves in the innermost recesses of my mind.
Forgetting myself, I merged in a golden dream
Which arose within me. As noble aspirations
Clearly manifested themselves in my mind,
The Divine Mother, with bright, gentle hands,
Caressed my head. With bowed head, I told
Mother that my life is dedicated to Her.

Smiling, She became a Divine Effulgence
And merged in me. My mind blossomed,
Bathed in the many-hued Light of Divinity
And the events of millions of years gone by
Rose up within me. Thenceforth,
Seeing nothing as separate from my own Self
A single Unity, and merging in the Divine Mother,
I renounced all sense of enjoyment.

Mother told me to ask the people
To fulfill their human birth.
Therefore, I proclaim to the whole world
The sublime Truth that She uttered,
"Oh man, merge in your Self!"

Thousands and thousands of yogis
Have taken birth in India and
Lived the principles visualized by the
Great Sages of the unknown past.
To remove the sorrow of humanity,
How many naked truths there are!

Today I tremble with bliss
Recollecting Mother's words,
"Oh my darling, come to Me,
Leaving all other works.
You are always Mine."

O Pure Consciousness,
O Embodiment of Truth,
I will heed Your words.
O Mother, why are You late in coming?
Why did You give this birth?
I know nothing, O Mother,
Please forgive my mistakes.

At this point Sudhamani developed a strong aversion to the visible world. She would dig big holes to hide in, so as to escape from the diverse world and sensuous-minded people. She spent her days and nights enjoying the perennial Bliss of God-Realization and avoided all human company. If anyone had considered her mad before, they were firmly convinced of her insanity now. Who could conceive of the plane of consciousness in which she was established? Though internally Sudhamani had crossed the threshold into the Absolute, externally she was the same crazy Sudhamani who was possessed three nights a week by Krishna as far as the family and villagers were concerned. The only recent change, if they had noticed any at all, was that instead of rolling in the sand, she was now digging big holes.

ADVENT OF THE DEVI BHAVA

One day Sudhamani heard a voice from within her say,

"My child, I dwell in the heart of all beings and have no fixed abode. Your birth is not for merely enjoying the unalloyed Bliss of the Self but for comforting suffering humanity. Henceforth, worship Me in the hearts of all beings and relieve them of the sufferings of worldly existence..."

It was after this inner call that Sudhamani began manifesting *Devi Bhava*, the Mood of the Divine Mother, in addition to the *Krishna Bhava*. At these times, she revealed her oneness with the Divine Mother, though for the devotees, she had now merely become possessed by Devi as well as Krishna. The following incident marks the advent of *Devi Bhava*.

Only six months had passed since the beginning of *Krishna Bhava Darshan*. It was now late in 1975. One night as the *Krishna Bhava* was going on and the devotees were entering the temple one by one, an unexpected incident changed the whole atmosphere.

As usual, some devotees were singing *bhajans* outside the shrine room on the verandah. Sudhamani was manifesting her inner identification with the Sri Krishna aspect of the Supreme and was receiving the devotees joyfully. An enchanting smile lit up her bright face, and the devotees were delighting in the Divine Presence. At that moment, a devotee entered the small temple completely distraught. Apparently, he had been severely harassed by one of the antagonistic villagers.[32] Unable to bear the sharp remarks, he burst into tears and appealed to Krishna to find some remedy for the situation.

Without warning, the gracious smile vanished. Sudhamani's entire facial expression changed and became fierce, as if the final dissolution had come. Her eyes looked like two smoldering iron balls. Burning with anger, they seemed to emit shooting flames. Her fingers were holding the Devi *mudra*.[33] All present both

inside and outside the temple were shocked to hear
boisterous laughter issuing from her whole being. They
had never heard such laughter in their lives. Seeing
the sudden change in Sudhamani, those standing in
the temple began trembling out of fear. Some scholars
who were present began loudly chanting peace mantras
and devotional songs in praise of the Divine Mother,
while some others performed the ceremony of *Aarathi*.[34]
After much prayer and chanting of various mantras,
she became calm and peaceful, but the *Bhava* had been
transformed from that of Krishna to that of Devi.

Sudhamani later confided, "Seeing the distress of
that devotee, I felt like destroying all the unrighteous
people who persist in ridiculing the devotees. Unknow-
ingly, the Devi of fierce nature[35] manifested to grant
refuge to the persecuted." Thenceforth, in addition to
Krishna Bhava, the Holy Mother, as we will call Her
now, regularly gave *Darshan* to the devotees as Devi.

The Holy Mother was the embodiment of Universal
Love. Those virtues obvious since early childhood such
as the urge to love, help and serve people, fully un-
folded. The Mother accepted the worldly and the spiritual, the illiterate and the educated, the rich and the
poor, the sick and the healthy with the same equal
tenderness and compassion. Patiently listening to all
the problems which they came to unburden, She would
adapt Her counsel to the nature and maturity of each
one. According to each one's need, She would guide
and comfort them in all their difficulties.

Soon after the beginning of *Devi Bhava Darshan*,
there occurred certain changes in Mother. During Her
Devi *sadhana*, She was generally aloof and uncommu-

nicative. All Her time was devoted to prayer and meditation on the form of the Divine Mother. If Her parents or brother abused Her physically or verbally, She kept silent. Now She became more daring, and even Her facial expression changed. Her nature became fearless and unyielding when it came to dealing with Her parents and brother over the issues of the *Bhava Darshan* and Her association with the devotees in particular. She now began mingling more with the devotees and instructing them spiritually. This marked the beginning of the Mother's spiritual mission.

MY OWN FORMLESS SELF

"From that day onwards[36] I could see nothing as different from my own Formless Self wherein the entire universe exists as a tiny bubble..."

So saying, the Holy Mother conveys a wealth of insight. Although established in the ultimate state of God-Realization, the Mother performed additional *sadhana* to demonstrate that all the different forms of gods and goddesses are facets of the same non-dual Reality. Having attained perfect control over the mind, She found that She could identify Herself with any aspect of the Divine which She chose by Her own will. Mother has narrated various experiences which She had while performing these sadhanas:

"One day at the end of *sadhana*, I felt that a large canine tooth was coming out of my mouth. Simultaneously, I heard a terrific humming sound. I perceived the form of Devi with large canine teeth, a long protruding tongue, thick black curly hair, reddish bulging

eyes and dark blue in color.[37] I thought, 'Quick! Escape! Devi is coming to kill me!' I was about to run
away. Suddenly I realized that I myself am Devi. The
humming sound also was being produced by me. The
next moment I found that I was holding Devi's *veena*.[38]
I had Her crown on my head and I was wearing the
Mother's nose ring. After a couple of minutes I thought,
'What is this? How have I become Devi? Maybe this is
a trick played by the Divine Mother to obstruct my
sadhana.' So I thought, 'Let me meditate on Siva and
see what happens,' but the moment I began meditating
on Lord Siva's form, I became Him, matted hair, snakes
on my neck and coiled on my upper arms. I thought,
'Maybe Siva is also testing me,' so I stopped meditating on His form. Now I fixed my heart and soul on
Lord Ganesha, the remover of obstacles. Immediately
my being changed to that of Ganesha, an elephant's
face with a long trunk, a pair of tusks with one half
broken, and so on. Whichever form of god or goddess
I contemplated, I became. Then I heard a voice from
within, "You are not different from them. They have
all merged in you long ago. Then why should you call
on all these gods and goddesses?"

Thenceforth, the Holy Mother's meditation on God
with form naturally subsided. The all-pervasive sacred
syllable 'OM' sprang forth from within Her, and Her
whole being was forever merged in That. Even then, to
set an example, She would sit and meditate. When asked
about this, the Holy Mother explained, "During meditation, Mother approaches all the children, especially
those who are intensely thinking of Mother or those
who are suffering."

A similar incident occurs in the great epic, *Srimad Bhagavatam*. One day, when the renowned sage, Narada, visited Dwaraka, the Abode of Sri Krishna, he found the Lord sitting in deep meditation. Narada reverentially bowed to the Lord and asked, "O Lord, on whom are You meditating?" The Lord smilingly replied, "I am meditating upon my devotees."

Although the little one had become "Mother" in the eyes of many, She remained Sudhamani to Her family. Her natural abidance in the Supreme Self was far too subtle for Her parents and elder brother to understand. They continued to doubt and misinterpret Her behavior as schizophrenia. They feared that Her contact with the devotees would result in Her deviating from the path of morality and thereby bring disrepute to the family. Her brother Subhagan was especially fanatical in his aggression against the Mother, and his behavior toward Her became violent. One day, Subhagan and a few of his cousins called the Mother to a relative's house under a false pretext. When She arrived, they locked Her in a room and one of Her cousins began threatening Her, suddenly pulling out a long knife which he had hidden in his clothing. Subhagan announced, "This behavior of yours has gone too far! You are bound to spoil the family name. Since you cannot stop mixing freely with all sorts of people and persist in your singing and dancing, it is better that you die." He was enraged to hear the Mother laugh and retort, "I am not at all afraid of death. The body must meet its end sooner or later, but it is impossible for you to kill the Self. Now that you are determined to put an end to my physical existence, I will express a last wish. You are obliged to fulfill it. Let me meditate for a while, and then you may kill me while I am in meditation."

Hearing Her daring answer, they became still more infuriated. One among them exclaimed, "Who are you to command us? Are we here to kill you or not kill you according to your wish?" Mother smiled and boldly retorted, "It seems that nobody but God alone can put an end to my life!" Another of the cousins shouted, "God! Who is your God?" Though they verbally threatened the Holy Mother, none of them was courageous enough to do anything to Her after hearing Her bold reply and seeing Her unperturbed. Suddenly the cousin who had brandished the knife jumped forward and pressed the knife against Her chest as if to stab Her. But he could not make another move, as he was immediately stricken by an excruciating pain in his own chest at the exact point where he had pressed the knife against the Holy Mother's. He fell to the floor in agony. Seeing this, the others in the room were filled with dread. At this moment Damayanti arrived, having seen Sudhamani leaving with Subhagan and his cousins. Hearing the uproar, she began pounding on the door, shouting. When the door was opened, Damayanti took the Holy Mother by the hand and led Her home, taking the path by the shore. On the way back to Idamannel, the Mother told Damayanti, "Your people are dishonored by me. This ocean is my Mother as well. She will accept me happily with outstretched arms. I am going to Her lap." Hearing Her words, Damayanti became mentally unbalanced. She began screaming, "Don't say that, daughter! Don't say like that, daughter! During *Krishna Bhava*, Bhagavan told me that if you happen to commit suicide, all my

children will go insane..." Succeeding in dissuading
the Holy Mother, she took Her back to Idamannel.

The episode does not end here. The cousin who had
raised the knife against the Mother to stab Her was
taken in pain to the hospital. Though provided with
excellent medical treatment, he finally died, continuously vomiting blood. As his disease was in its acute
stages, the Holy Mother visited him in the hospital.
She lovingly consoled him and fed him with Her own
hands. He was deeply repentant toward Her for his
grave mistake, and burst into tears experiencing Her
compassion and forgiveness.

The Holy Mother had no enmity toward Her cousin
who had attempted to murder Her, nor had She made
any resolve to avenge his evil act. He simply suffered
the fruit of his action. The Mother explained, "Just as
human beings have intense love for Mother, numerous
subtle beings love Her as well. If somebody attempts
to harm Mother, Mother does not react. Mother faces
such a person without any excitement and does not
even think any harmful thought regarding him who acts
out of ignorance. But these subtle beings get angry and
take revenge. Do you understand how this is? Suppose
someone's mother is attacked by a man. Do the children sit back indifferently? Even if their mother tried
to stop them, they would find the man and take revenge."

Transcending the constraints of worldly existence,
the Holy Mother would receive devotees without differ-
entiation of caste, creed, class or gender. In the eyes
of ignorant nonbelievers, the equal vision and broad-
mindedness of the Holy Mother was just the manifes-

tation of a mental aberration. The miscreants continued to enter the temple during the *Bhava Darshan* to
question the Mother antagonistically. Though the Mother
remained unaffected and calm, Sugunanandan became
very depressed by their insolent remarks. Furthermore,
although all his attempts to arrange the marriage of his
daughter had ended in failure, he still could not completely let go of this idea. He now began to feel the
Bhava Darshan was a great impediment to the fulfillment of his wish. He joined Subhagan in his firm belief that the *Darshan* was a shameful thing. Something
else also worried him. His daughter's body would become stone-hard after the *Bhava* and only hours of strong
massage would return it to normal.

Sugunanandan's mind was resolved to join Subhagan
to somehow put an end to the *Bhava Darshan*. Entering
the temple during the next *Devi Bhava*, Sugunanandan
told the Holy Mother, "Devi should go away from the
little one's body. We don't need this *Bhava Darshan*
here anymore. We want to give her in marriage. I want
my daughter back!"[39]

The Holy Mother addressed him as stepfather[40] and
asked, "Is she your daughter?" Already agitated, he
became more furious hearing himself addressed that
way and angrily retorted, "Yes! She is my daughter.
Do gods and goddesses have stepfathers? I want my
daughter back!"

The Holy Mother calmly replied, "If I give back
your daughter, she will be nothing but a corpse and
will soon be decomposing. You will have to bury her,
not marry her." Not being in the mood to listen,
Sugunanandan demanded, "Let the Goddess go back to

Her own place! I want my child back!"

The Mother said, "If so, here is your daughter. Take her!" Instantly the Mother fell to the temple floor. Within a few moments Her body became stiff and Her heartbeat stopped. Though Her eyes were wide open, there was no sign of life to be seen. She was dead.

A great wailing arose. All those who had come for the *Darshan* became overwhelmed with grief. Damayanti and her other daughters fainted on the ground. The news flashed that Devi had taken away Sudhamani's life because of some error committed by Sugunanandan. Everyone accused him of being the cause of the untimely death of the Mother.

Oil lamps were lit around the body. Even Nature became silent in that moment. Some of the devotees burst into tears, others blabbered like idiots with sudden uncontrollable emotion. Others sat solemnly near the body, testing to see if there were any breath coming from the Mother, by holding their hands near Her nostrils. There was nothing. A doctor checked Her pulse. She was dead. It was a terrible moment.

Coming to realize the horror of the situation caused by his indiscriminate action, and unable to bear the excruciating pain in his heart, Sugunanandan also fell unconscious. A mournful silence reigned. Thinking that the impossible had truly happened, all hope of reviving Her was given up. Eight ominous hours dragged by. Regaining his consciousness only to confront the dreadful scene, Sugunanandan cried aloud his prayer to the Divine Mother, "O Devi! I beg You, forgive me for speaking words which I uttered in extreme ignorance! Please bring my daughter back to life! Forgive

my fault! Never again will I repeat this despicable
action!" Imploring, he fell on the ground, weeping
uncontrollably in full prostration before the temple.

Suddenly one among the devotees noticed faint signs
of movement in the Holy Mother's body. With soaring
hope, the devotees watched Her as their tears of sorrow were transformed into tears of joy. The Mother came
back to life, but in *Krishna Bhava*! Addressing
Sugunanandan, who was an ardent devotee of Krishna,
She told him, "Without Shakti[41] there can be no
Krishna!"

This incident brought about a great change in the
father's attitude toward God and his daughter. From
that time on, he left Her to do as She liked and never
again tried to arrange a marriage for Her. Later, the
Mother remarked about this particular incident,
"He was adamant about getting his daughter back from
Devi. But if She had really been their daughter, they
would have had the power to bring Her back to life as
well. That they could not do. At the most, this body is
theirs. When he demanded his child back, this body
was given."

CHAPTER NINE

THE SWORD OF TRUTH

Children, even when a man is cutting a tree down from its root, it gives him shade. A spiritual aspirant should be like this. Only he who prays even for the welfare of those who torment him can become a spiritual person. The spiritual aspirant's greatest weapon is the sword of Truth.

- MATA AMRITANANDAMAYI -

Durvritta vritta samanam tava dēvi sīlam
Rūpam tadhaitadavi cintyamatulya manyaih

Vīryam ca hantr hritadēvaparākramānām
Vairisvapi prākatitaiva dayā tvayēdham

*O Devi, Your nature is to subdue the conduct of
the wicked; this Your peerless beauty is inconceiv-
able for others; Your power destroys those who
have robbed the gods of their prowess, and You
have thus manifested Your compassion even toward the enemies.*

DEVI MAHATMYAM
CHAPTER 4, VERSE 21

It seems that all Great Souls must endure the persecution of the mediocre minded. However, the Great Ones
seem to thrive on it, as every obstacle thrown in their
path adds to their glory. The lives of Sri Krishna, Sri
Rama, Jesus Christ and Buddha offer abundant illustration of this fact. The Holy Mother's life is also a
magnificent example. Three years had now passed. By
1978 the number of devotees was growing rapidly, and
people were flocking to Idamannel from all parts of
India for the auspicious *Darshan* of the Holy Mother.
As Her admirers increased, the miscreants intensified
their evil campaign, but no worldly power could obstruct the spiritual mission of the Holy Mother.

At this time, certain bad omens were seen which
forebode a catastrophe at Idamannel. Subhagan was not
at all deterred by the ill consequences of his attempt
to have his sister murdered in cold blood. He now became

more openly arrogant and hostile toward the Holy Mother.
He tried to impose his own selfish ideas on the whole
family. Even they were afraid to oppose him because
of his volatile, hot-tempered nature. The increasing
number of devotees and the unabated slander of the
rationalists set his mind on fire with restlessness. He
began accosting devotees coming for the *Bhava Darshan* and severely abusing them, hoping to dissuade them
from partaking in the *Darshan*.

At this point, either due to fate or as a result of his
vile actions bearing fruit, Subhagan became afflicted
with the terrible disease elephantiasis. Symptoms of
this disease appeared on both his hands and legs.
Although he underwent various medical treatments, none
had a curative effect. The thought that he had become
terminally ill plagued him constantly. He became severely depressed and developed suicidal tendencies.
Several times he expressed his mental anguish to his
close friends. He developed insomnia as a result and
resorted to taking sleeping pills. The cumulative effect
of his physical and emotional afflictions took its toll
and gradually Subhagan lost his mental balance.

One day the Holy Mother called Damayanti and told
her, "It seems that brother Subhagan is nearing the
end of his life span. To avert this you can take a vow
of silence, but certain obstacles will arise to try to
break your vow. Therefore, be careful when you take
the vow." Adhering to the Mother's words, Damayanti
observed a vow of silence one day. However, halfway
through the day, one of the cows broke its rope and
started running from their cowshed. Damayanti completely forgot her vow and shouted, "There goes the

cow! Catch it!" The family took this as a bad omen, especially since Damayanti had been forewarned by the Mother to attend her vow with care. This inauspicious occurrence filled the family with fear and anxiety.

One day Subhagan, in a fit of fury, severely harassed a Muslim woman who had come to Idamannel for the *Bhava Darshan*. Unable to bear Subhagan's vicious remarks, the lady rushed to the temple, burst into tears and began beating her head against the threshold of the shrine room. She was crying out, "O Mother...O Mother...is this the fate of those who come to see You?"

Hearing the Muslim woman's distraught cries, the Mother's radiant and smiling face underwent an immediate transformation. With a terrifying appearance, She stood up from the sacred seat holding a trident in one hand and a sword in the other. In a solemn and deep tone the Mother said, "Whoever has caused this undue grief to this devotee will die after seven days."

When the Mother's prediction reached the ears of Sugunanandan, he rushed to the temple seeking forgiveness for his son's grievous behavior. He pleaded to the Mother to spare Subhagan's life and take his instead. Mother calmly said, "I never punish anybody. If I am abused or harassed I don't care at all. But when a devotee suffers such abuse even God will not forgive. Each one must experience the fruit of one's actions. There is no other way."

Seven days had passed. It was nearly midnight on June 2, 1978 when Subhagan, who had been informed of the Mother's prediction, committed suicide by hanging. He had written a suicide note giving the reason as unbearable stress caused by his incurable disease. Subhagan's suicide created chaos and distress at Idamannel house. The miscreants immediately seized this opportunity to strengthen their campaign against the Holy Mother. They began spreading fabricated versions of Subhagan's death. They accused Sugunanandan, who loved his eldest son like his own life, of murdering Subhagan.

For all their effort, the miscreants were unable to gain any ground with their unrighteous accusation since there was ample evidence that the death was a suicide. In addition to the suicide note in his own handwriting, Subhagan had also sent letters to some of his friends and relatives informing them of his intention. The post-mortem report also verified the death as suicide. Thus, the question of legal action did not arise.

Subhagan's suicide caused a stir among the family's relatives. They openly expressed their hatred and non-cooperation by completely ignoring the whole family as if it never existed. The family was no longer invited to attend or participate in public functions, festivals, marriage ceremonies or religious rites and rituals. All the relatives abandoned them. They would come to visit the house next door, but would not even look in the direction of Idamannel. If the relatives came to the seashore near Idamannel to perform rites for the ancestors, they would leave immediately after making the offering. This treatment was very hard on the family and added additional weight to their already heavy hearts.

Sixteen days after Subhagan's death when the *Bhava Darshan* was resumed, Sugunanandan approached the Holy Mother with a heavy heart. He complained that the Mother had not saved his dear son from a horrible death and burst into tears. Consoling him, the Mother said, "Do not worry. Your deceased son will again take birth as a devotee in this same house after three years." A few years later the eldest daughter, Kasturi was married. When she conceived her first child, the Holy Mother named the child 'Siva' while it was still in the womb. As the Mother had given a male name, the family was convinced that the child would be a boy. The child was in fact a boy. After his birth the Mother once said, "For the three years since Subhagan died, his soul has been around this Ashram atmosphere. Having heard the devotional singing and Vedic mantras, he was again given a birth as 'Siva' in this same house." Sivan grew to be an intelligent young boy. Since his infancy he would chant the sacred syllable 'OM' and sit in meditation without being asked.

THE RETURN OF THE RATIONALISTS

After the beginning of the *Devi Bhava*, the rationalists became more arrogant and antagonistic. They began using the news media to try and mislead people into thinking that the Holy Mother was a lunatic and that the *Bhava Darshan* was a fraud. However, the greater their efforts were to defame the Mother, the greater too were their failures. Their persistence was really a wonder!

One night, the miscreants decided to try again their old but unsuccessful tactic of catching hold of the Mother during the *Darshan* to humiliate Her and thus make a mockery of Godly power. Two of the rowdier members of their group appeared on the scene, fully drunk and

eager to create trouble in the shrine room. They joined
the other devotees in the queue in order to enter.

At that time, the Mother was already seated for the
Devi Bhava and told some of the devotees who were
sitting near Her in the shrine, "Just watch, Mother will
show you a good joke." With these words, She looked
directly at the drunkards and cast an enchanting smile
at them. By this time, they had reached the doorway of
the shrine room, but the one who was standing in front
became unable to move as if he was paralyzed. He
could not take another step and stood there frozen for
a couple of minutes. His cohort immediately behind
him became infuriated at this and asked in a harsh
voice why he was not entering the temple. "Can't you
see how many people are already standing inside the
temple ahead of me!" he retorted. The other man shouted,
"You've been just standing like a pile of wood for a
long time! Have you also been hypnotized by this girl?"
This sharp verbal exchange escalated into a fierce fight
between the two rowdies as they left Idamannel, as the
Holy Mother had already foreseen.

As previously mentioned, in those days some of the
householder devotees used to invite the Holy Mother
to their homes to conduct worship and devotional singing. Coming to know that the Mother would be visiting
a certain house, the miscreants would also gather there.
One evening the Mother visited a house situated in the
village Panmana which is about twenty kilometers from
Parayakadavu. For a long time the family members of
this house had been suffering various physical and mental
ailments for which they had been unable to find a
solution. They had conducted various pujas to invoke

the help of different Gods and Goddesses but to no avail. Coming to hear of the Holy Mother, they had attended the *Bhava Darshan* and appealed to Her for help. The compassionate Mother agreed to come to their house and perform a special *puja* to eliminate their ailments.

As it turned out, some of the family members were against the worship and joined up with the miscreants who were making preparations to disrupt the worship. On the evening of the Mother's visit one of the family members, full of arrogance, told the Holy Mother, "Let me observe the worship. I will keenly watch everything, and then I have certain questions to ask." Then the Mother asked him, "Is this 'I' something limited only to your body? Is it under your possession?"

It was now two o'clock in the morning and the Mother was preparing all the items for the *puja*. The person who had made the pompous declaration fell back in an unconscious state as if in a deep sleep much to the relief of the devoted family members. Just as the last step of the *puja* was completed the arrogant fellow woke up with a start. He jumped up and exclaimed, "Oh, is the worship over? Oh, is it over...?"

The Mother replied, "Yes, it is finished. You said you would watch it keenly. Did you see it? Now do you understand that the thing we call 'I' is not under our control? When you were sleeping, where did your 'I' go?" The man turned pale and hung his head without uttering a word.

The miscreants who had also gathered there were not put off so easily. They began questioning the Holy Mother in a most rude and irrational manner. The Mother remained ever cheerful and unperturbed, but the *brah-macharin*[42] who had come to assist in the *puja* got fed up. He asked the Mother, "Please show them something to keep their mouths shut. Otherwise they won't cease their disturbance."

A few more minutes had passed when suddenly there rose up from the nearby graveyard a tremendous blazing fireball. Rays of fire emerged from it, dancing around the fiery orb. Now it was the Mother's turn to ask a question to the dumbfounded troublemakers. "Those of you who are courageous, why not walk to the graveyard and back?" Not one of them stepped forward to accept the challenge. After a moment, the frightened men-turned-boys stepped back and fled from the place.

Another similar incident occurred in 1980 in the home of Srimati Indira of Karunagapally, a town about ten kilometers from Vallickavu.[43] Indira was an ardent devotee and had invited the Holy Mother to visit her home to bestow sanctity there. As usual, the rationalists also arrived on the appointed evening. Upon seeing them the family members became frightened as their bad reputation was well known. They prayed to the Mother to disperse the band of non-believers.

The Mother became absorbed in meditation. Within a couple of seconds to everyone's surprise there appeared a brilliantly shining orb surrounded by many bright lights which looked like tiny lamps. This orb appeared at the northern side of the house and began moving in a southward direction passing through the front door. The devotees were filled with awe and reverence and uttered the Divine Mother's Name. Slowly the orb flew higher and higher and finally disappeared into the distance, but only after it had circumambulated the sacred bilva tree (*aegle marmelos*) growing in the southern yard. Astounded and frightened, the non-believers left the house. They never returned to disturb the devotional singing of the Mother and in fact, after this incident, many of them also became devotees.

BLACK MAGIC FAILS

There was a very egotistical sorcerer who lived nearby the before mentioned house. Somebody had told him of a young girl in Parayakadavu who was possessed by Krishna and Devi three nights a week. The black magician boasted that he would bring a quick end to the possession. He even described the incantation he would use. "I will split the midrib of a coconut leaf blade in two while uttering certain powerful mantras, and the visit of the God and the Goddess in her body will immediately stop," he declared. Thus he came to Idamannel one day. Try as he might, none of his trickery produced the boasted result and he had to leave after tasting a dose of his own ego. Still he persisted in his witchcraft against the Mother. On several occasions he sent Her ash which had been imbued with evil mantras, but all of his attempts failed. Shortly thereafter he himself went crazy and became a beggar in the streets. He would always be heard asking people, "Give me ten *paise*, give me ten *paise*..."

There was a priest who lived in Arickal, a village on the same island where the Holy Mother lived. Besides being a temple priest, he was also a well known sorcerer who was particularly efficient in driving out

evil spirits and subtle beings that had possessed innocent people. It seems that one elderly woman who had
a strong disliking for the Holy Mother, secretly approached this priest. Her intention was to persuade
him to use his powers to bring the downfall of the Holy
Mother and the Divine *Bhavas*. In order to initiate the
conjuration the woman wrote the Holy Mother's Name
and birth star on a piece of paper and gave it to the
priest.

That same day, another woman devotee of the Mother
had a dream where the Holy Mother appeared and said
that she should go to a particular temple the next day
and offer her prayers there. The next day, the devotee
came to the Holy Mother and told Her about the dream.
The Mother said, "You go there and come back. Then
you will understand the significance of the dream."

Thus, having taken the permission of the Holy Mother,
the woman proceeded to the temple indicated in her
dream. Unknown to the devotee, this was the same temple
where the priest who had been persuaded to carry out
black magic against the Mother conducted the daily
worship. Having offered her prayers in the temple, the
devotee went to meet the priest to discuss a few things.
Seeing the devotee, the priest expressed his hospital-
ity and got up from the cot where he was sitting. He
began rolling up the mattress saying "Come, please sit
down...please be seated..." As he was rolling up the
mattress, a small scrap of paper fell on the ground in
front of the devotee. Picking it up, she saw the Holy
Mother's name and birth star written on the scrap of
paper. Immediately, she understood the import of the
paper and the priest-sorcerer and the dream. She be-

gan beating her chest saying, "What have you done? Have you done something to our Mother? If so, then we cannot live anymore!" Saying thus she burst into tears. The priest explained, "No, no, I have not done anything. An old lady came here yesterday telling me over and over that I should destroy that place. In order to get her to quit bothering me, I took this note from her and kept it here."

Observing the priest's sincerity, she calmed down and said to him, "Please, come and see for yourself what is happening there. Then you will understand the truth of the matter." The priest agreed to come there soon and observe the situation first hand.

As promised, the priest arrived at Idamannel during one *Bhava Darshan*. Hearing about the infamous priest's arrival, a big crowd of believers and non-believers gathered and anxiously awaited to see the sorcerer's meeting with the Mother. Some said, "This priest is a great magician. He will put an end to everything that is going on here." The devotees said with strong conviction, "He is not going to do anything."

The priest had come with an elderly woman and he gave her a packet of beaten rice[44] to hold while he entered the temple. The priest had already decided that he would become a devotee of the Mother if She could prove to him that She was really a Divine Being. The Mother was in *Krishna Bhava*. She gave him a handful of sacred ash and asked, "Are you not here to chant this mantra?" She then uttered an obscure mantra which was known only to the priest. The priest was taken aback. The Mother continued, "Aren't you a worshipper of Hanuman? You should not chant evil mantras with the same tongue which you use to chant His

Name." The priest stood there speechless. Nobody in the whole world knew that his *Upasana Murthi* (Beloved Deity) was Hanuman. The Mother had just revealed the greatest secret in his life. But the Mother was not finished with him. "Didn't you ask a lady to stand outside and hold a packet of beaten rice? Kuchela[45] went to Sri Krishna with an offering of beaten rice. Have you not come with the same offering of rice? Except Kuchela offered the beaten rice of renunciation and truth to Krishna. Even though the rice was full of stones and sand, the Lord couldn't see it. He looked and could only see Kuchela's pure devotion and open heart. He saw neither the stones nor sand. Everything was ambrosia. That is why the Lord ate it. Why did you borrow raw rice from your neighbor? And after husking the paddy, why did you mix it with stones and sand and bring it here?"

The priest was incredulous. Hearing all that he had done coming from the mouth of the Holy Mother in exacting detail, he burst into tears. With deep remorse, he sought forgiveness for his evil actions. From that day foreward, he became a true devotee of the Holy Mother.

FURTHER EXPLOITS OF THE COMMITTEE TO STOP BLIND BELIEFS

The Committee to Stop Blind Beliefs now launched more devious plans against the Holy Mother. They tried to influence high police officials and government authorities to make a move against the *Bhava Darshan*. The Committee's activity led to several investigations, both public and undercover, but the only outcome to be seen was that many of the investigators became devotees!

One evening as the *Devi Bhava* was in progress, the troublemakers ordered the girl who was singing devotional songs to stop. The girl retorted, "I will sing. I have faith in the Holy Mother." A wordy duel started from this incident which culminated in a quarrel between the devotees and the rowdies. Finally, Sugunanandan arrived on the scene and chased them away.

Soon after they left, the Holy Mother called Her father and warned him, "They have gone to lodge a petition against us. I will be the first defendant and you will be the second. You must go beforehand and inform the authorities of the true situation." Without heeding the words of the Mother, he said, "They won't lodge a case against us. The police won't come here." The Mother insisted several more times and at last, Sugunanandan went to the police station. He found that the Holy Mother's prediction was perfectly true and he presented his case clearly and sincerely.

"We are not cheating anybody. It is true that my daughter is manifesting Divine Moods. Only if you come there yourself will you really understand the truth of the matter. The devotees come and sing devotional songs. There is nothing artificial there. Water taken from the public tap and ash purchased from Oachira are the substances distributed as *prasadam*.[46] We never materialize flowers from the sky. We offer flowers plucked from the trees and bushes. No advertisement or publicity is given about the Divine Moods. People come after

hearing the experiences of others who have already
witnessed the *Bhava Darshan*. Above all, this takes
place in my house. It is nobody else's property. The
miscreants come to my house to fight and quarrel with
me. Is this justice? Therefore, I request you to protect
us from them!"

The officers could not utter a word after hearing
what Sugunanandan said and seeing his emphatic sincerity. The false petition was canceled. The miscreants were furious. In retaliation they launched their
next plot to harm the Mother. In those days during the
Bhava Darshan after the Holy Mother revealed Her
oneness with Devi, She would come out from the temple
and dance in bliss. One evening, the miscreants came
to Idamannel with a basket full of poisonous thorns.
These thorns were so sharp and poisonous that if even
one pierced a person's foot, they would fall down unconscious.

The thorns were entrusted to a group of local children who had been instructed to scatter them on the
ground where the Mother always danced. This was to
be done during the *Deeparadhana*[47] so that all the attention would be on the Holy Mother and not on the
children spreading the thorns. This is exactly what the
children did. When the Mother emerged from the temple
She gave an intimation to the devotees about what had
occurred and warned them not to move from where they
stood. With that, the Mother began Her ecstatic dance
holding the sword and the trident in Her uplifted hands.
It was an awe-inspiring sight. The devotees felt as if
Mother Kali Herself, the Destroyer of evil, was dancing before them. She was dancing along the verandah

at the front of the temple when suddenly Her sword severed the strings which held the pictures on the wall. They came to the ground with a crash scattering broken glass all over the verandah. Unmindful of the hazard, the Mother continued dancing, all the while trampling the broken pieces of glass as if they were merely flower petals.

Those who had come to harm the Holy Mother were wonderstruck at this sight but still waited full of hope to see Her feet bleeding full of thorns and witness the Mother collapsing on the ground unable to bear the excruciating pain.

Then the Mother stepped down from the temple verandah and came right to the place where the thorns had been scattered. She drew a line on the ground with the tip of Her sword and forbade anyone to cross over it. With that, She stepped over the line and danced for a long time trampling the poisonous thorns. The miscreants could not believe their eyes. Now they became extremely nervous seeing this blood-curdling sight and immediately left.

When Sugunanandan realized what was happening, he began running here and there full of dread thinking of his daughter's wounded feet. He came with medicine to treat the wounds, but much to his astonishment he could not find even a trace of a scratch or a prick.

Although the so-called rationalists witnessed many such miracles with their own eyes, they were not ready to relinquish their envy and enmity toward the Mother. From the viewpoint of the villagers and the devotees, the extraordinary happenings around the Mother were a source of wonder. But for the Mother, ever abiding in the Supreme Reality, these events were all child's play. When some of the devotees came to Her depressed by the endless stream of harassment imposed on their beloved Mother by the unrighteous miscreants, She said, "Children, there is no world without the dualities of pleasure and pain, light and darkness, etc. We should not be bothered by all these things. Mother's devotees are all around the world. They will not be deluded by all these actions."

The Holy Mother advised the devotees and family members to be calm and patient. They implicitly followed the Mother's advice and silently endured the dreadful behavior of the rationalists.

On another occasion, some of the younger members of the rationalist movement came to Idamannel with a mischievous intention. They had decided to imitate the dance of the Holy Mother during the *Bhava* thinking that they could deceive the devotees and make a mockery of the Mother.

By the time they arrived, the *Darshan* had already begun. The Mother was lovingly receiving the devotees one by one. At the same time, She called a few of the devotees and told them of the youths' intention to dance in imitation of Her. She forbade the devotees from harming them and sent them outside after giving the necessary instructions. These devotees waited with alertness. After some time, one of the youths started to make a show. He tried to imitate certain gestures which the Holy Mother manifested during the Divine Mood. The vigilant devotees surrounded the trickster and began questioning him. Unable to answer their questions, he became frightened and understood the seriousness of what he had done. All his friends immediately fled leaving this boy behind. Running in confusion, he finally jumped into the backwaters! The devotees dragged him out of the water. They gave him a stern warning not to repeat his foolish actions and sent him on his way.

At this time, the miscreants launched their most bold and macabre plan of all. They hired an assassin to enter the temple and stab the Mother to death during the *Bhava Darshan*. Concealing a knife under his clothes, he entered the temple. Seeing him, the Mother beamed a benign smile at him and continued receiving the devotees. Her smile had a strangely soothing effect on him. Coming to his senses and realizing his grave mistake, he fell at the Mother's feet begging Her forgiveness. When he left the temple, he was a changed man. Noticing the startling change which had come over him, his villainous comrades asked him whether he too had been mesmerized by the Holy Mother. He merely smiled at them and thenceforth became an ardent devotee of the Mother.

During this period, it became impossible for the Holy Mother to walk along the road or village path without being verbally abused by the uncouth troublemakers. They would stand on either side of the road and mock Her in a very coarse manner. They even encouraged the young village children to do the same. If it were early morning, they would hide behind trees and bushes and even throw stones at Her. These barbarians did not limit their torments to the Holy Mother. The whole family fell a prey to their deplorable pastime. Seeing a family member, they would call out,

"Here comes Krishna! Here comes Krishna!"

If the rationalists had no other plan for the evening, they would then enter the temple and make false claims to the Mother hoping to expose Her as a fraud. One man came to the Mother and told Her that he was blind. She immediately shot out Her forefinger as if to poke out his eye. The man jumped back and cried out, "Oh!" Thus, the Mother exposed the fraud of the one who came to defraud Her.

On another occasion, a young man came to the Mother and said that he had severe pain in his arm. He expected the Mother to massage his arm believing his words. Instead, She asked a *brahmacharin* standing nearby to rub the man's arm. As soon as the *brahmacharin* touched his arm, the man experienced severe pain in the exact place that he had described to the Mother. Unable to bear the racking pain, he sought Her forgiveness for his childish prank. Without fail, those who came to defraud the Mother were themselves exposed as frauds.

"TODAY'S ENEMY IS TOMORROW'S FRIEND"

Sugunanandan became fed up hearing and seeing this perpetual nonsense and evil actions of the rationalists. Frustrated, one night during *Devi Bhava* he approached the Mother and said, "Is this the fruit which God has given me? People call me the murderer of my own son! I cannot walk through the village without constant reproach. This is a pitiful situation. Devi should punish the evildoers!"

The Mother replied, "Wait and see. Today's enemy

is tomorrow's friend. Then who should I punish? Those who oppose you today will come and marry your daughters tomorrow. Console yourself thinking that everything happens according to God's Will. If your one son is gone, thousands of sons will come tomorrow." Damayanti was steeped in sorrow over the death of her son. The Holy Mother told her, "Don't be sad. In future, many children will come here from all over the world. Love them as your own children."

Though the Holy Mother's days and nights were dedicated to bestowing solace and succor upon the devotees, She still found time to serve and extend help to family members who were facing critical moments in life. From a worldly point of view, She was a young maiden, yet She did perfect justice to thousands of Her devotees as well as Her own parents without even slightly deviating from the path of truth and righteousness. Her attitude toward Her family and the way She looked after them was a source of inspiration for the householder devotees. The Mother was an impeccable example of how one could be spiritual and still fulfill one's duty to one's family while remaining detached and pure.

Though Sugunanandan had a fish marketing business, it was not very profitable. He finally closed it when the *Bhava Darshan* began bringing large numbers of people from all over the country to his house. Also, he could not concentrate on his business due to the opposition of the villagers and other problems which had cropped up in connection with the *Bhava Darshan*. He was forced to spend all his time at Idamannel. Besides all this, he still had three daughters yet to be

married, though he seemed rather unconcerned. His
sons were all in school. Now and then someone in the
family would be afflicted with an illness requiring
medical attention.

At this point, perhaps triggered by all this stress
and strain, Sugunanandan was hospitalized in the beginning of 1979 and subsequently had to undergo surgery. The hospital was in Quilon, a city thirty five
kilometers south of Vallickavu. There was nobody to
help with the household chores or to tend Sugunanandan
in the hospital. All the relatives had disowned the family.
Kasturi was working in a distant place. Damayanti was
bedridden with rheumatic pain. The boys were either
too young or studying in school. All the burden fell on
the Holy Mother's shoulders.

On *Darshan* days the devotees began arriving at
one o'clock. By four in the afternoon the Mother would
sit for the devotional singing followed by the *Bhava
Darshan* which would sometimes go on until eight or
nine the next morning. The Mother would not leave
Her seat in the temple until everybody had been received. In between all this, She would give instruction
to the spiritual aspirants who came seeking Her guidance. After the *Darshan* ended, the Mother would attend to all the household chores just as She had done
for so many years. She would get all the younger ones
ready and send them off to school. Once all the work
had been accomplished, the Mother would go to Quilon
bringing food and necessities to Sugunanandan in the
hospital. She looked after him with utmost care and
sincerely served him throughout his illness.

The miscreants never missed an opportunity. When

the Mother walked through the village on Her way to Quilon, they would mock Her and throw stones. They would call out, "Krishna, Krishna..." Silently enduring all their misguided behavior, the Mother thought, "At least in this way they are chanting the Lord's Name." Once a rowdy even tried to seize the Holy Mother, but when he jumped forward to catch Her, he slipped and fell into the roadside ditch.

Gradually, Sugunanandan regained his health. However, shortly thereafter Damayanti was also hospitalized followed by Suresh. Throughout this period, it was the Mother who looked after all household duties and served the hospitalized family members.

Chaos and confusion prevailed in the family atmosphere but no matter what the situation, the Mother remained a solid pillar of support and sustenance, ever calm and compassionate. Imagine the situation. The uproar created by Subhagan's suicide, the noncooperation of the relatives, the antagonism of the rationalists, the flocking of thousands of devotees for the *Bhava Darshan*, and three unmarried daughters in the house. It is no wonder that nobody was eager to make a marriage alliance with this family! If somebody came with a marriage proposal from a distant place, by the time they reached Idamannel, certain members of the village had met up with them to discourage them from their proposal. Several prospective grooms had beaten a quick retreat.

And so it was that Sugunanandan again approached the Holy Mother and said, "Because of the *Bhava Darshan*, I have lost my honor. I cannot even show my face outside of Idamannel. The villagers as well as the relatives hate me and my daughters remain unmarried. What am I to do?"

The Holy Mother replied, "It is not the *Bhava Darshan* which is the cause of all your misfortune. Everything moves according to Divine Will. All will take place at the proper time. Do not worry." Sugunanandan was not to be consoled this time. He angrily shouted, "I will drink poison and die!" Hearing this, the Mother turned to a portrait of Devi and asked with tear-filled eyes, "O Compassionate Mother, am I bringing only sorrow to these people?"

Occasions were not rare when the Mother decided to leave Idamannel and even began making preparations to do so. But each time, this act was mysteriously blocked. Again Sugunanandan approached the Mother with his anxiety. Again She told him, "Do not worry. The marriage of your daughters will take place without much delay."

Within a month, the words of the Mother came true. A marriage proposal came for Sugunamma from the most unexpected family. This family had been staunchly against the Holy Mother and the bridegroom was one of the ringleaders of the rationalist movement. Ironically, now that the marriage was fixed, Sugunanandan dropped out of the picture. The total responsibility for arranging the actual wedding fell to the Holy Mother! Established as She was in a state of perfect equanimity, it seemed that there was nothing which could shake the initiative and efficiency of the Mother. The marriage ceremony went successfully despite the fact that Sugunanandan stood on the side lines casually observing the whole event.

The Holy Mother's words, "Today's enemy is tomorrow's friend," came true and the same was repeated for the other daughters' marriages as well.

There is a saying in Malayalam, 'The jasmine which grows in the front of the house has no fragrance.' The meaning of this is that a person who becomes great and famous will never be recognized by his or her own community. Many righteous souls have suffered the truth of the adage. The Holy Mother would say, "Suppose somebody was listening to a beautiful song on the radio. He was really enjoying the sweetness of the song's melody when his close friend came into the room and said, 'Do you know who is singing that song? It is our neighbor, Shankar.' Immediately, the one who was enjoying the song turned off the radio saying, 'Oh, what kind of a singer is he? It's terrible!' Children, this is the attitude of the people. It is difficult for them to accept a person who they have always known and moved closely with." Thus it was in the case of the Holy Mother.

The circumstances surrounding the Mother were far from kind. This young fisherfolk girl was supported by none. Since the devotees were from different parts of the country, they could do nothing against the ignorant and uncultured villagers who tormented the Holy Mother. Besides that, the devotees for the most part believed that the Mother was possessed by Krishna and Devi during the *Bhava Darshan*. They failed to understand the depth or fullness of the Mother's God-Realization. Not only that; most of the devotees in those early days came primarily for worldly achievements, not spiritual upliftment. If their desire was fulfilled, they would return only when another desire cropped up. If their desire didn't get fulfilled, they would never come again and their devotion to the Mother ended there. The Mother had neither an inch of Her own land nor a penny at Her disposal. Her own relatives were non-cooperative and strongly opposed Her. Her family members were unsupportive and neither helped nor encouraged Her in any way.

On one occasion, a devotee asked the Mother about the immensity of the trials and tribulations which She had to confront both during and after Her *sadhana* days. They wondered how their own Realization could ever take place if they had to undergo so much suffering which they doubted they could forbear. Mother was quick to point out that Her own life only showed that it was possible to realize God even under the worst possible circumstances.

CHAPTER TEN

THE MOTHER OF IMMORTAL BLISS

Always understand that Mother is omnipresent. Have the faith that Mother's Self and your Self are one. Children, the mother who gave birth to you may look after matters relating to this life; nowadays even this is very rare. But Mother's aim is to lead you in such a way that you can enjoy bliss in all your future lives.

- MATA AMRITANANDAMAYI -

Trailōkya sphuta vaktāro
  devādyasura pannagāha
Guruvaktra sthitā vidyā
  gurubhaktyā tu labhyatye

*The Guru's Wisdom cannot be learned from even
gods of the higher worlds; The Guru's Knowledge
awakens in him who serves his Guru with purest
love.*

GURU GITA, VERSE 22

*"Children, the coolness of the breeze, the beams
of the moon, the vastness of space and all things
of the world—these are all permeated with Divine
Consciousness. Knowing and experiencing this Truth
is the Goal of human birth. In this dark age a
band of youths, renouncing all, will set out to
disseminate spiritual light throughout the world."*

-MATA AMRITANANDAMAYI

A BAND OF YOUTHS

As early as 1976, a young boy of twenty named Unnikrishna from the village of Alappad came to meet
the Holy Mother. He was rather like a mendicant. Although he had a home and family, he only rarely visited them. After meeting the Holy Mother, he developed a strong thirst to lead a spiritual life. The Holy
Mother understood this and entrusted him, a year later,
with the daily worship in the temple, allowing him to
remain in Her presence at Idamannel. He spent his
days inside the small shrine performing the daily wor-

ship and reciting the *Sri Lalita Sahasranamam*[48], as the Holy Mother had instructed him. He did other spiritual practices as well, read scriptural texts, and wrote devotional poetry. At night, he slept on the temple verandah using only a thin towel spread on the floor as a mattress. He was so calm and quiet that none of the visitors knew he was staying there. In this way, he became the first resident of the future Ashram.

By the end of 1978, the nucleus of the Ashram grew when a group of well-educated young men, renouncing home and worldly life, took refuge at the feet of the Holy Mother with the one aim of God-Realization and service to humanity. Attracted by the magnetic personality and all-embracing love of the Holy Mother, these young men were inspired to lead a divine life against great odds. Most of them were from the town of Haripad[49], and came from upper class families. After meeting the Holy Mother, they knew with strong conviction that the path shown by the Mother was the ultimate goal that they could aspire to in their lives.

Within one month Sreekumar, Ramesh Rao, Venugopal, Harikumara Pai, Ramakrishnan and Balagopalan (Balu)[50] came to meet the Holy Mother and humbly requested Her to guide them to their chosen goal. However, Sugunanandan discouraged them from staying permanently near the Holy Mother. His reluctance was motivated by the fact that his other daughters were not yet married. These young aspirants were either still in college or holding jobs, except for Balu, who had just completed his college studies. They would come to see the Mother nearly every day or every other day while at the same time continuing to fulfill their responsibilities in the world.

For the most part, their sudden transformation from worldly youths to seekers of God created havoc among their family and friends. In their minds, the Holy Mother was a witch who had hypnotized their sons through the use of Her sorcery. Ever ready to find fault with the Holy Mother, the rationalists took up the cause. They began feeding the news media sensational stories in order to provoke public reaction against the Holy Mother.

The devotees and young men became worried about the appearance of these fabricated stories in the newspaper. When the Mother came to know of their anxiety, She burst into laughter and said, "We are not those letters and words printed on a piece of paper. Continue your spiritual practices without wasting your time paying attention to such things. Those who oppose today will become devotees tomorrow." As the days passed, this declaration by the Holy Mother became perfectly true.

In November of that year, a college student came to Idamannel to meet the Holy Mother. The first visit itself created a great transformation in him. He came to visit the Mother now and then whenever possible. He developed an intense desire to relinquish worldly life and asked the Holy Mother where he could stay in order to do his spiritual practices, since, in those days, it was Sugunanandan's habit to chase away any young aspirant who desired to stay in the presence of the Holy Mother. He also had to face Sugunanandan's scolding one evening and had been ordered to leave Idamannel. Greatly pained at heart, he asked the Holy Mother to

suggest a suitable place for him to continue his practice. She directed him to Tiruvannamalai, the abode of
the great Sage Ramana Maharshi, and instructed him
to observe a vow of silence for forty-one days.

Before leaving, he asked, "Mother, if Sugunanandan
continues to act like this toward the devotees, how will
this place ever become an Ashram? He is unkind to
you and to those who want to stay near you. Mother,
you are undergoing so many hardships nowadays! I can't
bear to see your sufferings. Is there no one to take
care of you and look after your needs?"

The Mother consoled him saying, "Do not worry.
Everything will become all right after you return from
Tiruvannamalai. In that place there are people who
will look after Mother and the future Ashram. My children from other countries are there anxiously waiting
to see me. The day will come when Sugunanandan will
welcome you with love and affection.

"He then asked the Mother for a watch so that he
could keep up his daily routine and for a rosary of
rudraksha beads[51] for repeating his mantra. The Holy
Mother said, "Do not ask Mother for such things or
even think of them. A good aspirant will never move
from his seat. Whatever he needs is bound to come.
Look at the spider and the python. They never go out
in search of prey. The spider quietly sits in its web
and the small insects come and get trapped in it. It is
the duty of God to take care of His devotees. Dedicate
everything at His Feet, go to Arunachala and everything necessary will come to you."

Cherishing the Mother's image in his heart and remembering Her boundless love, the young man left for

Tiruvannamalai using the money given to him by a friend for that purpose. Reaching the sacred abode of Lord Siva, he spent a few days in a cave on the sacred mountain Arunachala. The first two days he subsisted only on leaves and water. On the third day, in the evening, for lack of food he fainted calling aloud, 'Amma!' In a letter to the Mother he wrote, "It was about five o'clock in the afternoon when I fainted due to hunger. I was lying on the mountain in a semiconscious state. Just then, I clearly heard Mother's voice calling, 'My son!' I felt that my forehead was being gently rubbed by someone. When I opened my eyes I saw Mother standing before me in Her white clothes. I was extremely thrilled at the sight!"

After the Holy Mother received this letter, the devotees understood that it was exactly at that moment in Vallickavu when the Holy Mother had suddenly called out, "Oh my son!" and turned to a devotee sitting nearby saying, "My son is in Tiruvannamalai and has been starving for three days and now he is crying to see me!" After this incident, he never had any difficulty getting food regularly.

In the absence of a proper place to do his spiritual practices, the youth would spend his days on the mountain and his nights sleeping at the foot of the hill. Coming down from the mountain, the first person that he met was an Australian woman named Gayatri. After a couple of days he met Madhusudhana[52], a native of Reunion Island, whose descendants had come from India. All three felt a stream of love binding them together. Recalling the words of the Holy Mother, he had a strong feeling that both of them were Her children. He began talking to them about the Holy Mother and showed them a small photo of Her. Gayatri was enchanted by the blissful countenance and the glowing eyes of the Mother in the photo.

Although Gayatri would regularly try to meditate, she was not satisfied with her spiritual progress. After seeing the Holy Mother's photo and hearing about Her selfless love and compassion, Gayatri had her first spiritual experience. To put it in her own words, "I saw a flash of light within me and discerned the living form of the Mother in that light. Suddenly from within me arose the cry, 'Amma! Amma! Amma!' Then all thoughts subsided and my mind sank into stillness. When I opened my eyes and looked at the clock, I realized that twenty minutes had passed. I had been unaware of anything."

Madhu, eager to share the happiness which he experienced while hearing about the Holy Mother, introduced the young man to an American devotee named Nealu who was contemplative by nature. His spiritual teacher, who was a direct disciple of Sri Ramana Maharshi, had passed away four years earlier. Serving his teacher, Nealu had been living in Tiruvannamalai for the past eleven years. At this time, he was mostly bedridden, suffering from acute pain in the stomach and spine. He was hardly able to sit or walk even for a few moments. The doctors were at a loss as to the cause or cure.

Coming to know of his difficulty to find a place for meditation, Nealu offered his late teacher's cottage for his use. The boy told him about the Holy Mother but Nealu was at first not very interested. He had already seen many great saints and was only concerned to cure his illness so that he could continue with his *sadhana*. With that idea in mind, he asked him to take him to meet the Holy Mother after the completion of the young man's vow of silence. Then Nealu gave the young *sadhak* (aspirant) a clock and *rudraksha* rosary thinking that these items may be helpful in his spiritual practice. Recalling the Holy Mother's words that all would come unasked, the boy felt overwhelmed with emotion and earnestly started his vow.

One day while circumambulating Arunachala, he noticed a tall white man chanting Tamil verses while moving with a group of people around the hill. It was the day of Sri Ramana's birthday celebrations. When he glanced at the man, he also looked back at him, though with an air of pride. The young *sadhak* thought, "Though proud, he too seems to be the son of the Holy Mother." This man was, in fact, a devotee from France named Ganga who later came to stay near the Holy Mother.

After forty one days of silence had been observed, the young devotee of the Mother and Nealu journeyed to Vallickavu. Nealu's first meeting with the Holy Mother was highly significant.[53] As he himself describes, "The first four days I spent there, I felt as if I was in Heaven itself, such was the bliss experienced in the Mother's Presence! One evening at the end of *Devi Bhava*, Mother was standing at the door of the temple and I was standing outside gazing at Her with joined palms. I was overflowing with joy. At that moment, I saw Her physical form disappear into an expanding radiance which spread all around and engulfed everything visible. That expansive light suddenly contracted into a blazing pin-

point of unbearably dazzling light and then I felt as if
that light had entered into me. For three days I could
get no sleep due to the spiritual intoxication of that
experience. After this, I could think only of the Holy
Mother day and night. I decided to be near Her until
the end of my life in order to receive guidance from
Her and serve Her."

Nealu returned to Tiruvannamalai with the boy to
settle his affairs and then came back to Vallickavu
accompanied by Gayatri who was keenly desirous of
serving the Holy Mother. Strangely enough,
Sugunanandan welcomed all of them as if they were
his own children. For the first time in three years,
Nealu felt some relief from his sickness and could move
about doing small tasks.

When Nealu returned from Tiruvannamalai, he expressed his wish to the Holy Mother, "I do not want to
go away from here. I want to stay with you forever as
your humble servant." The Mother told him, "Son, I
don't have an inch of land that is my own. Ask the
father. Anyhow, we need a place to stay."

It was a great surprise to everyone when
Sugunanandan agreed to donate a small piece of land
on which was built a modest hut of woven coconut palm
leaves. All told, it measured nine by eighteen feet.
One corner was used as a kitchen for preparing drinks
for the Holy Mother, but daily meals were still prepared in the main house. This hut served as shelter for
the Holy Mother along with Nealu, Balu and Gayatri.
This marked the informal beginning of the Ashram.

After his first meeting with the Holy Mother, Balu
left his home and spent most of his time with the Mother.

He was fortunate to get the permission of Sugunanandan to remain at Idamannel on a permanent basis. Thus, when Nealu came from Tiruvannamalai to stay permanently, Balu also settled there.

After the arrival of Nealu and Gayatri, Ganga and Madhu also came and settled at the feet of the Holy Mother. Even though they offered their wealth to the Holy Mother with total devotion, She declined to accept it saying, "If you attain a pure character and become perfect spiritually, that will be my wealth. If one realizes the Essence within himself, he will see It in all. The whole world will become his own."

One night, a man from a neighboring house woke up Ganga in order to borrow his flashlight. The man's daughter was suffering from an acute asthma attack and had to be rushed off to the hospital in the dark. After a few hours, the man came back and returned the flashlight. The next morning Ganga told Mother about the incident and added that he had felt like breaking the man's head for disturbing his sleep. The Mother scolded him saying,

"What kind of spiritual aspirant are you? What have you gained by leading a spiritual life for so many years before coming here? Is this the fruit of that? Being a follower of the Path of Knowledge as you seem to think you are, you should see everything as your own Self. If this is so, how could you be angry with that man? If your foot was pricked by a sharp thorn, would you not feel the pain and be restless to remove it? Imagine that man's anxiety to relieve his daughter of her suffering. The pain and suffering of all living beings should be felt to be your own. Only then will your mind ex-

pand and become as the sky which accommodates all
equally. For that, your mind should become innocent
like a child's, and this is possible only through pure
devotion to God."

Ganga replied in a mocking tone, "Devotion is not
at all intellectually satisfying. To follow the Path of
Devotion shows a certain weakness. Why all these
emotional expressions like weeping and singing? I cannot
do that. Sri Ramana never prescribed the Path of Devotion. He would only prescribe the Path of Knowledge
to his devotees. I prefer the Path of Knowledge as it
appeals to the intellect. It is more convincing." Such
was Ganga's misconception of devotion at the time of
his coming to the Mother.

Mother smilingly retorted,

"I have just seen the fruit of your practice of the
Path of Knowledge. If this is the result, then you need
not bother about leading a life of sacrifice and renunciation. You may as well enjoy all the pleasures of the
senses! Did you read all the writings by and about Sri
Ramana? If not, then please do so, for there are many
works which are full of devotion. In fact, he himself
was an embodiment of devotion to Lord Arunachala.
Even the mere mention of that Name would bring tears
of Divine Love to his eyes. Devotion is not an indica-
tion of mental weakness as you seem to think. It is the
greatest achievement that a human can attain. It is
perceiving God in all beings equally; it is pure love of
Selfless Existence. Son, you should cultivate love within
yourself."

Not convinced by the Holy Mother's words, Ganga
went to Tiruvannamalai. Much to his surprise, he hap-

pened to come across a devotional work of Sri Ramana's.
Recollecting the Mother's words, he was filled with an
overwhelming feeling of love and began weeping. He
prayed to the Mother to call him back to Her Holy
Presence. It was at this time that the Mother, knowing
his mental state, wrote a letter asking Ganga to return.
Clearly realizing Her greatness, he surrendered himself at Her feet with all humility.

Madhu had met many saints before coming to the
Holy Mother, but when he saw the Mother for the first
time he felt as though he had come to the end of his
journey. Dedicating his heart and soul to the Mother,
Madhu began to collect all the existing commentaries
on the *Srimad Bhagavad Gita* and to translate them
into French for the spiritual benefit of French devotees. Inspired by the Holy Mother, he spread Her spiritual
mission in his native land of Reunion and built a beautiful Ashram there dedicated to Her. With the blessings of the Holy Mother, he has been instrumental in
bringing many people to the spiritual path.

In those days, the Holy Mother spent most of Her
nights outdoors. Therefore, everyone preferred to sleep
beneath the coconut palms in the sand. Even if the
Mother happened to take rest in the hut, by the middle
of the night She would get up and walk outside to lie
down on the open ground. It continued to be the case
that the Holy Mother slept very little, ate very little
and gave unstintingly of Herself. Even after sitting in
the temple receiving the devotees three times a week
for the entire night, She always made time during the
day to receive the devotees and to instruct the spiritual aspirants who sought Her guidance.

In the beginning, Nealu and Gayatri had a lot of language problems. They always sought the help of Balu to converse with the Holy Mother, but before long, they slowly began to pick up the Mother's language, Malayalam. During this period, it was Balu's good fortune to serve the Holy Mother since there was nobody else to look after Her needs.

One day, Sugunanandan rudely remarked that he was unwilling to feed the *'saippus'* (foreigners). Thereafter, Gayatri began preparing food in the hut for the Holy Mother, Nealu, Balu and herself. The Mother ate almost nothing. Sometimes at the insistence of Nealu or Balu She would eat a little, for name sake only.

One day, Nealu kept on insisting that the Mother should eat some food. Finally, the Mother said, "Yes, I will eat. Bring something." Without delay, Nealu brought a plateful of food for the Mother. Strangely enough, She finished everything in an instant. Nealu again served food to the Mother. That also was consumed in no time. The Mother looked expectantly at Nealu without moving from Her seat. More food was served. This was also eaten. The Mother ate and ate but whatever was served seemed to leave Her unsatisfied! Nealu and the others looked at each other in astonishment. More food was purchased and brought from the nearby teashop. That also was rapidly consumed by the Mother. Nealu was exhausted! He turned pale. Never again did he insist that the Holy Mother eat!

During this period, family conflicts again cropped up. Only two months had passed since the marriage of Sugunamma when Sugunanandan hastily arranged the marriages of his other two daughters. Without anybody's consent, he fixed the marriage of his eldest daughter Kasturi. Even the Holy Mother was informed only after Sugunanandan's acceptance had been conveyed to the bridegroom's party.

The problem was, how to conduct the marriage without any money? Sugunanandan had no income and there was no money in the temple. As was his habit, Sugunanandan stepped out of the picture at this point. The Mother was unperturbed. Witnessing this, Balu became very sad and asked, "Mother, what shall we do? How can the marriage be conducted?" Nealu offered, "Mother, I will give whatever I have. It is the duty of the disciple to look after and discharge the responsibilities of his Guru. I have nothing to call my own; whatever I have is Mother's. Therefore, please perform Kasturi's marriage with the money which I have at my disposal."

The Holy Mother replied, "After the marriage, the girl will lead a worldly life. The wealth you have is meant for spirituality. It must be spent only for righteous purposes. If it is given to worldly people, they will incur sin. That will affect us and our path as well. If it is God who made the father fix the marriage, let God conduct it. We do not have to be concerned with it. Sugunanandan is not much bothered by it; then why should we worry? Children, we do not have to be anxious about the matter."

Though Sugunanandan was in a hurry to fix the marriage, when it came to the more important details like the finances, one could find him standing on the sidelines. The Mother began organizing the needful without uttering a word. Seeing this, Balu became pained at heart and told the Mother, "I will bring my inheritance from my house." The Holy Mother was in complete disagreement. Then Balu wrote to some close devotees requesting financial assistance. Later, when the Mother came to know of this, She scolded him saying, "Son, let us confront it calmly. There is nothing to be excited about."

At last, everything was ready except one thing, five thousand rupees. This amount was absolutely necessary to meet the expenses of the wedding. After a few days passed, a check for five thousand rupees was received from an anonymous donor from Madras who had recently heard about the Holy Mother. Thus, in mid-September of 1980, Kasturi was married.

Not three months had passed when Sugunanandan next fixed Sajani's marriage. That done, he repeated his disappearing act and left the hard part to the Holy Mother. The responsibility for accumulating enough money to give as dowry, pay for the wedding ceremony and craft the bride's gold ornaments all fell on the Holy Mother's shoulders.

Balu no longer felt sad, he felt angry! The Mother was also displeased by Sugunanandan's lack of discrimination. Though annoyed, She remained unruffled and efficiently executed the task. The bridegroom's party asked for more gold. As usual, money remained a big question. The Holy Mother was insistant that not a penny be spent from what had been put aside for righteous purposes. Nor would She allow any money to be borrowed. Then what could be done?

At this point, Kasturi returned to Idamannel from her husband's house due to some disagreement. Coming to know of the need for more gold she said, "For the time being you can take my ornaments to conduct Sajani's marriage. It is fine if you return them later." Now, everything was ready except one necklace and one ring. Two days before the marriage these items were still missing; yet the Mother was as calm and detached as ever. The next morning when the *Bhava Darshan* was over Gayatri, who was cleaning the temple, noticed a small package lying among the offerings. Opening it, she was surprised to find a necklace and ring fitting the exact description of what was needed for the marriage! Even the style of the ornaments was the same as had been selected a month ago! What other proof was needed to show that the Divine Will arranges for everything?

However, this was not the end of the difficulties which plagued this final wedding. Some of the local devotees raised an objection with Sugunanandan. Why had he fixed a marriage alliance with those who had previously been enemies? Were the sons of the well-wishers and devotees not good enough for him? Some young men who had been close friends of Subhagan had wished to marry Sugunanandan's daughters. Now they also turned against him. Thus, when enemies became relatives, those who were friends became enemies. They came to quarrel with Sugunanandan and conspired to create obstacles for Sajani's marriage. Hoping to annul the marriage, they spread scandalous stories and sent the same to the bridegroom. Even the day before the wedding everyone was full of doubt whether or not the marriage would be performed.

On the day of the marriage, the Holy Mother took

the *brahmacharis* to a neighboring house, as She had also done for the two previous marriages. This was for the benefit of the *brahmacharis* who should not attend such ceremonies.

The Mother explained,

"An aspirant should not take part in marriage ceremonies or funerals. At the former, everyone will be thinking of the marriage, which is a bondage. At the latter, the grief is about the loss of a mortal being. In both cases, the participants are dwelling on the non-eternal. These thought waves will be harmful to a seeker. The worldly vibrations will enter the subconscious mind. The seeker will become restless for unreal things."

Thus, the main impediment for the *brahmacharis* to take up permanent residence in the Holy Mother's presence had been removed. All three of Sugunanandan's daughters were now married. Not only that, the miscreants and rationalists, accepting utter failure, retreated one by one. Some among them understood that their irrational actions were meaningless and left the organization forever. The remaining members began fighting among themselves and thus the 'Committee to Stop Blind Beliefs' was totally dissolved. Those who came to fight against Truth and Righteousness became the cause of their own destruction. These developments marked the beginning of a new phase in the Holy Mother's spiritual service to relieve and uplift ailing humanity.

Mother's attitude toward all the trials and tribulations which She suffered from Her relatives and miscreants over the years is unique. One day She narrated,

"It was their misguided conceptions that made them speak and behave the way they did and also because they could not realize the significance and purpose of spiritual life. Such being the case, why should we be angry with them or dislike them? It would be our ignorance to do so and as a result our minds would only get polluted. Look at these fresh roses. How beautiful they are! What a fine fragrance they exude! But what do we give them to make them grow? Just a little used tea leaves and cow dung! What a vast difference between these beautiful flowers and the manure given to them! Compared to their beauty and fragrance, is this manure befitting them? In the same way, impediments are the fertilizer which makes us grow stronger spiritually. These obstacles will all help our hearts to blossom fully. Chirping at night is the nature of crickets but that sound never disturbs anybody's sleep. Likewise, to create trouble is the nature of the ignorant. We must therefore pray to God to forgive them and lead them to the right path. Dedicate everything to God and He will look after you."

THE MOTHER OF IMMORTAL BLISS

It was now possible for the first group of *brahmacharis* to settle at the feet of the Holy Mother due to the relative peace of mind that Sugunanandan enjoyed since the marriage of his daughters. Due to the *brahmacharis'* keen interest to be in the company of the Holy Mother, they took no notice of the fact that food, clothing and shelter were minimal. Most of the time, they had to live outdoors and sleep on the bare ground

without even a mat. Whatever was received came unasked and was shared amongst themselves. Having no
money, if any of them had to go somewhere, they would
walk. Even though they had only one set of clothes
each, somehow they learned to manage.

Feeling a bit depressed one day that his only set of
clothes was dirty and worn, one of the *brahmacharis*
complained to the Mother about the lack of necessities. The Mother replied, "Son, do not ask for such
small things from God. Surrender yourself at His Feet
and He will give you whatever you really need." The
Holy Mother had lived that way Herself and therefore
spoke only from Her own experience. The very next
day a devotee brought a new set of clothes for all the
brahmacharis although he had been unaware of the situation at the time.

These boys received an all-around training in renunciation as a result of the austere circumstances in
which they lived during the early days of the Ashram.
In order to give them courage, the Holy Mother told
them, "If you can withstand these conditions, you can
be at home anywhere. If you can overcome any adverse
situation now, then you will easily cope with any crisis
or challenge of life."

As the number of devotees and resident *brahmacharis* continued to increase and the lack of facilities
remained the same, the idea to formally incorporate as
an Ashram was born. However, the situation did not
look very promising. The Holy Mother had neither land
nor wealth at Her disposal. Even the land where Nealu
had built the hut belonged to Sugunanandan. Although
he had given permission for Nealu, Balu and Gayatri

to stay at Idamannel permanently, Sugunanandan had never entertained the idea that his home would become a future Ashram. The thought of accommodating more and more people did not hold his fancy either. Once when the Holy Mother was discussing the idea of an Ashram, he angrily made his point very clear, "What is this! Do we have any wealth or riches here? How would we run an Ashram? Where shall we (the family) go if this becomes an Ashram? No! I shall not agree to register an Ashram here!"

Initially, the Holy Mother was also opposed to the idea to become a formal Ashram. When some devotees approached Her with the proposal, She replied, "Mother has heard a lot about 'Ashram'. Mother does not need an Ashram. Is it not a bondage? Haven't you seen the palmist walking with the caged parrot? In the end, Mother's situation will also become like that (i.e. being bound for another person's purpose). I cannot do that. Mother has Her own freedom. There should be no obstacle for that."

However, as the flow of devotees and disciples swelled, it was soon an unavoidable necessity to have an organized Ashram. Furthermore, the Holy Mother's foreign disciples, according to the law of the land, were prohibited from staying in a private house for any appreciable length of time. At this point the Holy Mother Herself became convinced of the need for a government approved spiritual center. The Mother's opinion was sought as to how to proceed. She mischievously replied, "Anyhow, the family members will not establish an Ashram. Their *samskara* (mental makeup) is different. Let us not wait for their permission; they will never cooperate. But we may have to hear a little of their scolding!"

Thus, on the 6th of May in the year 1981, with a view to preserving and propagating the ideals and teachings of the Holy Mother, the Mata Amritanandamayi Math and Mission Trust was founded and registered under the Travancore-Cochin State Literary and Charitable Act of 1955, at Quilon, Kerala, South India. From this time onward, the Holy Mother officially adopted the name 'Mata Amritanandamayi' which was given to Her by one of Her *brahmacharin* sons. Already being the Mother of Immortal Bliss, as Her name denotes, it was indeed befitting.

Around this time, one of the *brahmacharins* who was in need of some scriptural books, asked Mother to select a number for him from a lottery in which the winner would be presented with some books. Mother told him, "Why crave such things? You will soon receive plenty of books." It was shortly after this incident that Nealu, who came to stay permanently with Mother from Tiruvannamalai, decided to shift his library of more than two thousand books in English and various Indian languages from there to the Ashram in Vallickavu. Thus, the Ashram Library came into being.

On the 27th of August, 1982, a *Vedanta Vidyalaya* (School) was started in order to impart traditional Vedantic and Sanskrit knowledge to the residents of the Ashram. Still, Mother always reminds the *brahmacharins* of the importance of meditation instead of mere book learning. The Ashram routine consists of six to eight hours of meditation for all the residents. Those who would like to devote all of their time for meditation are by all means encouraged and there are a few such in the Ashram. Mother says,

"Scriptures are just like signboards. They are only a means and not an end in themselves. The end is something beyond them. A student of agriculture knows how to sow the seeds, when and how to fertilize, how to get rid of pests and prevent their return, etc. Likewise, study of scriptures gives us directions as to how to do our spiritual practices."

A word should be said about the vast change which has come over the Holy Mother's family and the villagers. Realizing Her to be divine, they now feel proud that they are related to Her or living in the same village. Sugunanandan and Damayanti often wonder what meritorious acts they performed in their past lives in order to become the 'parents' of the Divine Mother Herself! They are now exemplary householders and lovingly play the role of a father and mother to all of the *brahmacharins* who stay in the Ashram, regarding them as their own children.

Today, Mata Amritanandamayi Math and Mission Trust is a growing spiritual center headed by the Holy Mother who is very particular to see that it is run according to the ancient traditions of the holy land of India. All the Ashram work is attended to by the residents themselves who each put in at least one hour of work each day for the maintenance of the Ashram, cooking, cleaning, tending the cows, etc. The Ashram is looked upon by Mother's many devotees as their spiritual home and as a fertile field where noble spiritual qualities can be abundantly cultivated, and the fruit of God-Realization reaped.

Responding to the repeated requests of Her children from abroad, the Holy Mother made Her first world
tour during May-August 1987. She traveled widely in
the U.S.A. and Europe. The impact was wonderful. The
Holy Mother inspired and transformed many people who
experienced Her unique spiritual charm and universal
love on a vast scale. Subsequently, the Holy Mother
has circled the globe every year since. A beautiful resi-
dential retreat center, the Mata Amritanandamayi Center, has also come into existence about a forty-five minute
drive from San Francisco, California. In December 1987,
the Holy Mother visited Reunion Island and Mauritius
at the request of the Amritanandamayi Mata Ashram,
which has been functioning there since that time under the leadership of one of Her disciples.

To those blessed souls who find their way to Mother's
Holy Presence, She graciously advises them:
"Beholding a block of stone, a master sculptor will
see only the beautiful form latent in it ignoring its
rough exterior. Likewise, a God-Realized Soul sees only
the ever-shining *Atman* or Self in all without distinc-
tion, ignoring the external differences. A drunkard cannot
propagate prohibition of liquor. He should himself ab-
stain from drinking first and then only can he ask others to do the same. Likewise, my children, only after
you yourselves become morally and spiritually perfect
and behold Divinity in all, can you teach others to
become so."
Let this biography of the Holy Mother be concluded
with Her loving call to the entire human race:
"Come quickly my darling children, you who are the

Divine Essence of 'OM'. Removing all sorrows, grow to be adorable and merge with the sacred 'OM'!"

PART TWO

*The Meaning
of the
Divine Bhavas*

The Divine *Bhavas* of the Holy Mother as Krishna and Devi are a subject beyond the reach of the human intellect, yet a thoughtful study of them gives us a glimpse into the Holy Mother's infinite spiritual power. Responding to the sincere call of the devotee, a Perfect Master slowly reveals His infinite attributes to the heart of the devotee. When the process of purification becomes intense, the Guru's greatness, which is nothing but the True Nature of the disciple or devotee, will gradually be revealed by the grace of the Master. Grace, of course, is the primary requisite for beginning to grasp the significance of the Holy Mother's Divine Moods.

The Great Masters of India have classified Divine Incarnations in three main categories: 1) *Purna Avatara* (full or perfect), 2) *Amsa Avatara* (partial manifestation), and 3) *Avesa Avatara* (temporary overshadowing by divine power). The word *'Avatara'* means coming down or descent. A *Purna Avatara* is the descent of the nameless, formless and immutable Supreme Energy, assuming a human form and manifesting infinite power without any limitations. The intention of such a One is to restore and preserve righteousness (*dharma*) and awaken humanity by making people aware of the higher Self. *Amsa Avatara* is the coming down of God while partially manifesting some of His power in order to fulfill a particular purpose or goal. The Incarnations of Lord Vishnu as Vamana (the Dwarf) and Narasimha (Man-lion) are typical examples of *Amsa Avataras*.

Avesa Avatara is entirely different from these two types of Incarnations. This is the temporary visitation or possession by divine beings, who use the body of

some people in order to fulfill certain tasks. Lord
Vishnu's Incarnation as Parasurama, as depicted in the
epic *Srimad Bhagavatam*, is an example of this type.
Here, the Lord entered the body of Parasurama, who
was a great warrior, in order to destroy the cruel *kshatriya*
kings who had become very arrogant and egotistic. Soon
after he had fulfilled this task, the power left him. It
is said that Sri Rama, another Incarnation of Lord Vishnu,
took the divine power back from Parasurama while
returning to Ayodhya after his marriage with Sita.
The scriptures say that demons or ghosts sometimes
possess the body of people who are mentally weak.
People who are predominantly virtuous and good in
nature (*sattvic*) will be possessed by devas (minor gods),
those endowed with creativity and vigor (*rajasic*) may
be possessed by celestial being (inferior to minor gods),
and people whose nature is full of darkness and obscu-
rity (*tamasic*) may be possessed by evil spirits. The
scriptures also mention that in the body of rare souls
who are extremely pure, Divine Power may manifest
for a short period of time. This is why Parasurama is
considered to be an *Avesa Avatara*.

The following is an illustration which might help
the reader to gain insight into the Holy Mother's Divine *Bhavas*. Once when Lord Krishna was living in
Dwaraka, he cherished a desire to see his dear devotee, Hanuman. His vehicle, *Garuda*, the king of birds,
was sent as his messenger to Kadali Vanam, where
Hanuman was residing, but Hanuman refused to go.
He explained, "I won't go to see anyone other than my
Lord Rama". When the reply of Hanuman was conveyed to Lord Sri Krishna, He once again sent the bird

AMMACHI

chief to Hanuman saying, "You tell him that Lord Sri
Rama with His holy consort Sita have come to Dwaraka
and They would like to see Hanuman."

While *Garuda* was fetching Hanuman, certain events
were taking place in Dwaraka. Lord Krishna, by His
mere Will, assumed the form of Lord Rama, who had
lived many centuries earlier. Rukmini, Krishna's consort, became Sita. By this time, Hanuman had arrived
in Dwaraka. Having seen His beloved Sri Rama and
Sita and having offered worship to Them, He returned
to His abode.

Though Sri Rama was also one of the Incarnations
of Lord Vishnu, He had lived in Ayodhya thousands of
years before Sri Krishna's lifetime. Yet Hanuman, the
great devotee of Lord Rama, did not doubt that Lord
Rama and Sita could appear in Dwaraka, even though
the all-knowing Hanuman was fully aware of the fact
that Krishna was the Lord of Dwaraka. Certainly Hanuman knew that no one except Krishna could manifest Rama *Bhava*. What really happened was that Hanuman was determined to use this opportunity to see
his Lord with Sita in human form once again. Lord
Krishna, the servant of His devotees, happily fulfilled
His great devotee's wish and blessed him.

Only a *Purna Avatara* can become one with any
other God or Goddess. Being such an *Avatara*, Krishna
easily manifested Rama *Bhava*. One day, Lord Krishna
asked His wives including Satyabhama, one of His dear
ones, to assume Sita *Bhava*, but none were able to.
Finally Rukmini, an Incarnation of Goddess Lakshmi,
effortlessly assumed Sita *Bhava*.

In the case of an *Avesa Avatara*, godly powers enter

into a particular person and withdraw after fulfilling the intended goal. This was not the case with Sri Krishna and Rukmini. What Lord Krishna did was to manifest Rama *Bhava* or the attributes of Rama which were already latent in Him.

There is a similar incident in the life of Lord Chaitanya of Bengal. One day Pandit Srivasa, an ardent devotee of Lord Narasimha, was performing his usual chanting (mantra *japa*), while sitting in his family shrine room. Suddenly there was a knock on the door. "Who is that?" the pandit asked. "Behold the Beloved Deity whom you are worshipping," came the reply. Pandit Srivasa opened the door and beheld Lord Chaitanya standing before him on the threshold of the house in a divine mood. He entered the shrine room and sat on the seat which was specially made for worship. The pandit saw the Lord Narasimha shining within Lord Chaitanya and with great devotion worshipped Him in Lord Chaitanya's form. Lord Chaitanya blessed the pundit's family by permitting all of them to take part in the worship.

After everyone had received his blessings, Lord Chaitanya fell unconscious. On regaining his external awareness after a few moments, he asked the pandit, "What happened? I cannot remember anything. Did I say anything wrong?" With all humility, Srivasa prostrated before his Lord and said, "O Bhagavan, please do not delude this humble servant of Yours anymore. By Your Grace I was able to see who You are!" Hearing this, Lord Chaitanya graciously smiled in a gesture of confirmation. Many such incidents in Lord Chaitanya's life reveal that he gave darshan to his devotees in diverse *bhavas*.

From these illustrations one can clearly glimpse what *Bhava Darshan* is. *Bhava Darshan* is the manifestation of different *Isvara Bhavas* or Divine Moods by an Incarnation of God according to the wishes of the devotees. Anandamayi Ma, who lived in Bengal, used to manifest Krishna and Kali *Bhavas* while singing *bhajans*. These *Bhavas* manifested by Incarnations took place only on certain occasions to fulfill a particular end, especially in response to the ardent desire of their devotees. Moreover, they would last only for a short time. The Holy Mother Amritanandamayi manifests the Divine Moods three nights a week lasting for long periods of 10 to 12 hours depending upon the number of devotees present for *Darshan*. This is the Holy Mother's way of serving humanity, plunged as it is in the deep quagmire of worldliness.

Lord Chaitanya is said to have had two *bhavas*, that of a devotee, in which mood he was most frequently seen, and *Bhagavat Bhava*, during which he would reveal his real state of Self-Abidance. Sri Ramakrishna Paramahamsa also revealed more than one *bhava*. It is said that he even developed a small growth like a tail during the period of his spiritual practices in Hanuman *Bhava*.

During the Holy Mother's Krishna and Devi *Bhavas*, She brings out That which is within Her and manifests those Divine Beings in order to bless Her devotees. The Holy Mother once said regarding the *Bhavas*: "Mother is not manifesting even an infinitesimal part of Her spiritual power during the *Bhavas*. If it were to be manifested as it is, no one could come near!" She continues, "All the deities of the Hindu Pantheon, who represent the numberless aspects of the One Supreme Being, exist within us. A Divine Incarnation can manifest any of them by mere will for the good of the world. *Krishna Bhava* is the manifestation of the *Purusha* or Pure Being aspect, and *Devi Bhava* is the manifestation of the Eternal Feminine, the Creatrix, the active principle of the Impersonal Absolute. Here is a crazy girl who puts on the garb of Krishna and after some time that of Devi, but it is within this crazy girl that both exist. However, it should be remembered that all objects having a name or form are mere mental projections. Why decorate an elephant? Why should a lawyer wear a black coat or why does a policeman wear a uniform and a cap? All these are merely external aids meant to create a certain impression. In a like manner, Mother dons the garb of Krishna and Devi in order to give strength to the devotional attitude of the people coming for *Darshan*. The *Atman* or Self that is in me is also within you. If you can realize that Indivisible Principle that is ever shining in you, you will become That."

Even now some people believe that Lord Krishna and Devi visit the Holy Mother's body three nights a week, after which They leave Her body. This misconception springs from a lack of correct understanding about the Holy Mother's Divine Moods. These Divine *Bhavas* are nothing but the external revelation of Her incessant Oneness with the Supreme. They have nothing to do with possession or Divine Grace as it is commonly understood.

Answering the queries of the devotees, the Holy Mother has explained many points relating to the *Bhavas*:

Devotee: Many devotees say that Mother is the same during the Divine *Bhavas* and at other times. If this is so, then what is the significance of the *Bhavas*?

Mother: During the time of the *Bhava Darshan* Mother will remove two or three layers (veils, so to say), so that the devotees can obtain a glimpse of the Supreme. Different people have different kinds of belief. Mother's intention is to somehow help the people approach God. Some are interested only if they see Mother in the costume of Devi or Krishna. Not only that, very few people know anything about spirituality. Some people find it difficult to believe Mother's words during ordinary times, but if Mother says the same thing during the *Devi Bhava* they will believe.

Devotee: Mother, is there any particular time for manifesting this *Bhava*?

Mother: No, there is not. It can be manifested at any time. Mere will is enough.

Devotee: Mother, why do you wear these costumes of Krishna and Devi?

Mother: It will help the people to remember what *Bhava* is. Child, each attire is important in its own way. We are naked when we are born. Later, according to each country and social custom, people adopt different kinds of dress. Whatever the dress, the person is the same. In this age people give much importance to dress. Mother will make this point clear through an anecdote. One man was cutting down a tree which was growing by the side of a road. Another man who happened to see him doing this said, "Don't cut down that tree! It is wrong to do so, it is against the law." The man not only refused to stop cutting but also scolded him severely.

The person who tried to prevent the hooligan from cutting the tree was a policeman. He departed but soon returned in his official dress. Even from a distance the mere sight of the policeman's cap was enough to make the hooligan flee without looking back. See the different impact created when he came in ordinary and then official dress. Therefore, special attire is needed to teach ignorant people. Likewise, the costumes of Krishna and Devi *Bhavas*. Some people who still feel dissatisfied even after talking to Mother for hours will feel fully content after conversing with Her only for a couple of seconds during *Bhava Darshan*. They feel peaceful after having told all their worries directly to God.

All Incarnations are unique in nature. One cannot say that Krishna was greater than Rama or that Rama was greater than Buddha. Each of Them had Their own task to fulfill and adopted befitting ways to uplift humanity. But this does not mean that They had different visions of life. Their actions cannot be assessed using the measuring rod of our limited intellect and logic. We can get perhaps a glimpse of their greatness through pure intuition born of spiritual practice. The spiritual experiences gained by thousands of devotees through the Holy Mother throws much light on this Great Soul's inexplicable spiritual power. In the following pages we will share with the reader some of the divine experiences of the Holy Mother's devotees as related by them.

PART THREE

Experiences of Devotees

Dr. D.N. Srivastava, Scientific Officer at the Bhabha Atomic Research Center in Bombay, writes about his experience with the Holy Mother:

"In my student days I had studied accounts of the life of Sri Chaitanya Mahaprabhu which vividly described the flow of divine love from his lips, from his face, and from his actions, when he used to utter the Holy Names. For many years I had aspired to see someone with devotion that intense. I met many saints, admirable and worthy of respect, but I failed to find the intensity of radiant bliss that I was seeking.

However, when I met Mata Amritanandamayi and heard Her songs, even though I could not fully understand the words, I knew that I had found it. Just by sitting beside Her, I could feel the spiritual current that one experiences in deep meditation. Her address of the Most High by various Names reveals different facets of the Infinite kaleidoscopically. Her simple explanations of many complex questions show the clarity of Her vision of Reality. Her spontaneous words impart wings to one's intuition which enable one to fly to the world of inner light where there are no doubts.

Even in this age of hypocrisy, the number of dedicated seekers is not small, but complete dissolution in Universal Love, which Mata Amritanandamayi manifests, is an extremely rare phenomenon."

Sheeja is a seven year old girl to whom the Holy Mother has given the pet name, "Takkali", which means "tomato". Once she cherished an intense desire in her innocent young heart praying, "O God, if only I were fortunate enough to wear the crown which Amma wears during *Krishna Bhava*, I would be so happy!" But she knew that the fulfillment of her wish was all but impossible.

That year during Lord Krishna's birthday celebrations, Takkali came to the Ashram. The Holy Mother, who was waiting at the boat jetty, took her by the hand and walked with her to the Ashram. There a group of children, dressed in colorful costumes, were preparing to perform a folk dance portraying Krishna's childhood sports in Vrindavan. Mother took Takkali into the temple and dressed her in beautiful clothes and finally put Her Krishna crown on Takkali's head. Now she looked like Krishna when He was a child! Placing her in the middle of the other children, Mother asked them to dance around her. Takkali was thrilled with her great good fortune! Her dream had come true. Even without being asked, Mother had understood her innocent wish and fulfilled it. God knows and fulfills the longings of the pure in heart.

❀

Nambisseri Bhargavi Amma was an ardent devotee of Lord Krishna, who had appeared to her one day in a dream saying, "You are burning Me up." She hadn't understood the meaning of the Lord's statement. Shortly after the vision, she came to the Holy Mother's Ashram. During *Krishna Bhava* Mother told Bhargavi Amma, "You have locked Me in the cupboard, so you are burning Me up." Bhargavi was very much amazed to hear the same words from the Holy Mother which she had heard

from the Lord's mouth during the dream. Suddenly she
realized the meaning of Krishna's words. The portrait
of Sri Krishna which she had worshipped for a long
time was locked in the cupboard. Some time ago, when
she had gone to stay with her daughter, she had locked
the portrait in the cupboard to protect it from insects.
Bhargavi had forgotten to retrieve it and to resume her
worship when she returned. It had been lying in there
for a long time. Hearing these words and understanding her mistake, she burst into tears and sought forgiveness from Krishna. Now Bhargavi was fully convinced that there was no difference between Lord
Krishna, her Beloved Deity, and the Holy Mother.

✿

The Holy Mother always loved the company of small
children with whom She often played merrily like a
small child Herself. One little girl named Shayma, who
lived nearby, suffered from breathing trouble. Once when
she had a severe attack, her grandmother rushed her to
the hospital, but unfortunately too late. Hearing the
doctors pronounce her dead, the grandmother was overcome by grief. Wailing uncontrollably, she fled with
the child to the shrine and laid her dead body on Mother's
sacred *Darshan* seat. Mother, who was absorbed in singing *bhajans* in a villager's house, immediately felt restless
and stopped singing abruptly. She hurried to the temple.
There She found the old grandmother raving wildly and
the dead body of the little girl on the seat. "Oh Mother,
please save the child!" begged the old lady. Mother
then sat on the floor and, taking the child on Her lap,

meditated for a long time. After some time, the little girl opened her eyes and gradually revived. Tears of joy coursed down the grandmother's cheeks, as she embraced the Holy Mother again and again with profound gratitude.

❧

Bindu, a fourteen year old girl, and her parents were very devoted to the Holy Mother. They were from a village named Kattoor, which is about seventy kilometers east of Vallickavu. A devotee one day pressed them to recount their inspiring experiences with the Holy Mother. After some coaxing, Bindu revealed,

"Whenever I called Mother, She would come to me. One day father and mother went to Vallickavu, leaving me alone at home. That evening while I was offering my prayers in the family shrine room, I was crying, imploring Mother, 'Is it not because I am a girl that I have no freedom? If I were a boy, I could have visited my Mother all alone without anybody's help.' What happened next was unbelievable. To my astonishment, Mother appeared right in front of me. I was overcome that the Holy Mother Herself was standing in flesh and blood before me. In my excitement I couldn't say even a word to Her. I even forgot to prostrate to Her. Before I could say anything, She disappeared. I felt very happy and blessed thinking that even though my parents did not take me to Mother's Ashram, the compassionate Mother, hearing my prayers, mercifully came to me."

Bindu's mother narrated her own experiences of the Holy Mother.

"Several times I have suddenly smelled the same

fragrance one smells in the temple where the Holy Mother sits in *Bhava*. One day I had a wonderful experience. You may find it difficult to believe, but it really happened. I saw it with my own eyes. There is no greater proof than that. It was daytime and I was standing on the front verandah of the house. Unexpectedly a woman in white clothes approached the house through the front gate. Her head was also covered with a white cloth. I watched Her closely. To my amazement, I realized that the Holy Mother Herself was coming to our house. My hairs stood on end. I was so thrilled that I could not even move. There wasn't anybody else with Her; She was alone. I clearly saw Her coming into the front yard and then suddenly disappear. Flying out of the house, I looked all around for Her, but could not see Her anywhere."

After a short pause She said, "Bindu's experience while taking her exams is still more wonderful." The devotee's curiosity was aroused, and he begged Bindu to tell what had happened.

"Of all the subjects I had to study," she said, "chemistry and physics were too difficult for me to grasp. I was really perplexed when I received the exam on science. Sitting in the examination hall, I sincerely prayed to the Holy Mother to help me. The next moment I was startled to see Mother sitting beside me. I thought that my eyes were playing tricks, so I looked again; Mother was really sitting next to me. Nobody else in the examination hall seemed to be able to see Her. Again, I had the feeling that it must be a hallucination or projection of my own mind. The next moment, as if to convince me, Mother talked to me. She

encouraged me and explained how to answer the difficult questions. The same thing happened the next day
as well. The Mother came and sat beside me every day,
instructing me how to answer the difficult questions
from the first day of the examinations until the last.
When the results were announced, I was even more
surprised to see that I passed, scoring higher marks
than I had expected." Returning to the Ashram, the
devotee related what he had heard from Bindu and her
mother to the Holy Mother. Mystified, he asked Her
how these things could happen. The Holy Mother smilingly replied, "Who knows? It might be that daughter's
innocent faith!"

✺

Nothing is impossible for God. By God's grace the
dumb speak, the deaf hear, and the lame climb
mountains. Both Mr. Ramankutty, a high school head-
master from Kayamkulam, and his wife, Saradamba,
have unshakable faith in the Holy Mother. They have
had a number of experiences revealing Her infinite
spiritual power.

In 1980 a theft occurred in Ramankutty's relatives'
family temple. The relatives took refuge at the Holy
Mother's feet. Mother told them that within a certain
period of time all the stolen articles would be returned.
They were, indeed, returned, as Mother had promised.
Encouraged by that incident, Ramankutty and his wife
decided to visit Mother to beg help for their youngest
daughter, Lekha, who had been deaf and dumb from
birth. Treatment after treatment had not succeeded in
alleviating her condition. Mother consoled them in a
loving and affectionate way.

A month after visiting the Holy Mother, Lekha began uttering the word, 'Amma', and gradually her speech
and hearing increased. The vast change in her condition caused her parents to become ardent devotees of
the Holy Mother.

Other miraculous incidents took place in the life of
Ramankutty and his wife after their coming to Amma.
In 1982, when Amma visited Cape Comorin at the southern tip of India, She asked them to accompany Her.
During *Krishna Bhava*, Ramankutty expressed his fear
that no one would be able to look after his house and
children. The Holy Mother reassured him saying, "Don't
worry. I will look after everything. Only I should be
offered My usual banana and milk everyday in the shrine
room." Before leaving the house, the couple cut down
a big unripened banana bunch from their vegetable
garden and, after covering it with a sack, hung it from
the ceiling of the store room to ripen.

After the pilgrimage everyone returned to the Ashram.
It was *Bhava Darshan* day. Both husband and wife decided to stay for the *Darshan* before returning home.
When Ramankutty approached Amma in *Krishna Bhava*,
She smilingly said, "I have tasted all the bananas. Don't
beat the children. I didn't eat any of them, but just
licked them all." Unable to understand the meaning of
Mother's words, Ramankutty went home remembering
the banana bunch left to ripen. Taking the storeroom
key from its hiding place, he opened the room. What
he saw was astonishing. The sack he had used to cover
the bananas was lying on the floor, and all the bananas
were forming a perfect circle on it! How could this
have happened? The sack had been securely tied around

the bunch with a rope! Thinking his children had done some mischief, he called them and questioned them. Disbelieving their professions of innocence, he tied their hands behind their backs and beat them.

The next *Darshan* day when Ramankutty entered the shrine room where Mother was standing in *Krishna Bhava*, he saw Her standing as if Her hands were tied behind Her back. "Go ahead and beat Me," She said. "I am ready to bear it. I am the one who plucked the bananas from the bunch, because the children didn't offer Me My usual banana and milk every day!" Mother was standing in the exact pose of Ramankutty's children when they had received his beating. Both he and his wife wept with joy, thinking of their great good fortune to have the Holy Mother as their God, Guru and Mother all in one.

🪷

Ramamurti of Madurai in Tamil Nadu was a truck driver. Occasionally he would visit Kerala in connection with his job, and would also go to various other pilgrimage centers in the state. Hearing about the Holy Mother in 1975, he came to Her Ashram. Nine years earlier, his five year old daughter had suddenly disappeared. All of his efforts to find her were fruitless. As he narrated his sorrowful tale to the Holy Mother, he heaved deep sighs. Lovingly consoling him She said, "Don't worry, you will get your daughter back." He believed Her words. Now and then, whenever he came to Kerala, he never forgot to visit the Holy Mother. One day Mother gave Ramamurti some flowers saying, "Within a month you will get your daughter back."

During his travels, Ramamurti stopped his truck one day in a market place in Madras. He saw a few people gathered around a girl of about fourteen or fifteen years of age, who was crying over lost money which she had been saving for some purchases. Some people tried to console her saying that they themselves would give her the lost amount, but she refused to accept it. The girl continued weeping miserably.

Ramamurti lovingly asked her name. On hearing it, he was astonished. It was the same name as his missing daughter's! He looked very closely at her face and was overwhelmed with joy to find that it was indeed his missing daughter. He said, "Child, I will take you back to your home. Don't worry about the money. I will tell your family all about it." The girl agreed, so Ramamurti drove her home. The house was big, owned by a rich landlord. With great hesitation Ramamurti told the landlord his story. After hearing it, the landlord replied, with feeling, "About ten years ago, as I was returning home after a short journey, I saw a crying child standing by the side of the road. I questioned her, but she would not tell me where she came from nor how she became lost. She told me only her name. She was alone, and I was moved by her plight. Since I had no children of my own, I brought her home with me and raised her as my own child. We sometimes send her to the market where you found her."

Understanding Ramamurti's feelings, the landlord gave him permission to take back his daughter, even though he was sad to lose her. Ramamurti was overjoyed. Mother's words proved true, as he now had his daughter back, indeed before the end of the month.

From the time of that great blessing, his faith in Mother has been deep and firm.

❀

Rukmini Amma lives in Quilon, about thirty-five kilometers from the Holy Mother's Ashram. The right side of her body became completely paralyzed due to high blood pressure, and she became bedridden in 1978. She underwent all kinds of allopathic and *ayurvedic* treatment for three years at great expense, but to no avail. Finally she and her husband, Achutan Pillai, and their entire family had succumbed to despair.

Finally they heard of the healings of the Holy Mother, and decided to take Rukmini Amma to the Ashram. After bringing her in a car, two strong men carried her into the Ashram on a chair. Mother gave her some sacred ashes as *prasadam*, blessed her, and sent her away without mentioning a word about her disease. Both husband and wife returned home, disappointed with the apparently fruitless journey. The car parked a few yards from their house. Carried as before, Rukmini Amma was brought to the door of the house, when suddenly an incredible sight stunned the family: Rukmini Amma stood up, pushed aside her attendants, and marched into the house! Unable to believe their eyes, her husband and the others stood dazed. Their happiness was overflowing. Thereafter, they, too, became ardent devotees of the Holy Mother. Rukmini Amma slowly regained her health. Seeing her today, one can hardly believe that she was ever completely bedridden with paralysis.

❀

Neelambaran is a pious man who is very devoted to the Holy Mother. He lives in the small village of Vavvakkavu, about four kilometers from Mother's Ashram. On *Darshan* days he used to come to the Ashram with a beautiful garland of fragrant flowers for the Holy Mother. Though his faith in Mother was unshakable, his wife was antagonistic. She would even scold him severely for going to the Ashram.

One day in 1975 Neelambaran was plowing a field near a road where some others were also working. Neelambaran was telling them about his difficulties making ends meet. "Today I don't have even a penny to buy rice or other food." Hearing this, the other workers teased him mockingly, "That girl in Vallickavu (the Holy Mother) will give you money. Wait till you get that!" Everyone looked at Neelambaran and burst out laughing. Neelambaran turned pale and kept silent.

A few minutes later a little girl appeared, walking toward Neelambaran. As if she were a close relative of his, she smiled at him and stretched out her right hand, offering him a twenty rupee note. Without a thought, Neelambaran accepted the money. "See you," the girl said familiarly, strolling away without another word. The workers speculated on the probable source of the money. Some thought it was a debt being repaid, while others thought that it was credit for some articles pledged. Yet the fact was that none of them had ever seen her before. One curious worker asked Neelambaran, "Who was that girl?"

Neelambaran hesitated. He was dumbfounded. He stood like a statue, holding the money in one hand, thinking of the strange girl. His eyes were fixed on the path she had taken. Hearing the question of his co-worker, Neelambaran answered as if in a dream, "I, too, am wondering about it." The girl had gone. Who she was remained a mystery for Neelambaran and his friends. The next day when Neelambaran visited the Ashram, the Holy Mother lovingly and with much affection said to him, "Did Mother Goddess give you a twenty rupee note yesterday? My child, it was Mother who came to you and gave you the money." Neelambaran's heart overflowed with Divine Love, and embracing the Holy Mother's feet, he wept like a child.

❀

Francis Daniel was an assistant locomotive driver, working for the Southern Railways in Quilon. He tells of a thrilling experience he had after meeting the Holy Mother.

"Before meeting the Holy Mother Amritanandamayi, I was an atheist. Indulging in all kinds of wicked deeds, I led a degraded life. Becoming closely associated with Railway Union politics, I actively participated in many strikes against the government. This created a lot of enemies for me, who accused me of several crimes and created false evidence in order to trap me. Because of their position and influence in the ruling party, I was suspended from service in March, 1978.

From then on my life deteriorated rapidly. Having lost my job, I was beset with difficulties from all directions. I found no way to make ends meet. I lost all hope and succumbed to despair. On the verge of a nervous breakdown, I heard about the Holy Mother from

some railway officers. Their persistence led me finally
to go see Her at Her Ashram in Vallickavu. At first
sight of Mother's radiant form, I fell at Her feet crying
loudly, 'O Mother, save me and grant me refuge!' With
great affection Mother said, 'Son, don't worry. Mother
will straighten out everything. All the false evidence
created against you will be burnt to ashes.'

Firmly believing in Mother's assurance, I peacefully sat at home making no further effort to get back
my job. I continued visiting the Holy Mother as a year
and a half passed. One morning an article in the daily
newspaper described an accident on a train en route to
Madras. A fire had broken out and destroyed many
things. Several passengers were killed. While reading
the paper I was not at all aware that Mother had bestowed a blessing on me.

Later I learned further details of the accident. It
was on that train that the officer who was appointed to
the case against me was traveling, carrying all the false
documents. In that accident the false evidence and forged
materials were all destroyed. As no documentation existed to prosecute me, the court suspended the petition
filed against me, and I was rehired. These incidents
wholly transformed my life, giving me perfect faith in
the unconditional power of God."

DATTAN THE LEPER

Boundless compassion is the nature of God. He discards none. His heart is like the expansive sky
which enfolds the universe with all its beings. The never
ending stream of His love and compassion embraces
every creature in the world.

All the great saints and sages of the past and present are embodiments of Divine Love and Compassion. One who meets the Holy Mother Amritanandamayi can experience this all consuming and all embracing love of God. The following story is a moving testament to that infinite love and compassion.

Dattan was born and grew up in Perumpally near Kayamkulam in Kerala. When he was very young he became a victim of the terrible disease of leprosy. His own parents and relatives turned him out of the house. Finding no other way to earn a livelihood, Dattan became a beggar. Begging his food, he spent his days and nights in a temple compound. As the disease advanced, his whole body was covered with infected wounds oozing pus. Dattan said, "My eyesight was almost gone. In place of my eyes there were only two small slits. The hair of my head fell out. Nobody would give me any food. I was not allowed to travel in a bus. I used to cover my body with a piece of cloth, but even that would stick to my body and stink from the pus and blood oozing from the putrid-smelling wounds. Even fellow beggars wouldn't allow me to eat or sleep near them. Insects always flew around me, disturbing me. At the mere sight of me people held their noses and shrank away. For years I heard no loving word nor saw a compassionate face. Everybody hated me and spat on seeing my ugly looking body and face. I led a dreadfully miserable and despairing life. All my hopes had ebbed away.

Then I heard of the Holy Mother in Vallickavu. I went to see Her on a *Bhava Darshan* day, but no one would let me go into the temple. Full of abhorrence,

people urged me, 'Go away, go away!' for my wounds
produced a foul smell. But the Holy Mother called me
to come to Her, consoled me, and treated me like Her
own child, just as She was treating everyone else."

For those who witnessed the healing, it was a chilling sight to watch the Holy Mother licking his pus
infected wounds, sucking the pus and blood from them.
Each *Bhava Darshan* day She gave him a bath, pouring
pots of water on his head. She smeared sacred ash all
over his body and treated him with the same love, affection and compassion which She showed to other devotees. Witnessing the Holy Mother's merciful way of
serving him, some devotees vomited, some fainted, others
watched with awe and reverence, weeping with love
and devotion on realizing that they were sitting in the
Holy Presence of the Divine Mother Herself. Who but
She could show such love? The Holy Mother said about
Dattan: "Who else is there to take care of him and to
love him? Mother doesn't see his external body. She
sees only his heart. I cannot discard him. He is my son
and I am his mother. Can a mother abandon her son?"

Now Dattan is transformed. Almost all his wounds
have healed. The Holy Mother's spittle is his divine
medicine. His eyes have opened and he can see clearly
now. Hair has grown back on his head. He can travel
in a bus, and people are willing to talk to him and
serve him food. Though the scars of the terrible disease still remain on Dattan's body, no more blood or
pus oozes from them, nor is there any putrid smell. He
can wear a shirt or a loincloth without its sticking to
his body and causing him pain. He is happy. The Holy
Mother has given him a new birth. He has found meaning and joy in life through Her blessings.

Kuttappan Nair, a retired head constable, narrates one of numerous experiences he has had with Mother.

"My family and I have been householder devotees of Mother for the past eight years. One night during *Bhava Darshan* five years ago, Amma pointed out to me that some of the planets were in an unfavorable position for me. When I requested a remedy for the problem, Amma advised me to observe a vow of silence on Saturdays. Since I had gone to the hospital on Friday to see my daughter in the maternity ward, I was unable to observe the vow of silence that Saturday. Oddly, a hen which had no disease died that day at my house. The following Saturday also, I was unable to observe the vow of silence. That day our puppy died. I could not observe silence on the third Saturday either. That day our year old calf mysteriously succumbed. Then I remembered Amma's instruction to observe a vow of silence.

The following day I returned contritely to Amma in Vallickavu. When I prostrated before Her during *Bhava Darshan*, Amma announced, 'You have not observed the vow which I advised. Already three deaths have taken place in your house. In the future, if you do not observe the vow, more unpleasant misfortunes will occur.' On the next Saturday, early in the morning after bathing, I offered prayers at the Devi temple near our house, came home and sat in meditation in the *puja* room. As Saturday was a school holiday, my grandchildren and nephew were all at home in the next room. When they started making noise I scolded them, forgetting about my vow. Then I resumed my vow of silence. I spent the entire day in the *puja* room except for brief breaks for breakfast, lunch, tea and supper.The next day during *Bhava Darshan* Amma caught hold of my ear and sternly rebuked me saying, 'Is this how you observe silence?' I begged forgiveness, dismayed that in my anger at the children I had forgotten about my vow. Amma admonished me further, 'It is not that. If you observe a vow without fasting, no good can come of it.' Again, I asked forgiveness, confessing that I did not know the rules of observing a vow. Amma then advised me to observe the vow only from morning till evening, and during that time to take only water, milk and coconut juice. If my hunger became unbearable, I might take some fruit. When I begged Amma to forgive my mistakes and remove all obstacles, She gave me a mantra. Ever since I started chanting that mantra, I have been able to observe silence on Saturdays without any difficulty.

Three years back in the month of May, on a Saturday at around eleven in the morning, I was meditating in my *puja* room. On seeing a crow pecking at a ripe jack fruit, my granddaughter interrupted me to ask me to pick it for her. I headed for the tree with a hacking knife. As I hacked the stem of the jackfruit, the knife missed its target, hit the tree and, slipping out of my hands, hit me a little above my left eye. The eye started bleeding profusely, so I covered the wound with my *dhoti*. Luckily my nephew, who was just passing by on his bicycle, carried me off to the hospital, where the wound was cleaned and bandaged. Throughout the entire incident I still managed to keep my silence.

At the same time in Vallickavu Amma called my son commanding him, 'Go home immediately. Father has had a minor accident. There is nothing to worry about though; Amma has averted the danger.' If the wound had been a little to the right, it would have been in the center of my forehead. If the knife had hit me a little lower, it would have hit my left eye. After I had returned from the hospital, my son came rushing into the house asking, 'Where is father? What has happened to him?' When we wondered how on earth he had heard about my accident, he related to us what Mother had told him."

Sri R. Reddiar, who lives in Quilon, narrates his experience with the Holy Mother: "One of our daughters had run away from home sometime earlier. Friends suggested we see the Holy Mother to confide in Her our anxiety about the missing girl. The Mother assured us: 'The girl will be back home seven days from today. You don't have to go anywhere to search for her.' Then She gave us seven wicks and instructed us to light one each day. She continued, 'On the seventh day, when you light the last wick, officials will inform you of the girl's whereabouts.'

Not fully trusting Mother's words, we continued to search for her, but could find no clue to her disappearance. We were very distressed, especially because she was an unprotected young girl. Greatly disappointed, we returned to the Holy Mother. She questioned us, 'Why did you waste so much money? Mother has already told you that the girl will return. Don't be anxious. You must be confident. As I told you before, you will get her back.'

Six days had passed, and we had burnt six wicks according to the Holy Mother's instructions. On the seventh day, we had lit the last wick during the twilight hour. While it was burning in the oil lamp the phone rang. A family member answered it, relaying the message: 'Your child is in the custody of the Madras Police.' The girl had gone to a goldsmith's shop to sell a gold ornament. Suspicious, the goldsmith had informed the police, who then held her for questioning.Thus at exactly the time the Holy Mother had indicated, we received word about the lost girl, who was immediately returned to us. From that time on we have surrendered everything at the Holy Mother's Feet. We firmly believe that Mother protects us."

Kunjamma lives in Kayamkulam, about twelve kilometers from Mother's Ashram. The following incident greatly strengthened her devotion to the Holy Mother.

A couple of years before she came to the Holy Mother, her husband had suddenly died, as his horoscope had foretold. Miserable after the death of her husband, she was still more disconsolate when she learned that her son's horoscope predicted his death at twenty-three from a snake bite. To save her son from his terrible fate, Kunjamma frantically sought solutions, finally seeking refuge at the feet of the Holy Mother. "Don't worry, daughter," Mother consoled her, "Mother will give you a mantra to chant daily. Once a week observe a vow for your son. Vows observed by mothers for their children have great power. Your son's death will be transferred to one of your domestic animals. Go and be peaceful."

Kunjamma was not fully persuaded by the Holy Mother's words. Every day she had dreams that her son had died from a snake bite. After the death of her husband, Kunjamma had raised a dog to guard the house. One day she heard barking and howling from the front yard, followed by the hissing sound of a snake. Full of dread, she opened the door a little and peeped out. The dog was desperately fighting with a snake. She immediately closed the door on the fearful sight and waited inside until the commotion had subsided. Terrified, Kunjamma slowly opened the door. To her amazement both the dog and snake lay dead.

Though she felt sad about her dog's death, she suddenly remembered the Holy Mother's words: "Your son's death will be transferred to one of your domestic animals." Her heart was flooded with gratitude to Mother. This incident occurred during the very period when her son was supposed to die. Full of love and reverence, Kunjamma saluted the Holy Mother mentally. Her faith in the Mother was greatly strengthened by this gift of grace. Her son is still alive and is leading a happy life with the blessings of the Holy Mother.

***

One day in 1980, Chandramati came from her home across the backwaters to the Holy Mother's Ashram to receive Her blessings. The Holy Mother was receiving the devotees one by one. Suddenly She closed Her eyes and sat in an strange exalted mood for some time. Her body was motionless. The devotees anxiously waited;

within a couple of minutes Mother returned to Her usual state. Calling Chandramati aside, the Holy Mother confided to her, "Your grandchild just died, but the anguished cry of your daughter led Mother to her. The child has just come back to life."

Chandramati did not fully understand the meaning of the Holy Mother's words until she learned of the incident which had occurred simultaneously in her daughter's house at exactly the same moment. Chandramati's daughter, Nalini, was also an ardent devotee of the Holy Mother. She had only one son, who was then six years old. The child had suddenly become acutely ill and had died before any medical aid could be summoned. An uproar arose in the house. Nalini, beating her chest, had loudly prayed, "O Mother, how long have I called on You and worshipped You sincerely? Is this the fruit of my prayers? Who else is there for me in this world? O Mother, why did You take this child, my only son? Why did you take this only son of mine?" Immediately a blaze of lightning had flashed near the body of Nalini's son. Within a few seconds, the child had come back to life, as if he were waking up after a deep sleep.

Chandramati then related to her daughter what the Holy Mother had told her in the temple, and they both realized that it was only by the grace of the Holy Mother that the child's life had been restored. Shedding tears of joy, they both reverently prostrated to the Holy Mother in their gratitude.

❧

The Holy Mother has blessed many couples who had remained childless for many years by giving them a baby through Her divine resolve (*sankalpa*). Such couples often used to take refuge at the Holy Mother's feet. Sincere prayer and unshakable faith in all circumstances are the two most important factors which enable the supplicants to receive the fruit of their life-long desire. They must also have self-confidence, mental strength and devotion to confront the trials which may occur during the course of pregnancy. The Holy Mother is very strict in choosing the people who deserve this rare gift. Her decision depends entirely on various subtle considerations which are beyond the realm of human intellect. The following are the stories of four couples who were fortunate enough to receive this great blessing from the Holy Mother.

SHAKTI PRASAD I

Vidyadharan and Omana from Vavvakkavu were deeply grieved to have no child, even after nine years of married life. They longed earnestly for a child, fearing that the sweet smile and prattle of a baby were a dream which they would never realize. Omana's elder sister, Sarasamma, was a devotee who advised her sister to take her grief to the Holy Mother.

In 1977 Omana came to the Holy Mother's Ashram. When her turn came, Omana entered the temple and approached Mother. Before she could mention anything about her unfortunate condition, the Holy Mother consoled her in these words: "Daughter, you came here to ask for a baby. Mother will take your sorrow. Within four months a child will take form in your womb."

Having full faith in the Holy Mother's words, Omana

happily returned home. The Holy Mother's words proved true. Within four months symptoms of pregnancy appeared. Vidyadharan, Omana and their relatives were overjoyed. For nine years they had been praying and dreaming of a child, and now their lifelong wish was materializing.

In those days Omana worked in a cashew nut factory. When she was four months pregnant, she saw a doctor who confirmed that the fetus was healthy. In the ninth month she was examined again and was astonished to hear the doctor report that she was not pregnant! The most surprising thing was that her belly had remained enormous. Omana, her husband, and other members of the family were extremely worried. She was taken to another hospital where several gynecologists examined her and found no sign of a baby in the womb. The doctors were astounded. It appeared very strange even to them: a woman with all external symptoms of pregnancy but no trace of a child in the womb. At last one doctor, a specialist in gynecology, took an X-ray of the mother's womb and was surprised to see dense smoke on the film instead of a fetus. All of them were amazed and curious to learn the reason. The perplexed relatives took Omana to still another hospital in Quilon. All the tests were repeated, yet the doctors still could not reach a conclusion. When there was no sign of a baby in the womb, Omana's relatives were terribly disappointed. Nevertheless, Omana had unwavering faith in the Holy Mother, and remained optimistic. When she told the Holy Mother about the doctors' report and the result of the X-ray, Mother smiled benignly, "Be courageous, daughter. That child is God's son, not an image. They cannot take his photograph." Omana believed the Holy Mother's words.

The divine play was not yet over. Omana was ten months pregnant, but still she didn't give birth. Days and months passed, one by one. Nothing changed. Omana was thirteen months pregnant. The villagers abused and teased her, mocking the Holy Mother saying, "She is going to give birth to a baby elephant!" Others cuttingly taunted, "O, this fishergirl has given her a great child; maybe it is a serpent!" Omana and her husband spent their days in prayer and meditation. Their only succor and support was the Holy Mother. The test was very hard for them. Sixteen months passed, yet Omana had not given birth. The villagers continued their abuses, sometimes peppered with vulgar expressions. Surrendering everything at the Holy Mother's feet and observing strict vows, Omana held to her unswerving faith.

Finally one day in the sixteenth month, the Holy Mother directed Omana's family to take her to the hospital. Heeding Mother's words, Omana entered Victoria Hospital in Quilon. A crowd gathered to hear about the extraordinary delivery. Everyone anxiously waited. Learning from Omana's family that she was sixteen months pregnant, the doctors examined her thoroughly and were amazed to conclude that there was no baby in the womb, even though they observed all the indications of pregnancy. They acknowledged they faced a dilemma. After much discussion, they decided on surgery. The C-section revealed a fully grown healthy infant in the womb! After sixteen months in the womb, the babe came into the world. Named Shakti Prasad (Blessing of the Supreme Energy) by the Holy Mother, he began meditating and chanting mantras when he was barely three. Mother gave him a *rudraksha* rosary and a small seat made of grass. Seated on it, he would meditate in a perfect yogic posture and would repeat the sacred mantras 'Om Namah Sivaya' and 'OM'. Whenever he came to the Ashram, he sought the Holy Mother's presence without being prompted. Picking up some flower petals, he would offer them at the Holy Mother's feet. Often Mother would say, "He has the eyes of a yogi." Today he doesn't speak much. He is not mischievous or naughty like ordinary children. In school he tells his classmates, "You must meditate on Ammachi's form or you will become sick!"

SHAKTI PRASAD II

Ratnamma and her husband, Krishnan, are another fortunate couple who were blessed by the Holy Mother with an auspicious child. Ratnamma first came to the Ashram in 1976, prompted by a friend's healing. Her Christian neighbor, Reena, had long suffered from chronic severe chest pain. Hearing of the Holy Mother, Reena went to see Her to beg relief. The sacred water and ash which the Holy Mother gave her completely relieved Reena of her pain. Her neighbor's experience led Ratna also to seek the blessings of the Holy Mother, for she had suffered pain in her stomach for years. When she came to Vallickavu, the Holy Mother, in the Divine Mood, offered her a banana to eat. Ratna's tormenting stomach pains ceased completely.

Ratna had married Krishnan in 1971. They were both extremely sad to have had no children after five

years of marriage. Ratna had never mentioned her desire
for a child to Mother. One day the Holy Mother asked
her sweetly, "Do you not wish to have a son? Mother
will grant your prayer. After ten months a son will be
born to you."According to the Holy Mother's words,
Ratna was confident she had become pregnant, even
though the doctors with their X-rays insisted she was
not. Believing the doctors and full of frustration, Krishnan
prohibited Ratna from going to Vallickavu until the
birth of the child. During this period Ratna's intense
prayers often brought her visions of the Holy Mother.

Finally her faith was rewarded by the birth of a
beautiful male child on the exact date that the Holy
Mother had predicted. Soon after he began speaking
his mother tongue, Malayalam, he proclaimed that his
real father was God, not Krishnan. Though born and
brought up in a fishing village, Shakti Prasad never
ate fish or meat. Without fail he meditated every morning
and evening. Sometimes he would sit for more than
half an hour. Occasionally someone had to rouse him
from meditation. Even from his infancy, Shakti Prasad
often played making temples out of clay and worshipping Lord Siva and Goddess Parvati.

One day a stranger came to Shakti Prasad's house
when Ratnamma's husband, Krishnan, was out of town.
According to the custom, Ratna invited the guest to sit
on the verandah and gave him a cup of coffee. Suddenly seven year old Shakti came forward and slapped
him. Ratnamma immediately pushed him away. Shakti
protested to his mother: "Mother, he is a thief. Don't
let him sit here, don't give him coffee." Astonished,
Ratnamma queried, "How do you know he is a thief?"

Shakti explained, "By looking at his face." Hearing
this, the thief who had come in the guise of a guest,
immediately fled.

Sometimes Shakti Prasad used to tell his mother,
"You are not my mother. My mother is in Vallickavu,"
(the Holy Mother). If anybody in his house or a neighboring house becomes sick, Shakti takes basil leaves,
sacred water and ash to the person who is ill. By his
sprinkling the sacred water, the symptoms of the illness vanish. Unless his own intuition tells him to do
so, Shakti does not do this even if asked.

One day, Shakti went to a neighbor's house where
he accidentally knocked a piece of cake off a table.
The daughter of the family struck him. The next day,
she and her parents came to Shakti's house. The right
arm, the one she had hit Shakti with, was swollen and
causing her great pain. She couldn't even move the
hand. Concluding that the pain was punishment for hitting
Shakti, they came to ask forgiveness. Ratnamma suggested that they go see the Holy Mother. The next day
they apologized sincerely to the Holy Mother, where-
upon the girl's arm and hand returned to a normal
state.

From childhood Shakti Prasad has been kind and
merciful to others. If people in the neighborhood are
starving, he brings them to his house to feed them. His
generous nature has sometimes disturbed his parents,
who are financially unstable. If the family is hesitant
to give a hungry person food, Shakti offers his own
share and fasts. Ratnamma considers herself Shakti's
foster mother. She raises him on behalf of the Holy
Mother whom she considers his real mother.

UNNIKANNAN (SHAKTI PRASAD III)

Sarasan and his wife, Tankam, live on the island where the Holy Mother's Ashram is located. Although many years had passed after their marriage, they were grieving about having no child. Told of the Holy Mother and Her divine powers, they took refuge in Her and prayed sincerely for the fulfillment of their desire. One day during Her Divine Mood the Holy Mother told Tankam that she would become pregnant soon, and within a few days she did indeed become pregnant. One night, when Tankam was three months pregnant, she suddenly had an attack of severe stomach pain followed by continuous bleeding. There were no hospitals or doctors nearby. The family was very distressed, not knowing what to do. Unable to bear the pain, Tankam groaned loudly. At that moment, to everyone's amazement, the Holy Mother walked into the room. She made some basil leaf extract and asked Tankam to drink it. Within a few seconds her stomach pain and bleeding stopped. How had the Holy Mother come to their house at that time of the night? The Holy Mother with some other devotees had been on their way to another part of the island by boat. When the boat neared Tankam's house, the Holy Mother's mood suddenly changed and She seemed very restless. The next moment, Mother insisted that She must stop at Tankam's house. The devotees in the boat tried to change the Holy Mother's mind, as it was dark and the destination was still far away, but Mother was firm, so the boat was anchored near Tankam's house. Divine plans are always mysterious.

During the course of her pregnancy, when Tankam

came one day to see the Holy Mother, Mother said to her, "You will deliver on a dark night and there will be thunder and lightning followed by a heavy downpour." Exactly as Mother had said, Tankam gave birth to a beautiful male child at the Alleppy Medical College on a gloomy night with heavy rain and thunder. The electricity went off in the hospital. The entire building was plunged in darkness. But everyone present near the child witnessed something extraordinary: the brilliant eyes of the child were shining in the darkness. Named Unnikannan by the Holy Mother, the baby grew to be an extraordinary child. He was endowed with a sharp intellect and a face glowing with spiritual radiance. Though born and raised in the fishing clan, he would never eat fish or meat. Sometimes he asked questions concerning the performing of worship and other religious practices. He always acted according to his own insights. Nobody scolded or struck him, even if he did some mischief. If by chance he were beaten or scolded, nobody would be able to sleep that night because of mysterious disturbances. The Holy Mother once said, "I will give him whatever he wants." Unnikannan's parents have strong faith in the Holy Mother's protection.

SHAKTI PRASAD IV

Hasanu Kunju had married Subaida when she was sixteen years old. Sixteen more years passed, yet no child was born to Subaida, who was by then thirty-two. Her husband went to see the Holy Mother in 1977 after having undergone many unsuccessful treatments for an

infected wound on his shin. When the wound had completely healed by the blessings of the Holy Mother, he
and his wife, Subaida became devotees of Mother.

Having lost all hope of having a child, Subaida never
opened her heart to Mother. The doctors believed that
she would be unable to conceive without an operation.
One day, understanding Subaida's heart, the Holy Mother
told her, "You are sad because you haven't had a child,
even after so many years. Mother will give you a child."
Within a short period of time Subaida became pregnant. Thus Subaida conceived her first child in 1978
at the age of thirty-two, after sixteen years of marriage.
This was a remarkable occurrence for the villagers and
for Subaida's relatives. Fearing abuse from the Muslim
community, Subaida and her husband kept the origin
of the pregnancy a secret.

In 1979, Subaida gave birth to a magnificent male
child. The parents named him Ansim. The neighbors
called him Manikantan. The Holy Mother gave him the
name Shakti Prasad. He is a phenomenal child endowed with brilliance and unusual vitality. He attracts
the attention of everyone. The Holy Mother alone knows
his bright future. About the birth and future of these
children, the Holy Mother says, "During meditation, a
power emits from me and enters into the mother's womb,
and in this way she becomes pregnant. Some of these
children will become perfect *sannyasins*. Others will
lead a family life. Wherever they may be, they all will
turn to spirituality." Hearing this truth, many of the
mothers of these children were dismayed to think that
after some years they would lose their sons to the service of mankind. Therefore, Mother promised them

another child who would fulfill all the expectations that parents usually have for their children, that they marry and lead a householder's life. Within the next few years, all of these mothers were blessed with another child.

❀

Sarasamma lived with her husband and children in Karunagappally, a small town to the south of Vallickavu. They were leading a happy family life when, unexpectedly, they experienced a great calamity. They lost all their property including their house and were forced to live on others' liberality and generosity. After a period of great difficulty, they heard of the Holy Mother. When they took refuge at Her feet, all the adversities which they had been facing for a long time were gradually resolved.

Sarasamma's faith in the Holy Mother was unshakable. She was confident that if a catastrophe were to occur in their house, the Holy Mother would warn them to take necessary precautions. To avert possible misfortunes Mother had given her a mantra to chant and had instructed her to take a particular vow every week.

One day when Sarasamma came to the Ashram, the Holy Mother told her, "Daughter, Mother can see a death in your family. Continue keeping your vow. Pray sincerely to God. Don't worry, Mother is always with you." Though Sarasamma was very worried, she had strong faith in the Holy Mother's saving grace. Soon the inevitable happened. A couple of days after the Holy Mother had given the warning, Sarasamma's eldest daughter was bitten by a viper. Immediately they brought the girl to Mother's Ashram. By this time, the girl's whole body had turned blue. A mucilaginous saliva was trickling from her mouth. Some were sure she was dying; others believed she was already dead.

The devotees tried to console Sarasamma who was sitting near her daughter, sobbing uncontrollably. During *Devi Bhava* the Holy Mother sent word that the girl should stay overnight in the Ashram. Accordingly she was taken to a building on the north side.

The next morning the girl seemed unchanged, as if there were no life in her. Surrounded by a group of devotees, Sarasamma was still sitting beside her daughter. Though she seemed utterly overwhelmed, her strong faith in the Holy Mother enabled her to gather some inner strength and continue to hope.

Suddenly a snake appeared in the yard of the building and crawled straight toward the cot where the girl was lying. Terrified, everyone shouted "Snake! Snake!" The girl opened her eyes. By that time the snake was very close to her. Seeing the dreadful snake with its hood raised, the girl was horrified and leaped up immediately. To everyone's astonishment, all the symptoms of snake bite disappeared from the girl's body as she came back to life. The snake immediately crawled away from the spot. Later Sarasamma and her daughter prostrated with overflowing devotion and love before the Holy Mother.

At the insistence of her relatives, Sarasamma later went to see a very famous astrologer. She gave him the necessary details, but did not mention that she was seeking information about her daughter. She asked him about the girl's future. After making the astrological calculations, the astrologer said with great conviction, "This girl has died from poisoning." Sarasamma replied, "No, this is my daughter's horoscope, and she is still alive." The astrologer, who had strong faith in his science and ability, could not believe her words. He thought for a moment, made further calculations, and proclaimed, " I am certain that she was bitten by a poisonous snake during the time of her predestined death. If she is still alive, then it is a wonder and a rare blessing of God."

Sarasamma added, "Later we found that even in the horoscope written during her childhood, mention was made of her dying by poisoning at the age of nineteen. It was exactly at that age that she was bitten by the snake. Clearly the boundless compassion of the Holy Mother always protects us."

In 1981, Sarasamma had another unforgettable experience of Mother's grace which she narrated with deep emotion.

"In those days, the devotees who came for Mother's *Darshan* used to leave the Ashram around four a.m. in order to reach home by early morning. All the devotees used to go in a group to the bus stand about a half mile away, where they took buses to their respective towns. On a new moon night my son, Madhu, and I boarded the bus and headed home. Although it was five o'clock in the morning when we neared the village, it was still pitch dark. I got out at a stop which I thought was close to my house, thinking my son was right behind me.

"The conductor rang the bell, and the bus drove away into the darkness. Looking around, I could not

find my son and realized that I had made a foolish
mistake. I was in a lonely place about two kilometers
from my house. In the meantime, my son was shocked
to find me gone. He got off at the next bus stop and
ran back to rejoin me, but I was some distance away.
Perplexed and not knowing what to do, I remembered
Mother's parting words, 'Be very careful today.' I held
Mother's prasad tightly in my right hand. Then I noticed a truck stopping a short distance away. Seven or
eight men emerged and walked straight toward me.
Perhaps they had seen a woman getting off the bus in
this lonely place. Surrounded by burly looking rowdies, I was trembling with fear as they shot questions
at me, using vulgar language. I thought they might as-
sault me at any moment, and a terrible panic rose inside
me. 'Is this the fate of those who go to see the Holy
Mother? Is this the fruit of my lifelong devotion?' Such
thoughts burned in my mind, blanking out the threatening voices, and I screamed wildly, '*Yedi*!' (O Mother!).
This shocked the rowdies who surrounded me.

What followed is difficult to express. Instantly the
effulgent form of the Divine Mother appeared before
me in the sky with countless arms holding many weapons in Her hands. She was seated on an enormous
creature, and Her face, hair and crown exactly resembled
those of Mata Amritanandamayi during *Devi Bhava*. The
Holy Mother had assumed the terrible form of Kali in
order to save Her devotee! Overcome, I started to lose
my external awareness. The Divine Mother stretched
out Her hands toward me. My eyes were fixed on Her
radiant form and started to bulge. My tongue stuck out
like Mother Kali's, and I felt a tremendous power per-

vade my body. Uproarious laughter burst from within me, the mere remembrance of which sends shivers through me. The air trembled with the terrible sound of my laughter. The rowdies, who were about to pounce on me, were stunned to see that frightening form with disheveled hair, bulging eyes, protruding tongue and roaring laughter standing before them fearlessly. Perhaps they thought I was an evil spirit, not a human being! Losing their nerve, they moved to escape, and, slowly backing up, jumped into their truck and fled into the darkness. Even after they had vanished, I was unable to move. Gradually, I started to regain my normal consciousness as the enchanting form of Mother Kali also disappeared. My body felt numb, as if paralyzed. After a few minutes I could move a little, and the protruding tongue withdrew into my mouth. I could not yet move my bulging, transfixed eyes, but after massaging them for some time, they returned to normal. My throat pained severely from the roaring laughter. Looking down, I found that Mother's *prasadam* was still clenched in my hand.

A few minutes later my son, Madhu, came running up to me. 'Mother, what was that terrible roaring sound? Who were those men driving away in the truck? Did they hurt you?' But I could not answer him, as I was still struggling to get back my speech, which took some days to return to normal." Although this incident took place in 1981, when Sarasamma narrates it she trembles even now with fear, her throat chokes up with emotion, and tears stream down her face as she repeats over and over, "Amma, Amma, Amma..."

K.S. Gangadharan Vaidyar is a well known and proficient *Ayurvedic* doctor who lives in Alwaye, a town about a hundred and thirty-five kilometers from Vallickavu. Both he and his wife are ardent devotees of the Holy Mother. In 1986, Dr. Gangadharan was suffering from an attack of severe neck pain. Day by day the pain increased until it became unbearable. He recalls, "Though I was myself an experienced *Ayurvedic* doctor, I was unable to diagnose or relieve the severe pain. To reduce it a little, I wore a neck support. Finally the racking pain became too much to bear and I decided to consult a bone specialist. The day before my appointment I visited the Holy Mother's Ashram. It was a Sunday and was very crowded. When my turn came, I entered the temple where the Holy Mother was seated in *Devi Bhava*. Prostrating to Mother, I hesitantly told Her about the severe pain which I had been suffering from for a long time and for which I had undergone several treatments. The Holy Mother very affectionately rubbed my neck a couple of times with Her left hand and comforted me. Having received the Holy Mother's blessings, my wife and I returned home. At midnight the excruciating pain continued to persist, but I was so exhausted that I was able to fall asleep immediately. The next morning when I woke up I was amazed to find that the pain had disappeared, and for years since it has not returned."

Dr. Gangadharan resumed, "For the last thirty-five years I have worked as a doctor; though I underwent different kinds of treatments to cure my neck pain, I could find no remedy. The Holy Mother, by Her mere touch, completely removed my pain forever."

Dr. Gangadharan's sister, Sumathi, had long suffered severe pain in her stomach. She was fifty-seven years old and the mother of five children. Many eminent doctors had prescribed treatments. None of them were effective. Finally she was taken to a hospital near Trichur, well known for the treatment of cancer. After examining the patient thoroughly, the doctors concluded that she was suffering from cancer of the uterus.

During this period, Dr. Gangadharan and his wife were traveling in Europe visiting friends and were unaware of his sister's condition. On their return from Europe, they were informed of Sumathi's diagnosis. Dr. Gangadharan tells the story: "Hearing about my sister's condition, my wife and I rushed to the hospital. When she saw us, she burst into tears. After consoling her, we returned home and visited her again a week later. By that time she was failing rapidly. Helplessly watching my sister dying in excruciating pain, we could find no way to comfort her. The doctors believed that removing the uterus would be useless, as the disease had advanced too far and her whole system was affected. They decided to treat her using radiation and chemotherapy. Soon the news spread to the relatives that Sumathi had cancer and was expected to die. After the treatments, Sumathi was brought to my house for complete bed rest. Still the racking pain continued, disturbing her continuously and preventing her from sleeping. We had abandoned all hope of restoring her health and saving her life.

At last my wife suggested we seek refuge in the Holy Mother, who is forever our stay and support, and who has always stretched forth Her blessed hands to protect us from such miseries. One Sunday we took Sumathi to the Holy Mother's Ashram. The Holy Mother lovingly caressed and consoled her, rubbing her stomach. Sumathi felt great relief by the mere touch of the Holy Mother's hand. The Holy Mother asked us to bring some *tulasi* leaf extract during our next visit to the Ashram. The next *Darshan* we brought it according to Her instructions. Blessing the extract and handing it over to the patient, Mother asked her to take one teaspoonful every morning and evening. Sumathi followed Mother's advice. Within a week her pain disappeared and her disease was completely cured! Both of these stories are my own personal experiences. There is no greater Guru than one's own experience. Even though these experiences seem astounding to me, they are nothing for the Holy Mother, who is the embodiment of Infinite Power, and who can cure the fatal disease of worldly existence itself."

❁

Mr. Gopakumar is the personnel officer in a big fertilizer company at Alwaye. He tells this story of his experiences with the Holy Mother.

"My meeting with the Holy Mother was quite unexpected. The devotees had arranged a reception for Her in a temple in Ernakulam. The Mother's devotional singing followed by the reception had a great impact on me. I simply gazed at Her loving face and keenly listened to the poignant devotional songs which revealed the great truths of life. I could not control my tears. When the *bhajans* were over, Mother was receiving the devotees one by one, when I overheard some people commenting on Her spiritual power. 'She can do all the things God can do,' some devotees said. While receiving *prasadam* from the Holy Mother, I told Her my problem which I felt even God could not solve. 'Mother, I am suffering from terrible mental depression. For the last fifteen years I have been unable to sleep even one hour at night. From lack of sleep my face has turned black and dull, and I have become very weak. Many nights I have sincerely prayed to God to give me sleep. All my prayers have been fruitless.' The Holy Mother smiled at me and affectionately smeared some sacred ash on my forehead. She did not even utter a word.

I returned home when the darshan was over. It was midnight when I had my supper, after which I felt very tired. As sleep was beyond my imagination, I simply lay down on the cot. I opened my eyes when I heard my servant calling me, "Sir, please get up. What kind of sleep is this?" I was shocked when the servant boy told me that it was nine o'clock in the morning. Fortunately, since it was Sunday, I didn't have to go to work. The boy served me a glass of tea, yet I was unable to stay awake. Effortlessly I again went back to sleep. When I woke up again, it was one o'clock in the afternoon. Getting up from bed, I came to the dining room and saw both my breakfast and lunch sitting there on the table. It was like a dream. It took me a couple of minutes to realize that a miracle had changed my life. Ever since that day I have been able to sleep soundly. The Mother's blessings and Her boundless compassion have given me new vigor and strength.

Not long afterward, I visited the Holy Mother again

at Her Ashram. I still had a lot of family problems. During my first visit to the Ashram I had not told any of them to the Holy Mother. After seeing Her that day in *Devi Bhava*, I felt that my difficulties were diminishing.

Three years earlier, I had chided my father-in-law for some rude behavior. In protest, he had pressed my wife, a bank employee, to get a transfer to Trivandrum where he lived. He was so persistent that my wife felt obliged to obey him and to take my only son with her. Thus he succeeded in dividing our family. I was miserable, crushed by the grief of separation. My wife's family was trying to cut off our relationship by slowly turning my wife and son against me. During my second visit I prayed to the Holy Mother to save me. She smilingly consoled me saying, 'Son, don't worry, Mother will look after it.' Though Mother had reassured me, I did not have total confidence in Her words.

The next morning at my job I felt an unusual mental calmness and delight. I was able to discharge all my duties sincerely and easily. At noon I received a telegram containing the following message from my wife concerning my son: 'Balamurali seriously ill, admitted to hospital...Ammini.' Even after reading the message I felt no anxiety or sadness at all. I left work immediately and went to tell the news to one of Mother's devotees. When I reached his house, I found another devotee also present. I still remember their words, 'Gopakumar, don't worry, this is just Mother's technique to reunite all of you. Your son's illness is a ruse to make you go there.'

I reached Trivandrum at ten o'clock at night and

went straight to the hospital. When I entered the room where my son was lying, he suddenly jumped up calling out, 'Mother, my father has come.' He seemed to be all right. Then my wife briefly told me everything that had happened. 'In the morning his temperature was a hundred and five degrees. All of us were very worried. But later in the evening the temperature dropped, and he returned to normal.' Then I remembered the words of my friends and bowed my head at the Holy Mother's feet for showering so much grace on me. I happily spent two days with my wife and son in the hospital, and on the third day I returned to Ernakulam after getting my son discharged.

The following Sunday as usual, I went to Vallickavu to visit the Holy Mother during *Devi Bhava*. As it was crowded that day, I didn't get a chance to tell Her about my meeting with my wife and son. Anyhow, I thought, She knows everything. She would say, 'Mother knows the problems of Her children without being told. She can see their aching hearts.' As usual, the Holy Mother gave me an incense stick and sacred ash as *prasadam* and said, 'Son, when you reach home all your sorrows will be removed.' That night when I returned home and entered my bedroom, I was overwhelmed with joy to see both my wife and son lying fast asleep on my bed. When I realized they had returned after three years of forced separation, I stood in front of the portrait of the Holy Mother, lit some incense, and prayed with joined palms, 'My dear Mother, you can do those things which even God cannot do!'"

K.K. Damodaran Nair had a relative who was a devotee of the Holy Mother. The man came to visit him in his Bombay house, remaining for some months of employment. Often Mr. Nair noticed his guest sitting in front of a photo of a lady in white, worshipping, crying and singing *bhajans*. "What a waste of time to cry to a photo!" he thought. "Who is this so-called Mother?" He never expressed his skepticism, however, nor interfered with his relative's worship.

During this period, Mr. Nair returned for a visit to his family home, which was about a hundred and seventy kilometers from the Holy Mother's Ashram. Finding his eighty year old father working in the garden, he protested, "Father, you are so old, why should you be doing such strenuous work?" His father replied, "All my life I have been accustomed to doing hard work. I don't feel any strain." Mr. Nair then visited the family of the relative who had been staying with him in Bombay. That man's father was also a staunch devotee of the Holy Mother. The two of them decided to pay a visit to the Holy Mother, Mr. Nair primarily out of curiosity. They arrived to find Mother in *Krishna Bhava*. Entering the temple, Mr. Nair was astounded to see the shining face and mischievous smile of Krishna. While standing before Krishna during darshan, he suddenly found himself dancing. He could not control himself. Krishna teasingly asked him, "Now do you believe?" He felt humiliated and very confused, but still not ready to believe fully in the Holy Mother. He replied, "Give me an experience, then I will believe." With a smile on Her face, Mother assured him, "You will get one."

After returning to Bombay, Mr. Nair was working a

night shift one night when he fell asleep on his desk around midnight. Suddenly at two a.m., he felt someone tapping him on the shoulder. Startled, he woke up to see the Holy Mother before him saying, "Did you know that your father has died? Look and see." Suddenly he saw the corpse of his father, lamps lit both at his head and feet, surrounded by crying relatives. The Mother then asked him, "Now do you believe?" Mr. Nair did not know what to think of this experience. How could it have been a dream when he had seen Mother standing before him with his own eyes? Then again, how could it have been real, since only a few days earlier he had seen his father as strong and healthy as ever working in the garden? After completing his work, he returned home and related the incident to his wife. She told him, "Don't pay any attention to a silly dream. It must be only a figment of your imagination. Go to sleep." A couple of hours later a telegram arrived announcing, "Father died at one a.m. Come immediately."

After this incident, Mr. Nair had full faith in the Holy Mother's divinity, and he, too, became a devotee. He now worships the photo of the Holy Mother, just as his relative used to do.

Puvampuzha Swami was well known in his village near Quilon. When he heard about the Holy Mother and Her Divine Moods as Krishna and Devi, the Swami decided to test Her spiritual power. After his first visit to the Ashram in 1976, he could not return to the Holy Mother for some time following the death of his mother.

During his second visit the Swami thought, "If She really has the power of Krishna, let Her tell me any one of the doctrines of the *Bhagavad Gita*. Only then I will believe that She is genuine."

The Swami entered the temple with that *sankalpa* in his heart when the Holy Mother was in *Krishna Bhava*. He told Her, "My mother's death has prevented me from coming here for some days." The Holy Mother retorted, "That which is not never comes into being, and that which is never ceases to exist. Forget not this great truth." Hearing this, the Swami was overcome with awe and reverence. These words of the Holy Mother, though not learned from any scripture, were an exact translation of the sixteenth verse of chapter two of the *Bhagavad Gita*. Hearing this, the Swami became fully convinced of the Holy Mother's greatness and became Her ardent devotee.

Radha Bai, from Calicut, was a devotee of Sri Satya Sai Baba. On the twenty-third of January, 1985, she had a dream as she slept. Sri Satya Sai Baba appeared to her, along with a holy woman dressed in pure white clothes. Both of them were standing in front of a big house. Pointing to the holy woman, Baba told Radha Bai, "You must go see this Mother." Then both of them disappeared without another word. As her sleep was now disturbed, she got up thinking, "Where shall I go to meet this Mother? How can I know where to find Her?"

The next day Radha Bai found an article in the newspaper with a picture of a holy woman, announcing

Her arrival in Calicut that very day. She easily recognized Her face; it was the face of Mother whom she had seen with Baba in the dream. The article mentioned the house where She would stay during Her visit. Radha Bai was overwhelmed with joy.

That very day Radha Bai and her family went to meet the Holy Mother. When they arrived at the house where the Holy Mother was staying, Radha Bai was even more amazed, because it was the very house which she had seen the previous night in her dream. Everyone had darshan of the Holy Mother. While taking darshan, Radha Bai related the story of her dream to the Holy Mother. Mother quietly listened and then gently smiled as if to say that She was already aware of the fact. Radha Bai and her family returned home feeling exhilarated and singularly blessed.

❁

During the Holy Mother's first visit to Calicut, many devotees had the good fortune to have inspiring spiritual experiences. Mrs. Kunjukutty Amma, whose Chosen Deity was the Divine Mother, had worshipped Devi for many years as Mookambika, (an aspect of the Divine Mother). Along with her family, she came to see the Holy Mother on the twenty-fourth of January, 1985. The following is her experience with the Holy Mother in her own words.

"When I approached the Holy Mother, Her penetrating glance fell on me. That first look made all my hairs stand on end. I even felt that I was losing body-consciousness. I prostrated to Mother and pleaded loudly,

"O Mother! Great Enchantress! Mookambika! Protect me, O Mother! Give refuge, give refuge!" Most affectionately the Holy Mother placed my head on Her lap. Slowly raising my head from Her lap, Mother applied sacred ash on my forehead between the eyebrows with Her left forefinger. As soon as Mother touched my forehead, I experienced a terrific jolt all through my body like an electric shock. The next moment, I clearly saw my beloved Deity, Mookambika, adorned with gold ornaments, sitting in the lotus posture on the Holy Mother's seat." In a God-intoxicated mood, Kunjukutty Amma began dancing and singing. The Holy Mother asked, "Child, what do you want?" In the same rapturous mood she replied, "Blessed am I for having touched Thy Lotus Feet. I have seen *Parashakti* (the Supreme Energy)! O Mother, please do not abandon me!" She continued dancing blissfully and weeping with joy. Preventing some devotees from carrying her out of the room, the Holy Mother said, "Nobody should touch her. She is enjoying bliss." Kunjukutty Amma continued in her blissful mood for half an hour. Having seen her beloved Deity's beautiful form, she returned home with an overflowing heart.

Kunju Raman, a high school teacher, gives the following account of his experience with the Holy Mother:

"Having been initiated into *Siddha Vidya* (a type of spiritual practice) by His Holiness Swami Sivananda Paramahamsa, I have been following the instructions of my guru as well as I could as a householder. I have

been doing this for the past twelve years. Fully trusting that *Siddha Vidya* and scriptural texts like the
Bhagavad Gita would take me to my Supreme Goal, I
had decided not to go to anyone else for guidance.

In 1985 a lecturer friend and neighbor told me of
his experiences in Calicut with Holy Mother Mata Amritanandamayi. He told me that he had spiritual experiences when Mother merely touched him. He showed
me a booklet containing Mother's sayings, and I also
had a chance to listen to a cassette of Her *bhajan*,
'Manase Nin Svanthamayi'. Even though I was not in
good health, I decided that I would take any amount of
trouble to have darshan of this Holy Mother. I discussed the matter with a close friend and yoga practitioner, Sri K.S. Nair, who agreed to accompany me. We
reached Her Ashram on October 20,1985, at four in
the evening.Amma was giving darshan in the hut. When
my turn came to meet Her, She kindly asked my name
and where I lived saying that we would meet again
during *Bhava Darshan*. During the darshan, Amma forcefully pressed the center of my forehead and asked me
to sit by Her side and meditate.

The next day, while Sri Nair and I were standing in
front of the shrine totally at a loss to find a solitary
place to meditate, Amma suddenly appeared in front of
us saying, "Come, sons!" Amma touched us and took
us to the meditation hall on the southern side where
some of the *brahmacharis* were meditating. Amma
made us sit down and began to meditate with us. We
were very surprised. From somewhere in the Ashram,
Amma suddenly appeared in front of us, knowing our
desire to meditate. This incident revealed to us Her

high state. We believe that this experience we had was instrumental in our later success in gathering a group of devotees in Ambalapara.

In November and December I was having occasional difficulty with nose bleeding. Even after frequent treatments with a doctor, the bleeding continued to trouble me. We learned that Amma was appearing at Sri Ramakrishna Ashram, Pallapuram, on the fourth of January, so my friend Sri Narayanan Nair and I decided to go have Her darshan as well as finalize the details for the program to be held in Ambalapara on the seventeenth. After having Mother's darshan, we realized that we had forgotten to mention my nose bleeding problem. As an act of faith, I threw out all the medicines saying, 'If it is Amma's will, the problem will disappear of its own accord.' The problem did vanish and has never recurred.

When Amma visited Ambalapara in 1986, we had the good fortune of welcoming Her to our home. During the *pada puja* (worship offered to Amma's holy feet) the imprint of Her holy feet remained clearly visible on the plate in which they were washed. That plate is now kept in our meditation room where we and Her devotees continue to worship it. The imprint is still clearly visible today."

🪷

Seshan, a devotee from Madras, is an electrical engineer. After retirement he dedicated his life to organizing spiritual discourses and serving *sannyasins*. Even though he had done a lot of spiritual practice, he felt he was making no progress, until he met the Holy Mother in 1984. After his first meeting with the Holy Mother, Seshan prayed to Her to initiate him with a mantra. Mother did not pay much attention to his request. Nevertheless, Seshan persisted. During this period the Holy Mother visited Tiruvannamalai, the abode of Ramana Maharshi. Seshan brought his family to visit Mother there. This time, when Seshan expressed his cherished desire to Mother, She responded that She would initiate him during his next visit to Vallickavu.

As the Holy Mother had promised, Seshan received his initiation when he next visited the Ashram. Though a *Bhava Darshan* day, the crowd was not too great. At eleven at night, just before the end of *Devi Bhava*, Seshan was initiated by the Holy Mother. Before leaving the temple, She instructed the devotees: "This son should neither be touched nor called by anyone."

Soon after the initiation, Seshan plunged into deep meditation. After three hours had passed, he was still sitting in the temple unmoved. Following the Holy Mother's instructions, two Ashram residents guarded the temple doors to prevent his being disturbed. Just after two in the morning, Seshan opened his eyes and looked around perplexed. "Where is everybody? Where is Mother? Why is there no *bhajan*? I have meditated for only a few minutes, but what has happened?" The resident exclaimed, "A few minutes! Three hours have passed. Mother initiated you at eleven o'clock and now it is two o'clock. The *Bhava Darshan* finished long ago."

Hearing these words, Seshan was overcome with amazement and happiness. "The Mother's grace!" he exclaimed. The resident's curiosity was aroused and he asked, "If you don't mind, would you tell us about your experience? As spiritual practitioners, we would be inspired to hear it."

Seshan responded eagerly, "How can I express it through words? After imparting the mantra, the Holy Mother touched the spot between my eyebrows with Her forefinger. The impact of that touch was wonderful. I felt something like a very strong electric shock permeate my whole body. The temple and the entire world revolved at high speed until they disappeared from my sight. After this, I could feel only bliss. You told me that I sat for three hours in meditation, but it felt as if only three minutes had passed. What a wonder! There was neither space nor time!" After hearing this story, the resident's curiosity increased. With some hesitation he asked, "May I know the mantra which was given to you? If you think it proper, please do tell me. I am inspired to ask this, because from your explanation it is clear that you were transported to a formless state soon after the initiation."

Seshan replied, "A *sadhak* is not supposed to reveal these things to anybody else. A mantra should be kept secret. But I can tell you this much. I am a *Vedantin*, a worshipper of the formless Supreme Consciousness. For many years now I have been chanting a mantra, but without having had any experience. The Holy Mother initiated me with the same mantra. Not only did She give the mantra to me, but She blessed me by bestowing the experience of it as well."

M r. P.O. Narayan Nambiar, from Calicut, one of the three major cities in Kerala, narrates his experience as follows: "A devotee of Lord Krishna from a very young age, I always used to chant His Divine Names and sing devotional songs about Him. At the age of seventeen, I was initiated by the disciple of a Great Soul, Sivananda Paramahamsa. From that time on, besides singing the glories of the Lord, I also practiced meditation. It was in 1960 that the following incident occurred. One night I went to bed after my usual singing and meditation. At three-thirty a.m. I had a dream in which I saw a big hall with a courtyard in front of it. In the courtyard there were different kinds of colorful plants, both in flower pots and on the ground. There I saw two figures; one was that of a holy man wearing a bright orange gown with a mop of tight curly hair. The other was a holy woman dressed in white who made a sign with Her right hand, beckoning me to follow them. The holy man neither looked at me nor gestured. Though I knew it was only a dream, I was firmly convinced that there must be some significance behind it. The Great Souls I saw in the dream have remained vividly in my mind.

It was not until two years later, when he was first becoming known in our area, that I discovered that the man was Sri Satya Sai Baba of Puttaparthi. Another twenty years passed before I realized that the holy woman whom I saw in the dream was Mata Amritanandamayi. In January, 1985, I saw Her for the first time at the home of a devotee in Calicut.

When I met Mother, I told Her with all humility, 'I have been practicing meditation since the age of seventeen. But until now I have not experienced the state of *samadhi*. Please bless me by bestowing that boon on me.' The Mother looked in my eyes and said, 'Son, intensify your *sadhana* and proceed.'

Having received Her blessings again while standing outside the house, I watched the Holy Mother with some of Her disciples getting ready to depart in order to participate in a reception and consecration ceremony in a temple. I stood a short distance away from the entrance gate, thinking I would leave only after the car carrying the Holy Mother had left the compound. She was about to step into the car, when suddenly the Holy Mother noticed me. Immediately She walked toward me. Joining my palms, I bowed down to Her. She touched the back of my palms with Her finger and said, 'Son, Mother has agreed to go, but She will return soon.' That touch of the Holy Mother was like a tremendous electric shock. My whole body was jolted from head to toe. My eyes closed and filled with tears. Four or five seconds passed. When I opened my eyes again Mother had already entered the car and was leaving. I stood transfixed until Mother returned. The touch of the Holy Mother had great impact on me. My spiritual practices have been strengthened and my concentration has increased. Above all, my craving for worldly pleasures, which had distracted me until that day, effortlessly disappeared from my mind. This state of mind continues today.

In April, 1985, while attending a seven day spiritual camp at the Holy Mother's Ashram, I asked Her, 'Mother, I have read in spiritual texts that if one could find the spiritual Master of his previous birth, he could quickly make spiritual progress. Mother, were you my Guru in a previous birth?' The Holy Mother smilingly confirmed this saying, 'Yes, son.' I humbly continued, 'Mother, as this is so, kindly initiate me.' The Holy Mother affectionately replied, 'During your next visit Mother will initiate you.'

As the Holy Mother had promised, during my next visit to the Ashram on the twelfth of May, 1985, She initiated me at the end of *Devi Bhava*. Then the Holy Mother put a trident in my hands and instructed me to meditate as much time as I wished. From the moment She handed me the trident until I placed it back in its place, the trident vibrated strongly, as if it were charged with electricity. In order to convince myself that I was not hallucinating, I released one hand several times and held it with the other. But the vibration did not stop; it was real. Even my hands shook with the vibrations of the trident. This continued for an hour and a half until I returned the trident to its original place. Now I was convinced that the Holy Mother was a Perfect Master, and that She could transmit Her spiritual energy even to an inert object. These experiences and many others strengthened my faith in the Holy Mother. Now I have dedicated my whole life at Her Lotus Feet."

EXPERIENCES OF SPIRITUAL ASPIRANTS

Unnikrishna was the first person to be fortunate enough to meet Mother and stay with Her for a long time. He did not continue his schooling after the sixth grade. In him we see a wonderful example of Mother's kindness and grace. With the Guru's grace, even a semiliterate young boy can become an inspiring poet. Unnikrishna's life is testimony to this.

After completing his brief schooling, the young Unni wandered freely, engaging himself in a variety of activities. In 1976, when he was twenty years old, he heard about the Holy Mother and came to see Her. He felt great faith and devotion for Amma from that very first meeting. Thereafter, he visited Her frequently, seeking Her instructions. A year had passed when one day Mother asked him to stay with Her in order to perform the daily worship in the temple. She instructed him to chant the *Lalita Sahasranama* (the Thousand Names of the Divine Mother) every day.

From then on his life took a dramatic turn. The mere presence of the Holy Mother inspired him with a strong desire to realize the Truth. His days were filled with the practice of austere penance, formal worship, conversations with Amma, reading of scriptures, and other spiritual activities. As a result of this disciplined way of life, he gradually realized that the glorious Mother of the *Bhava Darshan*, and the sweet Mother in Her more usual moods were, in fact, one and the same, two facets or manifestations of the same infinite Divine Power, played out for the good of the world. This insight greatly stimulated his desire to perform *sadhana* (spiritual practices) and he surrendered himself fully at Mother's feet, regarding Her as his sole support in life. As time passed, his spiritual disciplines took an even more rigorous turn; he came to eat, sleep and speak less. On occasion, he fasted for several weeks at a stretch. He used to sleep on the bare ground without so much as a blanket to cover himself during the winter and the rainy season. When he went on pilgrimage, as he occasionally did, he traveled on foot the whole way, without recourse to any vehicle.

One day, with tears in his eyes, he asked Mother with overflowing emotion, "Who is my real Mother?" Regarding him with great tenderness, the Holy Mother took his head on Her lap and replied, "My child, you are my son, and I am your mother." Unnikrishna was overwhelmed with inexpressible bliss welling up from within. As he silently gazed at Mother's radiant face, he wept with joy.

By the infinite grace of Mother, Unnikrishna has become a prolific poet whose works are filled with philosophical truth and devotional sweetness. Once, when his parents had sent some relatives to bring him back home, he replied with the following poignant verse:

> Having left my home long ago,
> If I were now to lead a worldly life, would I gain
> Peace of mind thereby?
> What profit has there been in such an existence
> Even from time immemorial?
>
> When I am struggling to free myself
> From the utter folly of the world,
> Why do you pave a fool's path straight
> To the servitude of the beggar?
> Can I ever agree to such a fate?

Unni describes his first meeting with Mother in the following evocative way:

> In a distant temple a glowing flame burnt
> Without getting extinguished.

The Mother with infinite compassion was
Seated there as a guiding light for those
Wandering destitute in the darkness.

One day while I wandered there,
That embodiment of mercy called me aside.
Opening the inner sanctum
She dabbed sandalwood paste on my forehead.

Melodiously singing the exalted praises of the Lord,
She made a place for me on
Her soft and sacred arm.
Coming near, a wondrous divine
Dream whispered this truth in my ear:

"What need is there for tears? Don't you know
That you have come near the
Mother of the Universe?"
With a sigh I awoke, Her Lotus Face
Indelibly impressed on my consciousness.

Once when Unnikrishna experienced some inner conflict, he fasted for several weeks. When the Holy Mother learned of it, She also stopped eating and drinking. Unni, unaware of Her fasting, continued his vow. After a couple of days, while doing his daily worship, the Holy Mother's father scolded him for not taking food and thereby making Mother starve. Soon after the worship was over, he came to the doorway of Mother's hut with a heavy heart and eyes filled with tears. Calling him to Her side, She caressed him with great love and looking at his shivering body said, "Unni, my son, if you are feeling some inner agitation, you should come tell Mother about it. Don't torture your body like this. To do *tapas*, the body is needed. Eat at least for the sustenance of the body." Saying this, She asked for a plate of rice and fed Unni with Her own hands, eating out of the same plate Herself.

A few months after his settling in the Ashram, Unni, who had the temperament of a wandering mendicant, decided to go away. Without informing anyone, he made ready for his journey. As he was about to depart on a *Darshan* night, a man suddenly came to him with Mother's counsel, "Mother says that even though you are getting ready to go, you should not depart now." Unable to disobey the Holy Mother, he canceled his journey. Once more some time later he tried to leave, but the same thing happened. Finally, he did actually leave, but had to return after two days. He thereby became convinced that without Mother's knowledge and blessings, he could do nothing.

Mother once said that "Unni's songs spring from his meditation." What greater recognition could there be? The following is a translation of two of his songs:

> *I have wandered in distant lands carrying a heavy burden of sorrow. At last, coming to You I have surrendered myself at Your Lotus Feet. O Mother, won't You kindly wash away my endless afflictions and tears with the waters of Your Love?*

> *Consider not this poor one as a sinner, for no one else is there in this world as my stay and support. O Embodiment of Compassion, please caress me with the moonlight of Your beautiful eyes.*

> *O Mother, throwing away this heavy burden of thoughts let me sit near You and merge in*

*meditation. O You who are described in the
Vedas and Vedanta! O Mother of all the Gods
and Goddesses! Won't You fulfill this wish
springing from my soul to gain the Supreme
Self?*

*O Mother, when will that time come when I will
renounce all taste for pleasure-seeking and become
one with Your Holy Feet?*

❁

Balu (Swami Amritaswarupananda) tells of the following experiences of Mother's grace:

"When my B.A. final examinations were over, I heard
about a girl endowed with supernatural powers, who
gave darshan in the forms of Devi and Krishna. Though
my faith in the existence of God was deep-rooted, I
was not much interested in seeing Her. Some of my
relatives and friends, who had visited Her, spoke very
highly of Her and continued to press me to visit Her
Ashram. Finally, with a skeptical mind, I came to the
Ashram one evening, accompanied by my uncle. As I
approached the grounds, the melody of a moving devotional song sounded in my ears, capturing my attention. Approaching a small shrine, I saw a girl in white
clothes singing songs poignant with love and devotion.
Listening to Her song, I could see that Her heart was
overflowing with divine bliss and love. The vibrations
of Her singing pierced my heart, evoking the most tender
feelings.

When my turn came, I entered the shrine room where
She was seated on a *peetham* or stool. I prostrated before
Her, and when I got up, She took hold of my hand and

looked into my eyes. Her eyes were beaming like the full moon. That look penetrated me; that smile bound me and made me motionless. Infinite compassion manifested on Her face. Slowly She put my head on Her shoulder and softly but emphatically said, 'Child, I am your mother and you are my child.' That sweet voice entered deep into my heart and I became enraptured with inexplicable joy. This is what I had been searching for! I burst into tears. Love in all its purity, Motherhood in its universal essence had assumed a form. Thrilled by this experience, I sat near Mother the whole night.

When I reached home the next day, I realized the great change which had taken place in me. I became totally indifferent to all my usual activities. My desire to see Her again intensified. All my thoughts were fixed on Her. That night I was unable to sleep. Whenever I tried to close my eyes, Mother appeared in front of me. The next day I returned to the Ashram. After the second meeting with Mother, my desire to break off the fetters of worldliness became still more intense. Thinking of Mother, I became like a madman. I forgot to eat, to sleep and to take bath. I abandoned my fancy way of dressing and combing my hair. My parents and other family members were worried by the change in me and forbade me from going to Vallickavu.

The next day after participating in the *bhajan*, I entered the shrine with this resolve: 'Mother, if I am your child, please accept me.' Placing my head on Her shoulder, Mother lovingly said, 'Son, when Mother heard you singing, She understood that this voice is meant to merge in God. At that moment Mother came to you and made you one with Her. You are my very own.'

One night when I was half asleep, I smelled a peculiar sweet fragrance pervading the room. I opened my eyes and found that the fragrance was real, not just a dream or imagination. Suddenly, I felt someone's hands stroking my forehead. I looked up and to my astonishment I saw Mother standing at the end of the cot above my head. I couldn't believe my eyes. She smiled at me and said, 'My son, Mother is always with you, don't worry.' Saying this, She disappeared.

Next morning I rushed to Vallickavu, but Mother was not there. She returned only at four in the afternoon. Without a word, She ran to the house and emerged with a plate of rice which She fed me as a mother would her son. While feeding me She said, 'Last night, Mother came to you.' Overwhelmed with happiness, I cried like a small child. I had not in fact eaten anything yet that day.

After Mother initiated me with a mantra, I was unable to stay at home. My yearning to live in Her presence and to seek Her instructions increased day by day. Disregarding all the obstacles my relatives created, I left home and joined the residents of the Ashram.

Two years later, as we were sitting in a devotee's house, She suddenly said to me, 'My son Balu, you must get a Master's degree in philosophy.' I had previously told Mother that I was not going to continue my studies, but just wanted to be absorbed in thinking about Her. Now, two years later, She was asking me to study again. From my experience, I knew that She would not say or do anything without a purpose, so I enrolled in the graduate program. Now a real problem arose;

who would teach me? I would have to prepare eight papers, four on Indian philosophy, with which I was somewhat familiar, and four on Western philosophy, which was an entirely new subject for me. I asked Mother where I was to find some one to teach me.

'Don't worry about it. Someone will come here to instruct you. Wait patiently and see,' She said. But I was restless and frequently disturbed Her with the same question. A week later, a devotee directed me to a man who was a philosophy professor. I went to see him to explain my predicament. He was willing to teach me, but refused to come to the Ashram. I tried to make him understand my difficulty in leaving the Ashram to study. At last he agreed to visit the Ashram but said, 'I cannot stay there or give you classes there. If you want to study, you must come to my house. If not, drop the matter right now.' I thought that since I had no other choice, I would let him at least come to the Ashram to see Mother.

The following Thursday I went to fetch him from his home. When we reached the Ashram, I invited him to come see Mother, but he refused. When Mother sat for Her usual singing before the *Bhava Darshan*, he was watching from a distance. Even after the *Darshan* began, he continued to observe from a distance. I approached him to suggest that, if he liked, he could go inside the temple and have Mother's *Darshan*. 'No, I have never prostrated to anyone before. I don't want to do that,' he replied. I left him alone and sat down to sing. A few minutes later I saw him rush into the temple and heard a loud cry. He had fallen flat in front of Mother and was weeping like a small child. An hour or two passed. Coming out of the shrine, he called me aside and said, 'She is a Great Soul indeed! Every week I will come here to teach you.' Thus, Mother Herself arranged a teacher for me.

Making references to various books, the professor dictated a lot of notes to me, but didn't explain anything. Unfortunately, for various reasons, we were not able to continue the course of study regularly, and Western philosophy still remained an unknown subject to me. Only three months were left before the examinations. The professor dictated some more notes to me and gave me a summary of the whole thing. As I was involved in different activities of the Ashram and was frequently traveling with Mother, I could not follow through with my studies. Now only one month remained before the exams. Mother asked me to write all eight papers in one sitting. I was really worried how I could possibly write both the first and final year papers together. I dedicated the project to Mother's feet and began reading. At last it was the day before my departure to Tirupati (a town in Andhra Pradesh, seven hundred miles from the Ashram) where I had registered my name in the university as a student of philosophy.

At noon I was about to pack my things. Suddenly, I heard Mother calling me from Her room. I ran to Her room and saw Her packing some things in a bag. She put the last item into it and closed it. Another big bag stood ready on Her table. With great affection She announced, 'Son, I have packed everything for your journey.' Pointing to the bag on the table She said, 'That bag contains *dhotis*, shirts, towels, two blankets and other clothes, and in this one there is coconut oil, soap, a mirror, comb, something to make a hot drink and other useful things. I have packed all these things so you might save time for your studies.' I was stunned. I simply gazed at Her loving face. My heart was overflowing with joy. My eyes filled with tears and I broke down weeping.

This was the first time that I was going to be away from Her, and it would be for an entire month. My heart was very heavy. In the train I sat in a corner to hide my tears. All the passengers were chatting cheerfully, but my mind was full of sorrow to be separated from Mother. Throughout the trip, I thought of nothing but Her. The following morning I reached Tirupati. My days were filled with the excruciating pain of separation. I felt like a fish out of water. I tried to concentrate on my studies, but failed. Each minute passed at a snail's pace. l was even unable to look at Mother's picture. Each object brought from the Ashram reminded me of Mother and Her gracious form. I forgot to eat and sleep. Each day dragged like a year for me. Now and then I collapsed. Unable to bear the separation, I burst into tears. By the time the final exams began, I somehow managed to write the papers. There was nobody to share my sorrow.

At that time, I received a letter from Mother. Several times I read and reread it. Soaked by my tears, the letter turned wet. Mother's letter to me read:

Darling Son,
    Your Mother is always with you. Son, Mother doesn't feel that you are away from Her. My child, Mother can

see your yearning heart. Mother can hear your cries. My son, this world is so beautiful. The flowers, the vast ocean, the chirping birds, the expanse of the sky, trees, bushes, forests, mountains and valleys are all here. God made this earth beautiful. See Him in everything. Love Him in all beings. Cut open the bond separating you from God. Let your mind flow ceaselessly toward Him. Son, nothing is bad in this world. Everything is good. See the good and virtuous part. Let your mental flower blossom and spread its fragrance all around.

That night I was sitting outside my room watching the trees and plants dancing in the gentle breeze. The sky was full of glittering stars, and the silver light of the moon flooded the earth with splendor. I thought, 'This breeze may blow to my Mother; it may be fortunate enough to caress my Mother's body. Yes, no doubt this is carrying my dear Mother's divine fragrance. If I had wings, I would fly to my Mother.' The following poem was written that night:

> *O stars, can't you please come down?*
> *Mother is here to sing a lullaby to you.*
> *She is the stream of never-ending love and*
> *She is the shade-giving tree for seeking minds.*
> *O cool gentle breeze who comes slowly humming*
> *Silent songs in the night, what did you whisper so*
> *Sweetly in my ears? The sweet stories of my Mother?*
>
> *The sun and moon slowly rise and set*
> *In the blue sky every day.*
> *Don't you have the desire to see my*
> *Mother who has given you this divine splendor?*

Trees and creepers grow in abundance in
The silent lonely valleys and hillsides.
As if to console me their tender branches dance
In the wind.

I was in an intense and unusual mood. I paced the floor like one gone mad. Somehow I controlled myself and decided to leave the next day. I had one more paper to write. I decided not to appear for the first year exams, which were to begin in four days. I thought, 'Mother has asked me to attend all the exams, but this time I am going to act against Her advice.'

Finally I decided to seek Mother's permission in a peculiar way. I took three pieces of paper of equal size. On the first piece I wrote, 'Son, you come back.' On the second one I wrote, 'You write all the papers and then come,' and on the third I wrote, 'As my son likes.' I rolled all three papers in the same manner, shook them, and took Mother's picture from the bag. With this prayer I humbly offered the papers to Her, 'O Mother, I am going to take one of these papers. Let me know your will, whatever it be.' With closed eyes, I took one of the papers with trembling hands. I opened it. Alas! it was the one on which I had written, 'You write all the papers and then come.' Not satisfied with the first attempt, I tried my lot again with three more pieces of paper, but again I picked the same note. My mind, however, was so yearning to see Mother that I finally decided to leave the next day.

The next day, after attending the last of the final exams, I rushed to pack my things and was about to leave. Suddenly I noticed some things lying in the corner of the room. They were some useless newspapers, which

I had used as a wrapper to bring things from the Ashram, and a broken piece of a soap box. I thought, 'How intense was my pain when I was separated from Mother. Perhaps these things, too, share that pain. If I leave them here, it will be a sin.' I carefully packed those things as well in my bag.

The following day I reached the Ashram. On the way to Mother's room, I saw my brother, Venu. Astonished, he said, 'Last night Mother told me that you are getting very restless and that you will come today.' I entered Mother's room and fell at Her feet crying. Mother lifted me up and consoled me saying 'Son, I know your heart. This love is good, but try to acquire more mental strength. A *sadhak* should be soft like a flower and hard like a diamond. You must go and write the other papers. Even if you fail, Mother won't mind. Tomorrow you go and come back when the exams are over.'

The next morning I went back to Tirupati. After a week when the last exam was over, I returned to the Ashram. I was not satisfied with my answers and even feared that I might fail. Mother calmly said, 'Forget about it. Don't doubt. You will succeed.' When the results were published, I was surprised to see that I had passed with a high second class.

Simply to be in the presence of the Holy Mother is a *tapas*. There is always something new and fresh. Every moment one experiences enlightening insights which lead the devotee through different realms of spirituality, evolving him from one plane to the next. In the beginning stages of my spiritual life, I sometimes used to feel that I had understood the Holy Mother. Later I realized that I had understood nothing about Mother at all."

Venu (now known as Swami Pranavamritananda) is Balu's brother. They were both infants when their mother died. After her death, Balu grew up in his father's house, and Venu was raised by his aunt, Saraswathy Amma, in a religious and spiritual atmosphere. Venu was the pet of the family and never experienced the loss of a mother's love and affection. After completing secondary school at age fifteen, Venu moved to his father's house to continue his education at a local college. Though he manifested an inclination toward spirituality at an early age, during his college years he led a worldly life. Even then, whenever he saw a devotional movie or a monk in ochre robes, he would feel again the stirrings of his dormant spiritual impulse.

By the time Venu was in college, his brother Balu had already met the Holy Mother and had dedicated himself to spirituality. Though Balu told his brother about the Holy Mother several times, Venu paid little attention. Moreover, he openly scorned the Holy Mother and asserted, "I won't come near that fishergirl." Nevertheless, even before meeting Venu, Amma predicted to Balu, "Your brother also is my son. He, too, will come here." Hearing this, Balu was worried because there was already an uproar in his family over his own decision to leave home and the worldly life. What would happen if Venu also followed in his footsteps? However, the Divine Will is supreme, beyond the realm of ordinary mortal vision. What was destiny would inevitably come to pass.

While Venu was studying for the final year of his Bachelor of Science degree, the Holy Mother visited his aunt's house. When Venu arrived that day, the Holy

Mother was standing on the verandah of the house. Without even looking at Her, Venu strode past Mother into his room where Sreekumar, Pai, and some other residents of Mother's Ashram were seated.

Suddenly and unexpectedly, the Holy Mother approached Venu and, holding his hands like a loving mother, said, "Aren't you my son Balu's brother? Mother has been yearning to see you." Venu's heart melted, and he realized in a flash that Mother was not an ordinary personality, but rather a fountain of motherly love and tenderness. Venu felt attracted to Her as a piece of iron is drawn to a magnet. In the afternoon when Amma fed everyone, Venu also got a ball of rice. He was profoundly affected to see Her infinite love, equal vision and childlike innocence. Her face was overflowing with spiritual radiance, Her lucid way of explaining spiritual mysteries, ecstatic and bewitching *bhajans*, and above all Her absolute humility impressed him deeply. Within a short period of time, Venu found himself being drawn to Mother. Even when the Holy Mother was talking to others, it seemed to Venu that She was actually responding to the doubts which had cropped up in his mind.

The first meeting with the Holy Mother left a deep impression in Venu's mind, and all the prejudices which he had had about the Holy Mother and spiritual life vanished. Each day his longing to see Mother increased. At last in February, 1980, he came to Vallickavu. When Venu saw Mother he burst into tears. The Holy Mother caught hold of him and made him sit near Her. That night, when Venu went into the temple during *Krishna Bhava*, he felt that he was standing before Lord Sri

Krishna Himself. His mind overflowed with joy and he could neither cry nor laugh. He prayed to Mother to bless him by bestowing pure devotion and knowledge on him. Mother said, "Son, you will get what you are seeking." Mother gave him a mantra written on a piece of paper and a garland of *tulasi* leaves.

After Venu's first meeting with the Holy Mother, he lost all desire to continue his studies. His only wish was to lead a spiritual life. On Mother's insistence, Venu prepared for his college examinations which were a month away. Professors and students were amazed to see Venu coming to the college with a completely shaven head and sacred ashes on his forehead. They thought he had gone mad. His mind was entirely immersed in the thought of the Holy Mother. Indeed, he was so focused on Her that he inadvertently prepared for the following day's examination, not for that day's paper. Somehow he did manage to complete the exams and came to stay with the Holy Mother in September, 1980.

One day in connection with a festival, sweet pudding was prepared in the Ashram. It was customary to offer it to God before distributing it among the devotees. Venu took a tumblerful and placed it in the small shrine before the temple. Finding nothing else to cover the tumbler with, and looking around to make sure that Mother was not nearby, he plucked a tender leaf from a small plant growing near the shrine. Mother noticed the act from a distance and called aloud, 'Hey Venu!' Hearing Mother's voice, he tried to hide the tender leaf, but in his haste he tipped the tumbler spilling the entire contents on the sand. By this time, Venu was completely undone, and, hoping to escape further notice, he scooped up the pudding from the sand and stuffed it back into the tumbler, knowing that it was wrong to put it back in the shrine.

Mother, who was observing the whole scene from a distance, approached him and said in a serious tone, "Son, even a dog won't eat this. What of human beings? Then how could you offer it to God? Son, will you eat it? No! This is a real sin. God will accept anything that is offered to Him with pure love and devotion, not caring what it is. He only sees the attitude behind the offering. If you were really ignorant of your deed, I would not have minded it, but with full knowledge that what you were doing was wrong, you proceeded to do it. Not only that. You have committed another error by plucking a tender leaf from that small plant. How merciless you are! I can see the plant crying in pain. If someone pinches you, how much pain you suffer. Son, even though you don't feel its pain, Mother does."

Venu realized his mistake and repented. He prayed for forgiveness. Mother said, "Son, whatever errors you commit, I take to be some fault of my own. Mother is not at all angry with you, but in order to lead you on the path to Perfection, She has to pretend to be so."

Venu says, "Nothing can be concealed from the Holy Mother. She knows everything. About five years ago I had an experience which illustrates this fact. One night during supper while everyone was eating *kanji* (rice gruel), I suddenly had a strong desire to have some mango pickles as a side dish. I had seen them in the Ashram kitchen earlier in the day but, as they were meant for the laborers and visiting devotees, we resi-

dents were not supposed to take them. Also, Mother
had told us that, as spiritual aspirants, we should not
eat things which were very spicy, sour, salty or sweet.
She would often come into the kitchen unannounced to
see whether Her instructions were being followed. Although I was fully aware of this, the desire for the
pickles got the better of me.

Without making any noise, I entered the kitchen
and stealthily stole two big slices of mango pickle. I
was about to leave when suddenly I heard Mother's
voice, 'Venu, what is in your hand?' I was shocked
and, to avoid being caught red-handed, I threw the
mango slices away. Mother then searched and found
the slices. Seizing me, She caught hold of my hands
and tied them to a post. I was ashamed and full of
fear."

Seeing his childlike fear and innocence, Mother burst
into laughter. Actually, the Holy Mother was enjoying
looking upon Venu as the child Krishna who was tied
to a mortar by His mother, Yashoda, for stealing butter
and milk from the *Gopis'* houses. After a couple of
seconds, Mother untied him and lovingly served him
some mango pickles. She said, "Son, only if the taste
of the tongue is controlled can one enjoy the taste of
the heart."

Mother has Her own ways to exhaust the negative
tendencies of Her spiritual children. Sometimes She
says, "I am a crazy girl who knows nothing." She pre-
tends that She is an ignorant, innocent village girl, but
Her eyes penetrate the truth of everything. Once the
mistake is detected, then the Great Teacher in Her
rises up and instructs the student befittingly, as She
temporarily conceals Her Motherhood.

Sreekumar (now Swami Purnamritananda) a resident in the Holy Mother's Ashram, was an electronic engineer before coming to Her. While studying for his B.A. in 1979, he heard about a woman who could assume divine moods and bless devotees in various ways according to their particular needs. Though believing in God, he doubted that Divinity could manifest through a human being. Observing the nature of this world where few are happy and the majority suffer, his faith in a beneficent God waned. Finally he decided to see for himself whether or not the Holy Mother possessed divine power.

With a skeptical mind, he came to the Ashram in March, 1979, and entered the shrine room, drawing close to the Holy Mother. Her loving and compassionate glance entered deep into Sreekumar's heart. Her mere presence transported him to another world where God, His Holy Name, and he himself alone existed and he became oblivious to his surroundings. This experience bound him to Mother, and his mind became filled with the thought of Her alone.

About his second meeting with the Holy Mother Sreekumar says, "I heard some people calling Her 'child' (*kunju*) while others called Her 'Mother' (Amma). After *Bhava Darshan*, She talked with the devotees. All of a sudden, She would behave like a small and innocent child. She would play with the devotees, and seeing Her innocent ways, their hearts would rejoice, forgetting everything else. Sometimes She would sing and dance and the next moment, while hearing a song, She would weep and sit motionless as if lost to the world. Some bowed down before Her and others kissed Her hand; still others sang devotional songs. Then, like one gone mad, She would roll on the ground and laugh." In the beginning, Sreekumar felt that Mother was being temporarily possessed by the Divine Mother Kali and also by Krishna, but gradually, in close association with Her, he came to understand that She was actually manifesting Her inner identity with the Supreme Reality.

Sreekumar's relationship with the Holy Mother strengthened day by day. It became very difficult for him to be away from Her. Whenever he could get time, he would spend it with the Holy Mother. Sometimes the Holy Mother would feed him with Her own hands and would give him spiritual instructions at the same time. One day She asked him, "Has Mother given you a mantra to repeat?" He replied, "Yes, it was written on a small piece of paper and given for the improvement of my studies." Mother then told him, "Son, during *Devi Bhava*, Mother will initiate you." That night, Sreekumar was initiated with a mantra. From that moment he decided to dedicate his life to spirituality under the Holy Mother's guidance.

Although Sreekumar's parents were devoted to the Holy Mother, they did not approve of his becoming a monk. Their objection was mainly that his father was retired and his sister still remained to be married. They therefore arranged a job for him in Bangalore, about six hundred kilometers away. On days when his breaking heart yearned painfully for Her presence, he would see a vision of Her. In order to console him, Mother used to send him occasional letters. It was at this time that he wrote the following song:

O Mother, even though You are near,
I am wandering, unable to know You.
Even though I have eyes
I am searching, unable to see You.

Are You the beautiful moon
That blooms forth in the blue winter night?
I am the wave that, unable to reach the sky
Beats its head against the shore.

When I came to understand the truth
That all worldly comforts are worthless,
I longed to know You,
Shedding tears day and night.

Won't You come to comfort me
Who am weary of the burden of sorrow?
With the desire that You will come
I am waiting always.

His intense desire to see the Holy Mother and to stay with Her led Sreekumar to return home, even before the end of his first month in Bangalore. Laid up with fever, he was hospitalized immediately upon arriving home. His longing to see Mother continued to increase until one morning at four a.m. he had a wonderful experience.

"My father had gone out to get some coffee for me. I was alone in the room when all of a sudden my hands and legs felt paralyzed. A cool, gentle breeze caressed me, and to my great surprise, I saw Mother entering the room. With a benign smile on Her face, She walked toward me. Like a small child, I started crying. She then sat beside me and put my head on Her lap. She didn't say anything. I was overcome with emotion. Words stuck in my throat. An effulgence from Mother's body flooded the room and She was surrounded by a divine light. At that moment, the door opened and my father walked in. The Holy Mother immediately vanished."

A few days later, Mother visited Sreekumar's house in the morning. She was sitting in front of the house playing with some children. All of a sudden, She got up and walked through the fields toward the east with Her hands forming a *mudra*. After walking some distance, She entered a forest grove where a certain family had been worshipping snakes. In a semiconscious mood and with half-closed eyes, She cast a bewitching smile on the family and sat on the small shrine built for the snake worship. Several people gathered to see this unusual sight. However, others were afraid to enter the forest which was known for poisonous snakes. Hearing the news, the owners of the grove also came and stood before Mother with joined palms.

They asked, "Mother, we are doing the worship without a break. Do we need to do anything more?" Mother replied, "Keep a glass of fresh water here daily. That will suffice." When the Holy Mother came back to the house, the family asked Her, "Mother, what made you go there?" She replied, "Worship of snakes has been going on there for a very long time. Mother went there to satisfy the desire of the presiding deities in that forest. From the moment that I arrived here, I had the feeling that they were beckoning me."

Shortly after this, Sreekumar's parents found him a job in Bombay. They insisted so firmly that finally Sreekumar had no other choice but to go there. With great reluctance he left for Bombay, once more separated from the Holy Mother. While traveling in the train, he felt the presence of the Holy Mother intensely. In a half-waking, half-sleeping state he enjoyed constant visions of Her and reveled in the bliss of Her Divine Presence. Finally, after eight months he was unable to bear the separation from Her any longer and submitted his resignation to his employer.

During his stay in Bombay, Sreekumar wrote this poem which revealed his aching heart:

> *The sun has set in the western ocean*
> *And the day has started its lament...*
> *It is but the play of the Universal Architect.*
> *So why should you, O closing lotuses, be dejected?*
>
> *This world, full of misery and sorrow*
> *Is but a drama of God, and I, the onlooker,*
> *Am but a wooden puppet in His hands*
> *Having no tears to shed.*
> *Like a flame, my mind is burning in*
> *Separation from You in this ocean of grief.*
> *I am getting tossed about,*
> *Unable to find the shore.*

Even before coming to Mother to take up spiritual life seriously, Sreekumar used to have experiences in the astral plane of existence. While lying down, he would feel his subtle body emerge from his gross body and travel around. During such moments, even though his eyes were closed, he could clearly see the objective world.

During his stay in Bombay, he had a thrilling experience. It was daytime and he was relaxing with his eyes closed after meditation. Suddenly, his body became stiff. He felt his subtle form separate from the gross one and immediately heard a thundering sound, followed by an outpouring of billows of smoke into the atmosphere in the midst of which he beheld the figure of the Holy Mother dressed in the colorful costume which She wears during *Devi Bhava*. The magnificent figure of the Holy Mother filled his mind with awe and reverence. A few minutes passed as he beheld this sublime vision, unable to move or open his eyes.

On the evening of the twenty-eighth of January, 1980, Sreekumar was about to go to his house to visit his parents when Mother stopped him saying, "Stay here; don't go anywhere today." In his own words, "I was happy to hear Mother's words and canceled my plans to go out. At around six o'clock in the evening I was standing outside talking to some people when suddenly something bit me on the leg. I cried out in pain, which Mother heard and came running to the spot. Immediately finding the wound, Mother sucked out the blood and poison and then spat it out. In spite of this, the pain became unbearable. Seeing me rolling in agony due to the excruciating pain, Mother tried to comfort me. Finally, due to the insistence of others, She allowed me to be taken to a doctor specializing in snake bites. The doctor told, 'The snake which has bitten you was an extremely poisonous one but strangely enough the poison does not seem to have affected your body or blood.' By Mother's loving and affectionate care, I at last fell asleep at three a.m. only after which Mother Herself retired.

The next morning Mother told me, 'Son, wherever you might have been, you were destined to be bitten by a snake. However, as it happened in Mother's presence, nothing serious has come of it. That is why Mother prevented you from going away from here yesterday.' Later, after reaching my house, I went through my horoscope and was surprised to find that something had been written concerning that would-be fatal incident. It said, 'At the age of twenty-two there is the probability of poisoning. Therefore, special worship and offerings in the temple should be made for good health'."

By the grace of the Holy Mother, Sreekumar had several spiritual experiences which always served as a source of inspiration for him to continue his *sadhana* with more and more enthusiasm. After making some provision for his parents and sister, he came to settle permanently at the Ashram.

❀

Pai (Swami Amritamayananda) and Rao (Swami Amritatmananda) were relatives who were also close friends. They were like one soul in two bodies. Pai was a devotee of Mother Kali. Hearing about the Holy Mother from his friend Rao, Pai came to see Her in 1979. Then he was twenty-one years old. Getting off at a nearby bus stand, he asked a bystander to tell him the way to the Ashram. Instead of answering Pai's question, the man abused Mother and even tried to prevent him from going there saying, "Don't go there, it is a place where all kinds of evil things go on." "Let me go and see for myself," Pai responded and then he proceeded toward the Ashram.

It was a *Bhava Darshan* day and a large number of

people had come to the Ashram. He was welcomed by the beautiful sound of Mother's voice singing, "O Mother, the knower of the beginning, the middle and the end (of Creation), the Eternal Virgin". Shortly after the *bhajan*, Mother revealed Her identity with the Divine Mother of the Universe in the *Bhava Darshan*. When his turn came, Pai entered the temple and approached the Holy Mother. As he gazed on Her face overflowing with motherly love, Pai burst into tears. He tried to control them, but could not. His heart was full of bliss and within a few minutes he experienced a rare calm and peace of mind. The Holy Mother then told him tenderly, "Son, I am your Mother." The moment She uttered these words, Pai again cried aloud like a small child. Pai was essentially an orphan. Though both his father and mother were alive, they had long ago separated and he had no contact with them, but lived with his grandmother and grandfather. Now, for the first time in his life, he heard a true mother's words of love. Deep within him, Pai felt that his relationship with the Holy Mother was not new but had existed forever.

That first meeting with Mother created a very strong impact on Pai's mind. The Mother's form became deeply imprinted on his heart. Many things would vividly remind him of Mother. If, while walking on the road, he happened to hear the tinkling of anklets, he would suddenly turn and look thinking that it was Mother who had come to him (Amma used to wear anklets with small bells attached in those days). If he happened to see a girl with a nose ring, he would feel as if it were the Holy Mother Herself.

With each passing day his devotion intensified. His

tender feelings knew no bounds. At that time he was
employed in a shop, but as he could not concentrate
on the work he soon resigned. However, not being able
to stay permanently at the Ashram due to lack of facilities, Pai obtained a job as a clerk in another shop
only to resign once more six months later after realizing that the company and atmosphere were not condu-
cive to spirituality. It was a place where one could
easily fall a prey to intoxicants and women. After meeting
the Holy Mother, a strong aversion developed in Pai's
mind toward all worldly enjoyments.

Pai's new way of life did not please his relatives,
friends or the villagers. Some tried to advise him against
going to the Holy Mother, but Pai utterly ignored them.
They spread rumors that it was Pai who took Rao to
the Holy Mother and that it was he who was respon-
sible for Rao's sudden change. This reached the ears
of Rao's parents, who also turned against Pai. Rao's
friends also joined them. They threatened Pai saying
that they would chop off his legs if he stepped into
Haripad. His unshakable faith in the Holy Mother gave
him the courage and mental strength to confront these
challenges.

In those days, Mother's parents would not allow most
of Her spiritual children to visit the Ashram except on
Darshan days. Having left his house and relatives, Pai
spent his nights on shop verandahs, in bus stations
and temple compounds. He wandered around like a
lost soul. Sometimes he would get something to eat;
sometimes he would starve for days at a time. A being
who thirsts to attain eternal union with God is indifferent to all these things. Days, weeks and months passed.

Still Pai came to see the Holy Mother on all *Darshan* nights and at other times when She visited devotees' houses.

At last, when an Ashram was formed, Pai also came and stayed with the Holy Mother. Instructed by Her, Pai continued his spiritual practices. Pai always meditated on the Holy Mother in one particular pose. He cherished a wish to get a photo of Her in this pose but was afraid to admit his desire to the Holy Mother. How could one ask Her to sit in a particular pose in order to take a snapshot? He did not open his heart to anyone concerning this.

One day Pai felt very sad about this and sobbed for a long time. Suddenly Mother walked toward him and smilingly said, "Son, Mother knows your desire. Mother will fulfill it." After a couple of days, Mother called Pai and went to the temple. She sat on the *peetham* (stool) where She usually sat during the *Devi Bhava*. Immediately upon sitting down, the Holy Mother became absorbed in *samadhi*. It was exactly this pose which Pai had held dear. Sreekumar arrived with a camera, took a photo, and Pai was overjoyed.

Even though a *sadhak* may not be well versed in the scriptures, by the Guru's grace he can become an expert speaker. One of Pai's experiences illustrates this mysterious fact.

Once a devotee from Trivandrum came to see the Holy Mother. He wanted one of Her children to give a seven day discourse on the great epic, *Srimad Ramayana*. He prayed to Mother to kindly send one of Her spiritual children to fulfill his wish. The Holy Mother told him, "None of the children have learned *Ramayana*.

Therefore, your request is difficult to fulfill." The devotee answered, "Mother, please don't say so. I have promised the people that I will bring someone. Please save me!" At last, Mother suggested Pai as the one to give the discourses. When he came to know of Her plan he was shocked. He thought, 'Without having read or learned the *Ramayana*, how can I give a discourse?'

Mother called Pai aside and asked him to bring the *Ramayana* from the library. She chose the *Sundarakanda* (one chapter in the book) and asked him to read it. Hardly had he read ten lines when Mother asked him to stop saying, "That is enough. Now go." Having perfect faith in Mother's words, Pai went to Trivandrum. He stayed there for seven days and delivered speeches on the *Ramayana*. They were a great success. Everyone appreciated Pai's deep insight into the subject. At the end of the seven days, Pai frankly told everyone the truth, that he had not even studied the *Ramayana*, and that all had happened by the Holy Mother's grace. No one believed him. Nothing can equal the boundless compassion and grace of a Perfect Teacher. It is that grace which shapes man into God.

Ramakrishnan (Swami Ramakrishnananda) is the son of *brahmana* parents from Palghat in Kerala. In 1978, when he was an employee of the State Bank of Travancore, he heard about the Holy Mother from one of his friends. One evening he and his friend came to see Her. Though brought up in an orthodox family, Ramakrishnan was heading for trouble, falling under

the influence of bad company in college. When he saw
the Holy Mother, he burst into tears. All his inner coarse-
ness melted and softened until everything was washed
away in those purifying tears. After this, he would come
for almost all the *Darshans* in order to see Mother in
the Divine Mood. He would cry like a small child and
pray to Her to give him the vision of Madurai Meenakshi,
his beloved Deity. He would even fast on certain days
in deep sorrow for having failed to gain that vision. On
those days, the Holy Mother would feed him with sweet
pudding without even mentioning his fast. Weeping with
intense yearning while lying on Mother's lap during
Devi Bhava, he would ask Her, "Mother, will you come
to me tomorrow? At least let me hear the jingling of
your anklets." Mother granted his humble prayers, giving him many visions of his beloved Deity. Some days
he would hear the jingling of Mother's anklets and see
the Divine Mother; at other times he would smell a
divine fragrance pervading the atmosphere around him.

There were two significant events which inspired
Ramakrishnan to abandon worldly life and take up a
life of renunciation and spirituality. The first was his
receiving initiation from the Holy Mother. On that
auspicious day he felt an inexpressible power trans-
mitted from Her to him, which totally changed his concept
of the meaning and goal of life. The second event was
as follows:

One day, while showing a picture of Sri Ramakrishna Paramahamsa to Ramakrishnan, Mother said, "Both
of you have the same name, yet you have become like
this." These words of the Holy Mother pierced the inner
depths of Ramakrishnan's heart like a lightning bolt

and strengthened his desire to become a real spiritual aspirant.

One summer evening Ramakrishnan came to have darshan of Mother during *Devi Bhava*. It was extremely hot inside the temple where Mother was sitting. Mother asked him to fan Her. He hesitated, however, as there was a group of young ladies standing just outside the temple. He thought to himself, "If a young man like me, an employee in the State Bank, fans a woman, they may laugh at me." Thinking this, he didn't fan Mother. But while coming out of the temple after *Darshan*, he hit his head badly on the wooden lintel over the door. Seeing his clumsiness, all the young ladies standing there burst into laughter. Ramakrishnan turned pale and felt ashamed. The next day, when Ramakrishnan went for *Darshan*, Mother called him and said, "Yesterday you wouldn't fan me even though I asked you to. Therefore I thought it would be for your good to make you a laughing stock in front of the young ladies whose laugh you feared!" From the next *Darshan* on, Ramakrishnan regularly fanned Mother without being asked.

At one time, Ramakrishnan was transferred to a branch of the bank about a hundred kilometers from the Ashram. One of his duties was to keep the key of the safe with him and arrive promptly at ten a.m. every morning. Leaving the Ashram the following morning after the Sunday night *Darshan*, Ramakrishnan boarded the bus and reached a bus stop about thirteen kilometers from his office. Inquiring about another bus, he learned that there would not be any bus going to his destination before ten a.m. He then tried to get a taxi but none were available. Worried and upset, he called out "Amma!" Within a few moments, a man came along on a motorcycle and stopped in front of him. He was a complete stranger. Turning to Ramakrishnan, he said, "I am going to Pampakuda (the very village where Ramakrishnan was working). There are no buses until after ten, so if you like, I will drop you there." Ramakrishnan gratefully climbed on the back seat, arrived at the village and walked into the bank at exactly ten o'clock! Replying to Ramakrishnan's subsequent query, Mother told him, "One call is enough if done with concentration. God will hear it."

In 1981, Ramakrishnan had an experience which taught him a good lesson of obedience to the spiritual Master. Out of fear that Ramakrishnan would become a monk if he were to live in the Ashram too long, his parents tried to get him transferred to a branch bank in his home town near them. Giving in to their constant pressure, he at last submitted an application for transfer without seeking Mother's advice or permission. After a few days, he changed his mind and sent a letter to the bank authorities requesting them to ignore his previous application.

One day Mother said to him, "Better inquire about the second letter you sent to the bank. It never reached the bank." Ramakrishnan replied, "That is not necessary, Mother. They must have received and accepted it." Mother insisted several times that he inquire about the second letter, but Ramakrishnan did not take Her words seriously.

Before long Ramakrishnan received his transfer orders from the authorities in Trivandrum, where the head office of the bank was located. He rushed to meet the officers in charge, but it was too late. As Mother had said, they had not received any letter asking them to ignore the previous application. It had somehow been lost. In this way Ramakrishnan learned the bitter lesson that even seemingly insignificant statements of one's Guru should not be ignored.

One day in the middle of a conversation, Mother turned to Ramakrishnan with a frown on Her face and said, "There are some who still look at girls, even after embracing a life of renunciation." Ramakrishnan asked, "Who is that, Mother?"

"You!" Mother replied. Ramakrishnan was shocked.

"What, me? I never look at women! Mother is scolding me for no fault of my own," he pleaded.

The next moment Mother uttered the name of a woman Ramakrishnan knew well and continued to narrate all the details of her husband's name, the names of her children and other family members. Ramakrishnan stood gaping, his mouth wide open. Hearing the exact description, whereabouts and other details of a woman the Holy Mother had no way of knowing, he stood dumbfounded. Mother again asked him, "Hey, Ramakrishnan, tell the truth! Don't you look at her every day?"

Ramakrishnan kept silent. It was true that he looked at that woman every day, but why? The woman's external appearance closely resembled the Holy Mother's. Seeing her, he felt as if he were seeing the Holy Mother Herself. When Mother saw him standing there speechless with his head hanging down, She burst into laughter. It goes without saying that after this, Ramakrishnan never again looked at that woman.

The above incident clearly shows how the Holy Mother closely observes the external actions and internal thoughts of Her spiritual children and instructs them accordingly.

Before the Ashram was officially registered as a charitable institution, only a few people were allowed to stay there. To look after the needs of many people was impossible since there were no adequate funds at that time. Some of the *brahmacharins*, who had left their jobs, looked to Ramakrishnan for food and clothing. As he was still employed, he would happily meet their needs even unasked.

In the beginning days of the Ashram, Ramakrishnan felt that Mother was two distinct beings, Her usual self and the Divine Being during the *Bhava Darshan*. This idea gave rise to a lot of confusion in his mind and he would often feel miserable while thinking in this way. He at last requested Mother to bless him and clear his erroneous way of thinking. One night he had a vision of the Holy Mother in Her usual mood, dressed in white clothes. This happened in the days before Mother was dressing in white. After this vision, Ramakrishnan believed that Mother was essentially the same person whatever Her mood.

Ramakrishnan's faith in Mother deepened and his mind gradually became fixed on Her divine form and name. This state created many troublesome situations at his work. Sometimes he made mistakes while counting out money or committed errors in the bank's accounts. In 1982, he came to live in the Ashram and, at the same time, somehow continued his office work as well. Later, in 1984, he resigned his job to live in the Ashram permanently.

Ramesh Rao (Swami Amritatmananda) was born in a wealthy *brahmana* family in Haripad, Kerala. He grew up as a modern youth enjoying and indulging in worldly pleasures, following a wayward and misguided way of life. Though immersed in mundane life, he would go to a nearby Devi temple to pray and repent for his loose ways. Before undertaking any act, good or bad, he would go and pray in the temple seeking the blessings of the Divine Mother.

Once a friend of Ramesh's invited him to the Holy Mother's Ashram but he declined the invitation. Later, when he was trying to go abroad for employment, he decided to visit the Ashram in order to know about his future, as he had heard that the Holy Mother was endowed with divine powers and could foresee one's future. Thus, in June, 1979 he entered the temple and approached the Holy Mother during *Krishna Bhava*. Before he could say anything, the Holy Mother accosted him saying, "Son, you are trying to go across the ocean. Mother will make it possible if you wish. Don't worry."

At the very first meeting Ramesh was convinced of the Holy Mother's divinity and felt bound to Her by a strong feeling of divine love. Returning home, he tried to concentrate his mind on the textile business which he had inherited from his father but he could not for his mind was filled only with thoughts of the Holy Mother. On some days, his yearning to see Her would be so intense that he would close the shop and rush to the Ashram. One day, while taking leave of the Holy Mother to return to his house, She told him, "Son, where are you going? You are meant to be here."

One night Ramesh had a dream of the final disso-

lution of the Universe. Balls of fire were raining down
everywhere. The ocean's waves rose up to the sky and
threatened to inundate the earth. Gathering all his
strength, Ramesh called out, "Amma!" Immediately a
radiant light rose up from the turbulent ocean and
expanded in all directions. From that effulgence emerged
the enchanting form of Goddess Durga, dressed in a
red silk sari and seated on a ferocious lion. She held
divine weapons in each of Her eight hands. Ramesh
was full of wonder to find that the compassionate face
of the Goddess was the face of the Holy Mother. She
consoled him saying, "Why fear when I am with you?
You are My son. Don't worry." After this Ramesh had
many visions of the Holy Mother in dreams.

By his close association with the Holy Mother,
Ramesh's inner urge intensified to realize God and to
live in the presence of Mother. One day while sitting
in Her presence, he had an experience which fanned
the flames of his aspiration. It was four p.m. and Ramesh
had come as usual to see Mother, who was sitting in
the shrine. He entered the temple and, after prostrating before the Holy Mother, he sat down near Her.
While he gazed at Her radiant face, the whole atmosphere in the temple suddenly changed. The world of
plurality vanished from his sight and only Mother was
visible. He realized Her to be his own Mother and found
himself to be a two year old child. Intoxicated with
divine love, Ramesh forgot the world. The Holy Mother
lovingly placed his head on Her lap. Knowing that Rao
had become immersed in inner bliss, Mother gently
lifted his head and had some devotees lay him on the
floor of the temple. At nine p.m., Mother returned to

the temple and found him still lying in that state. Only upon hearing Mother call "Son", did he return to normal consciousness.

Following this incident, Ramesh's life changed dramatically. His longing to see Mother increased. He hardly cared for worldly matters. He stopped going to the shop. His visits to the Holy Mother became frequent. He spent days and weeks at the Holy Mother's place. This sudden change in Ramesh created anxiety in his family. His parents and relations concentrated their efforts on bringing him back to worldly life and persuading him to get married. But all their attempts ended in failure. One day Mother told Ramesh, "Son, your parents are longing to see you. Go to your house and get their permission to be here." Ramesh said, "Mother, are you abandoning me? They will make trouble for me." Mother replied, "A courageous man is one who can overcome all such difficulties."

The Mother sent Rao home with another resident of the Ashram. The family members used force to keep Ramesh in their custody. They thought that the Holy Mother had influenced him by using some malevolent power. In order to persuade their son to return to worldly life, they performed special rituals. The parents insisted that Ramesh eat a special type of ghee which had been prepared by a priest using particular mantras to make him leave the Ashram and return to worldly life. Ramesh sought the Holy Mother's advice about the ghee. The Mother said, "Son, eat it. If there is anything evil in it, let it be. Because of your spiritual tendencies you have come to me. Nothing will happen to you, even if you eat the ghee."

Obeying Her words, Ramesh ate the ghee, but nothing happened. His thirst for spiritual life did not weaken. Now the family changed their tactics and became more harsh and inhuman. They concluded that their son's sudden change was caused by some mental abnormality arising from his disappointment at not getting a job overseas. With the assistance of his friends, who also disapproved of his new ways, they forcefully took him to a psychiatrist for treatment.

Ramesh told the doctor, "I am not crazy. I will strictly abide by the words of my Guru. It is you who are crazy for this world. Therefore, you try to impose your madness on others also." At the insistence of his relatives, the doctor treated Rao for ten days. Their aim was to shift their son toward desiring worldly life. Immediately after the psychiatric treatment, they decided to send him to Bhilai to stay with relatives, thinking that a change in environment would help him regain his old way of life. In addition, they tried to find a suitable bride for Ramesh.

In a mental predicament, Ramesh wrote to Mother, "Mother, up to this moment I have not given in to their trivial temptations. Now, if Mother doesn't save me, I will merge with Mother in heaven. I will commit suicide."

After a month's stay at Bhilai, Rao was brought back to his house. His family was convinced by this time that he had given up his spiritual way of thinking and living. They urged him to continue his textile business. One day, without anyone's knowledge, he visited the Holy Mother pleading, "Mother, if you abandon me, I will die." Without waiting for Her reply,

Ramesh resumed staying in the Ashram. During his short stay of three days, Mother warned him several times about his relatives' intentions to create obstacles in his path. She even advised him to go back to his house and wait till they gave their consent to take up spiritual life, but Rao paid no heed saying, "If I return home they won't let me continue my spiritual practices."

By this time, Rao's father had lodged a petition against the Holy Mother requesting police intervention to regain his son who, he asserted, was being forcibly kept in the custody of the Holy Mother. On the third day, Rao's father and some other relatives came to the Ashram with a van full of policemen. Rao boldly said to the police officer, "I am mature enough to choose my way of living and am free to decide on my place of residence." They paid no attention to his words and, with the help of the police, his relatives decided to admit him to a mental hospital in Trivandrum. On their way, all of them stopped in Quilon to have their lunch. Rao refused to eat and sat in the car. Suddenly he heard a voice from within saying, "If you escape now, you will be saved. Otherwise you will be destroyed."

The very next moment an autorickshaw stopped directly in front of him. Without a moment's hesitation, he jumped into it. He told the driver the destination and asked him to drive fast. There was not even a penny in his pocket. At that time, one of the Ashram residents was staying in Quilon, preparing for his Master's degree in philosophy. Rao told him what had happened. That night with the help of some devotees, Rao left Kerala, and headed for Chinmaya Mission in

Bombay. Discovering that he was in Bombay, the relatives again tried to arrest him. To save his life, Rao departed for the Himalayas. He had hardly any money with him for his train fare and food, nor any warm clothes to protect him from the freezing cold. Somehow he reached the Himalayas, where he wandered from village to village. His clothes were torn and tattered as the young man became a wandering mendicant, begging his food and meditating under a tree or in a cave. Days and months passed. Finally he received a letter from the Holy Mother at an address which he had given Her. She simply told him, 'Son, come back. No more problems.'

Rao returned to the Holy Mother's Ashram. She then sent him to visit his parents who had learned a good lesson. They seemed to have relented and were happy to see their son back home. Yet they still tried to tempt him. When they realized that their antagonistic approach was foolish, they attempted to change him in a loving manner. But all their efforts were consumed in the fire of Rao's intense dispassion. On the twenty-seventh of August, 1982, Rao joined the Ashram as a permanent resident and continued his spiritual practices undisturbed.

Subhir (Shakti Prasad) gives the following account of his renunciation of worldly life achieved by the grace of the Holy Mother in the face of tremendous opposition.

"It was at the end of 1983 when I met Amma, after being directed to Her by the late Swami Vimalananda of Sri Ramakrishna Math, Nettayam, Trivandrum, in Kerala. During the first year of my association with Amma, She gave me a number of chances to confirm Her power as a Satguru. She blessed me with many spiritual experiences which established in me a deep bond of love and surrender.

One day I mentioned to Her my wish to join Her Ashram as a resident in order to receive Her teachings. This meant resigning my position as Project Engineer in the Electronics Research and Development Center, Trivandrum. The Mother agreed, yet warned me of a strong reaction from my relatives who belonged to the Muslim community.

On the fourth of May, 1985, I joined the Ashram. Many obstacles followed, which were overcome solely by Amma's grace and directions. On the eleventh of May my father and his friends arrived at the Ashram demanding that I accompany them home, saying that my mother was seriously ill. I was obliged to leave the Ashram in their company. The father and others seriously believed that I was mentally disturbed and could be salvaged by psychiatric treatment. I had no choice but to accompany them to many specialists in that field who, unfortunately, could not grasp the charm and greatness of the exploration of the Inner Reality through the ancient tradition of Ashram life.

On the night of the sixteenth, I escaped from their custody and spent two weeks in an Ashram in Trivandrum, where the people have great devotion to Amma. My parents then came to meet Amma and assured Her that they would not disturb me again. I returned to Vallickavu, where Amma confided that She did not believe their words.

Father came to our Ashram again on the fifth of
June and wanted me to leave with him, saying my mother
had been hospitalized. I discussed the matter with Amma,
and She commented, "Their plan is to take you to a
remote place for psychiatric treatment." Since Father
was not willing to go home without me, I asked Amma
to permit me to go, just to avoid any trouble to the
Ashram. While I bowed down at Her feet before leaving, She whispered in my ear, "You will be safe, I am
with you."

At the main road the car was waiting for me with
six people inside. Soon, the route was changed to Bangalore, not Edappally as I had originally been told. We
spent that night in a tourist bungalow in Mettur. I was
well guarded so as not to escape as before. This time
I was able to collect a few records revealing their intention to subject me to brainwashing and electric shock
treatment. I hid this documentation carefully, keeping
it to use as evidence before the Kerala High Court.

We took a room in a hotel near Subbaiah Circle in
Bangalore, and, when I made no attempt to escape,
Father and two others left the hotel to make arrangements for admitting me. Finding no way to escape, I
meditated for a while and then sought the answer from
Amma. Immediately on my mind's screen flashed the
whole operation for escape.

I requested those guarding me allow me to go to the
verandah and make a phone call to an old friend. They
refused. Again I repeated my request and finally commanded them in a loud voice. Almost mechanically they
unlocked the room. Once outside, I sprang ahead of
them and pushed the door with all my force, bolting it

from the outside, locking them all inside. I rushed to the main road for some vehicle. An autorickshaw sped by with a passenger inside. After fifty yards it stopped abruptly. The driver was trying to restart it with the cranking lever. Thanking Ammachi, I ran in that direction and dashed into the auto. That same moment it started and drove off. I could see through the back window that my captors were running about, frantically searching for me. At Majestic Circle, a travel agent arranged a ticket for me to Calicut (about eight hours north of the Ashram) by a tourist bus service that same night. I gave him my name to book the ticket, which I felt afterwards to be unwise. Reaching Mother's Ashram the next day, I was astonished to realize that the money Amma had arranged for me to take when I left the Ashram was exactly sufficient for my return. Seeing me, Amma commented, "Very good, but why should you give your name to those bus people?!"

One morning Amma warned me to expect something to happen and suggested that I not be sentimental in any way, just for the peace of the Ashram. She told me that She was dedicated to the *sadhaks* (spiritual seekers resident in the Ashram) and would act for their benefit alone when facing any adverse situation.

At eleven that morning a big group led by my father entered the Ashram demanding that I accompany them. As I refused, they threatened me with force. Amma remained calm and told them, "We will give him protection if he wants; that is our Ashram *dharma*." The atmosphere became tense as the residents also entered the scene. As a few local devotees also started gathering, the group left, giving me two weeks notice.

At three in the afternoon, Amma ordered me to leave
the Ashram grounds immediately. Of course, I left at
once. Within minutes after my departure, my father
and his cohorts were back with some policemen from
Karunagappally, accusing the Ashram of unlawful custody.

I spent those days hiding in various institutions
and friends' houses. After checking with Amma for permission, I headed for Cochin Arya Samaj and had the
necessary ceremonies performed, so that I could embrace Hinduism according to the Vedic rites. The details were published in the Gazette, a government jour-
nal.

The Governor and Inspector General of Kerala took
some action on hearing of my case, and warned my
family. They assured me that I could stay in the Ashram,
so I returned.

After one month, during *Devi Bhava*, Mother gave
me *mantra diksha*, initiation into the sacred mantra.
This greatly accelerated my progress in *sadhana*.

One day Amma was leaving for a reception and *bhajan*
program at a temple in Vypin, accompanied by the residents. On the way we visited our Ashram branch in
Quilon and spent an hour there. It is our experience as
disciples that, as a Great Master, Amma first gives
hints for right action from within, then from without,
and gives orders only if we miss the hint. Eight months
had passed since the last trouble with my family, and
we never anticipated any further action from them. But
a strange feeling within prompted me to consider halt-
ing my journey here in Quilon. This idea became stronger
until I was anxious about making a decision. I looked

to Amma for Her command; "Yes, remain here," She nodded meaningfully and went on to Vypin, leaving me in Quilon.

Two hours later Sreenivasan, a brother disciple, came running into the Quilon Ashram, telling me to flee immediately. At Karunagappally, thirty kilometers north of Quilon, the Ashram van had been stopped by the police who had a search warrant for my arrest, based on a lunacy act issued by the Quilon Chief Judicial Magistrate Court. In vain they had searched the van for me. I spent the following days staying secretly here and there. Many other instances of timely help occurred by Divine Grace.

At this stage of complete uncertainty, I thought I would have to leave Kerala, as a search warrant was still pending, reissued by the Court at my father's persistent request. Also, I felt guilty for creating difficulties for Amma and the Ashram. That same day Amma sent a message to me not to worry, assuring me that a favorable solution would come soon.

Two days later, a news article appeared in the Malayalam daily, 'Matrubhumi', that my parents had filed a Habias Corpus petition in the Kerala High Court, naming Amma the respondent. They charged Her with illegal custody and stated the need for expert psychiatric treatment for their son's mental illness.

After receiving instructions from Amma, I immediately moved on to Cochin. Through Advocate Govinda Bharathan of the Kerala High Court, I filed an Affidavit, stating all the facts. On the twenty-seventh of August, 1987, I appeared before the Kerala High Court with police protection. After a detailed discussion, the panel

of judges dismissed the original petition filed by my
father and issued orders for my protection. The presiding justice also issued a warning to those persons who
had been involved with my harassment during the last
two years

I had accompanied Amma and the *brahmacharins*
to Bombay for Her programs there, when we received
word that an appeal was being filed in the Supreme
Court of India questioning the ruling of the Kerala High
Court. They strongly argued that my sanity could be
proved only after a twenty-eight day observation by
medical experts. This claim had already been dismissed
by the High Court's ruling after they had examined all
the documents which I had produced, particularly the
testimonials from my previous employer. They had also
questioned me thoroughly about the reasons for my
embracing Hinduism and accepting Amma as my Master for spiritual life.

Assuring me of Her protection, Amma instructed
me to go to New Delhi. By Her grace, the appeal was
dismissed in the first hearing and argument.[54] I was
relieved from any additional complications and risks.[55]

Amma penetrates deep into our being, preparing us
also to contain the Infinite within. Let us continue our
journey to the Goal, experiencing and overcoming all
natural hurdles, in the soothing care of Divine Love."

PART FOUR

The Embodiment
of Perfection:
Mother as the
Spiritual Master

Who is a perfect person? If this question is asked to a modern youth he would say that an ideal person is a handsome, highly influential multimillionaire or perhaps a high ranking political leader; otherwise he would say the names of some romantic looking movie stars or cricket players. It is a pity that today the youngsters cannot conceive of a society without movies, politics and romance. It is a vital force for them. But do these have anything to do with our life and character building? What makes a person beautiful and perfect? What adds sweetness and attractiveness to one's actions? What is that factor which makes one immortal and adorable? Is it any of the aforesaid things? A mature person endowed with discrimination will undoubtedly say, "No, absolutely not!" Then what is it? To put it in a sentence, it is the integration of inner virtues which in turn will manifest as eternal virtues through one's whole being. This is what one can experience in the presence of the Holy Mother Amritanandamayi, the beautiful blending of unconditional love and bliss.

People from different walks of life, each according to their own level of understanding and mental maturity speak differently about the Holy Mother. For example, if you ask who Mata Amritanandamayi is to a person whose intellect always dwells at a gross level, he would say, "She is an extraordinary woman who can cure terrible and incurable diseases by a mere touch or look." He may also say, "She can also solve your

worldly problems and can easily fulfill all your desires." If the same question is asked to one who has a
more subtle intellect he would say, "Oh, the Holy Mother
is really incredible. She can bestow on you many psy-
chic powers. She is a master in telepathy and clairvoy-
ance. It is nothing for Her to transform water into
panchamritam and milk. All the eight mystic powers
are under Her sway," and so on. A true spiritual seeker's
answer to the same question would be, "The Mother is
the Ultimate Goal to be realized by an aspirant. She is
the source and support of true seekers and helps them
to cross the ever-changing Ocean of Transmigration.
Her very nature is love and compassion; She is a veritable witness to the truths expressed in the *Vedas* and
all other religious texts of the world. If you take refuge
at Her feet, definitely the Goal is at hand. She is a
Perfect Master and a Great Mother as well."

From the standpoint of a person who is following
the Path of Devotion (*Bhakti Yoga*), the Holy Mother is
a true devotee par excellence. In Her one can see the
different aspects of Supreme Devotion manifesting un-
impeded. When one who pursues the Path of Knowledge (*Jnana Yoga*) observes the Mother, he can perceive a perfect Knower of the Self in Her words and
deeds. For a person who is sincerely following the Path
of Action (*Karma Yoga*), the Holy Mother is unsur-
passed among *Karma Yogins*. These are all partial views
born of each one's limited experience and understanding. But through close association and observation devoid
of prejudice and presumption, one could clearly comprehend that the Holy Mother is an integration of all
these.

There is a proverb in Malayalam, 'As patient as the Earth.' The Mother Earth bears everything. People kick Her, spit on Her, till Her with a plow, dig into Her, and cut open Her breast using a pick ax for cultivation and other purposes. They even construct hundred story buildings on Her but She patiently bears everything. She has no complaints. She despises none but serves and nourishes all in the best way. Likewise, the Holy Mother shows an immense amount of patience in rebuilding the character of Her children. She patiently waits until the disciples become mature enough to be disciplined. Until then, She bathes them in Her selfless love forgiving all the errors which they may commit.

If one closely goes through the great lineage of the ancient saints and sages of India and observes the ways which they adopted to teach and enlighten their disciples, it is not difficult to understand the unique nature of the Guru-disciple relationship which cannot be seen anywhere else in the world. The Holy Mother would say, "In the beginning a *Satguru* (Perfect Master) won't give strict instructions to his disciple. He will simply love him. He will bind the disciple with his unconditional love. The strong impact created by the Guru's love will make the disciple fit for the Guru to work on his *vasanas* or mental tendencies. Slowly the Guru, with strict yet loving instructions, will discipline and remold the disciple's personality. In a real Guru-disciple relationship, it will be difficult to distinguish who is the Guru and who is the disciple because the Guru will be humbler than the disciple and the disciple will be humbler than the Guru." In the beginning the Guru, in addition to showing great love for the disciple, may even act according to the disciple's whims and fancies to some extent, but when he finds that the disciple is mature enough to earnestly start spiritual practice then the Guru will slowly start disciplining him. Once the disciplining starts however, though full of love for his disciple who is verily like a son or daughter to him or her, he will not express his love much. His sole aim will be to make the disciple aware of his own Pure Self. In other words, his disciplining itself is another way of expressing his love. That is real love, transforming the disciple into a pure jewel.

Pointing out and correcting the drawbacks of Her children the Holy Mother would say, "I am like a gardener. The garden is full of colorful flowers. I was not asked to look after the beautiful flowers which are in no way defective but I have been asked to remove the insects and worms from the pest-ridden flowers and plants. To remove the insects I may have to pinch the petals and leaves which is painful, but it is only to save the plants and flowers from destruction. In the same way, Mother will always work with the children's weaknesses. The process of elimination is painful but it is for your good. The virtuous aspects need no attention, but if your weaknesses are not removed, they will destroy your virtues as well. My children, you may think that Mother is angry with you. Not at all. Mother loves you more than anyone else and that is why She does all these things. Mother expects nothing except your spiritual progress."

One could never see the Holy Mother sitting on a royal seat commanding Her spiritual children and devotees to do this and that. She instructs and at the same time sets an example by Her actions. Humility and simplicity are the trademarks of greatness. The Holy Mother is a living example of this. She is humbler than the humblest and simpler than the simplest. She says about Herself, "I am the servant of servants. This life is for others. Her children's happiness is Mother's wealth and health."

The Holy Mother's method of exhausting the ego and other negative tendencies of Her children is wonderful. She is always the invincible warrior. The Mother Herself prepares the field to test Her children's mental maturity and spiritual progress by creating a suitable situation. Without causing the least suspicion She leads one to the field. By the time one realizes the seriousness of the situation, all the inner foes rise up and the discriminating intellect gives way to the emotional mind. At this moment the Holy Mother properly uses the opportunity to remove the egoism of Her children. Her mighty weapons hit the target without fail and in due course the negative tendencies of those who seek Her guidance become weaker and weaker. The following is one such incident.

Once, some years ago Brahmachari Nealu brought a portable typewriter from Tiruvannamalai where he had previously resided. Although Balu had not learned typing, he took a piece of paper and just for the fun of it typed, 'Mother, make me your slave.' Mother, who was sitting nearby talking to Nealu suddenly turned toward Balu and asked, "Son, what are you typing?" Balu thereupon translated the meaning of the sentence into Malayalam for Her. Without asking or saying anything more about it, Mother continued to talk to Nealu.

After fifteen minutes Mother said to Nealu, "I am going to send Balu abroad." It was a shock for Balu to hear those words from Mother's mouth as he had already quit two jobs with the intention of staying in Mother's presence forever. "What did you say, Mother?" he anxiously asked.

"Yes, we need money to run the Ashram. The number of residents is increasing and we have no income to support them all. So, you must go and work," Mother replied.

This was enough for Balu. His inner foes raised their hoods and with vehemence he said, "No, I don't want to work. I cannot go away from here. I came here to stay with Mother and not to do worldly work or earn money." However, Mother went on insisting that he must go until his anger knew no bounds. His negative tendencies stood ready to attack.

Suddenly in a soft voice Mother said, "Son, what did you type just a few minutes ago? If you want to become God's servant, you have to surrender all that is yours at His Feet. If the mind is not pure, God won't dwell in your heart. To become God's servant is to accept all experiences, good and bad, auspicious and inauspicious, with an equipoised mind. See everything as God's Will. Son, I don't want your wealth. When I see you crying for God I am so happy and my heart overflows toward you." As soon as She uttered the last word She became absorbed into a divine mood. Tear drops rolled down Her cheeks and Her body became still. This continued for an hour after which She slowly came down to this plane of worldly existence.

Balu's mind was full of remorse. He fell at Her feet and begged Her to forgive him. He prayed, "Mother, please purify my heart. Rid me of all impure thoughts and actions. Make me a perfect instrument in your hands." She consoled him and said, "Son, don't worry. You have come to Mother and now it is Her responsibility to look after you and make you perfect." Hearing these words, Balu felt full of peace and joy.

The Holy Mother once said, "Children, you are happy if Mother always shows a smiling face. If Mother says something against your wish, then you will think that Mother has no love for you, but it is not so. Mother is always trying to make you stronger. To reinforce you spiritually all mental weaknesses should be removed. To achieve that end sometimes She will make an external show of anger. Sometimes this is necessary in order to teach you. Take for example a cow that is merrily eating up the tender leaves of a young coconut tree. It is not enough if one says, 'Dear cow, please don't eat the tender leaves. The plant will wither away.' The cow definitely won't move an inch. But if you take a long stick and shout at it, 'Go away, go away!' the cow will immediately end its mischief. The same is true with Mother's show of anger. Children, Mother has not even an iota of anger toward you. Always remember that Mother has no selfish motives and acts only for your spiritual progress. If Mother always shows Her love and affection to you then you won't look inwards to seek your Real Self. Children, as far as a worldly person is concerned, it is enough for him to look after his wife and children, but a real *sannyasin* on the other hand, has to shoulder the burden of the whole world. Therefore you must grow stronger."

On one occasion after the usual *Darshan*, Mother could go for rest only at about four a.m. After She had entered Her hut and lay down, closing the door, one Ashramite slept in front of Her room as usual in order to ensure that nobody would disturb Her by going into the room. Exactly at that time a young woman who had missed the bus and had walked all the way from Quilon, a distance of thirty-five kilometers, reached the Ashram seeking Mother's blessings. When she learned that Mother had gone to bed she was crestfallen but still with a glimmer of hope she called Mother aloud a couple of times. Hearing the lady's voice, the Ashramite who was lying down in front of Mother's door got up and scolded the lady for disturbing Mother and even asked her to leave the place. At that very moment, Mother, who could understand what was happening, opened the door and came out to meet the devotee. After affectionate inquiries, Mother consoled her and assured her of solving the problems which she was facing.

Turning to the person who had slept in front of Her door, Mother spoke in a serious tone, "I am not here for enjoying any rest or comfort but rather to serve others and alleviate their sufferings. Their happiness is my happiness. I do not want anyone's service. I am here to serve all. I must be free to meet anybody at any time. I won't permit anyone to prevent me from meeting the devotees who come seeking solace and succor from me. Do you know with what great difficulty they come here with their meager savings just to unburden their aching hearts to me? If you repeat this rudeness and try to impose rules on me that I should meet devotees only at such and such times I will dissolve this organization. I do not want any such thing as a mission if it is not to serve ailing humanity. A mission should be for service." Saying this, She prohibited the Ashramite and all of the other residents from sleeping in front of Her hut.

On another occasion a sick lady who had come to the Ashram for Mother's advice had vomited on Mother's cloth. A resident, one of the girls who was personally attending Mother, picked up the dirtied cloth with a stick and was about to hand it over to the washerman. Seeing this, Mother scolded the girl and said, "If you are unable to see the one Divine in all and serve all equally, then what is the use of having done so many years of meditation and service? Is there any difference between me and this sick lady?" Saying these words, Mother took the cloth Herself and washed it, prohibiting the girl from attending Her for some days afterwards.

The Holy Mother's mere presence itself is inspiring to the devotees. She can inspire and give them the strength to do anything and everything at any time. For example, if there is some work in the Ashram such as carrying bricks, sand and other materials for construction purposes or even emptying the septic tank, cleaning the Ashram premises or assisting the masons in concrete work, etc., the residents would run here and there trying to gather some devotees to help. Sometimes it might be three or four in the morning when the *Bhava Darshan* had finished and all the devotees would be ready to go to sleep. Suddenly the Holy Mother would come to where the work was going to proceed. She would always be the first to start the work. Despite the fact that She had been sitting from six o'clock the previous evening until three or four the next morning, She would be seen working full of cheer and enthusiasm. Very soon word would spread that Mother is carrying bricks, water or whatever it may be and from all directions the devotees would come running. The most interesting part of it is that the work which normally would have taken six or seven hours to finish would be completed within one or two hours.

In order to make the devotees forget the strain of the work, the Holy Mother will make the devotees laugh with Her great sense of humor and will even make a small fire near the work spot and make drinks and roast peanuts for all those who are working and Herself distribute them to Her devotees. In the midst of the work the Holy Mother will instruct everyone saying, "Children, while engaged in any kind of work always try to chant your mantra or sing devotional songs. Only those actions which are surrendered to the Lord are counted as real action and then action (*karma*) becomes Yoga. Otherwise it is *Karma Bhoga* (action motivated by the urge to enjoy)."

"Even when the *Gopis* of Vrindavan went out to sell milk, buttermilk, etc., they would call out 'Krishna, Madhava, Yadava, Kesava...' Even in the kitchen they would write and affix Krishna's different names on all the spice bottles and other provisions. They also discharged the duties of a housewife. They never sat idle but always carried Krishna's form in their heart and His Divine Names on their lips. Children, try to be like them."

Whatever questions are asked and whoever is the

questioner, whether a theist, an atheist, a rationalist or
an antagonist, the Holy Mother gently, calmly, and affectionately answers them without hurting them or
belittling their ideas. For example, one day a young
man who visited the Ashram told the Holy Mother, "I
have no faith at all in spiritual philosophy and spiritual masters. Is it not better to serve humanity? Many
people are suffering from poverty and starvation. What
are these so-called spiritualists doing for them? Are
they not simply wasting their time sitting idle?"

The Holy Mother calmly replied, "Son, what you
say is correct. Of course, service to humanity is important. A true spiritual seeker's life must be dedicated to
that. Mother perfectly agrees with that point of yours.
But what is real service? Real service is extending
help without expecting anything. Who is doing that? If
somebody has an idea to help a poor family undoubtedly there will be a selfish motive behind it. Everyone
is after name and fame. Mother knows that spiritual
advice won't satisfy the hunger of a person who is plunged
in poverty. We must have compassion and love for such
people. Real compassion and love will come only by
practicing spirituality. We must have a high ideal in
our life. We must be ready to sacrifice everything to
uphold that ideal. This is genuine spirituality. Simply
providing food will not solve anyone's problems either.
Again one will be in want of food. So the best way is
to help others both externally and internally, i.e. feed
them and at the same time make them aware of the
necessity to develop internally as well. This is possible only through spiritual education. This kind of
service will help one to lead a happy and balanced life

in any circumstance even if one is starving. In reality spirituality is that which teaches us how to lead a perfect life in the world. Son, everything depends on the mind. If the mind is calm and tranquil even the lowest hell will become an abode of happiness but if the mind is agitated even the highest of heavens will become a place of tremendous suffering. That is what one gets from spirituality and spiritual masters, peace and tranquillity without which one cannot live."

Even the most notorious fellow, who in the eyes of his own parents and close relatives is cruel and who has been hated by them, is a darling son to the Holy Mother. Even such a person would say, "Mother loves me the most. I love Her more than my own mother who gave birth to me. I am Her child." This is the impression created by the Holy Mother in the hearts of Her devotees. Even about a rogue the Holy Mother would say, "What a good son he is. He is very innocent." Overlooking their bad qualities, She will speak highly of their goodness which in reality may be only infinitesimal.

Through our direct experience we can realize that the Holy Mother is a fountain of inexhaustible spiritual energy and dynamic creativity. Though the Holy Mother keenly attends to both the spiritual and material needs of Her devotees, She still remains detached and as pure as ever.

To express devotion and gratefulness, a devotee may remark, "O Mother, you are so compassionate to me. Because of your grace I am having good meditation and my mind is perfectly peaceful." Someone else will say, "O Mother, because of your blessings, all my family problems are now solved and many of my life-long wishes have been fulfilled." Hearing these words of the devotees, the Holy Mother sometimes will laugh loudly and reply, "Namah Shivaya! Who is Mother to bless anyone? She is just a crazy girl who is wandering around because there is nobody to put Her in a lunatic asylum. I am not doing anything. God does everything without doing anything."

There are many differences among the people who come to visit the Holy Mother. Some will ask questions about *Kundalini Yoga*, techniques to awaken the serpent power, while others are curious to know about *Nirvikalpa Samadhi*, the state of abiding in the Supreme Self. The next person may complain about bad health. Some parents will come crying saying that their only son is totally misled and doing all kinds of wicked actions and will ask Mother to save him. Some young people will complain that although they had finished their studies long ago, they couldn't find a job. They will say, "Please Mother, bless me to get a job." Husbands will come saying that their wife is not sincere. Wives will say that their husband is not loving them. There are some people who pray to Mother to punish their neighbor or who will tell Her that their cow is not giving enough milk or the coconut trees in their yard are not bearing an abundance of coconuts. Some seek Her blessings to pass their examinations while others will come with an incurable disease. Some parents are distraught because their son is showing a tendency to take up to a life of renunciation. There are a few who will become serious spiritual practitioners after meeting the Holy Mother and come to seek Her direct guid-

ance in order to proceed with their *sadhana*. In this
way one can see the whole world coming to seek Her
blessings. The Holy Mother discards none. Each one of
them will be treated equally, given the same amount of
love and affection and will be instructed in accordance
with their mental maturity and need. She not only listens to their problems but bestows fulfillment of all
desires.

Every morning around nine o'clock, the Holy Mother
comes to meet the devotees who come in large numbers to have Her darshan. Calling each one near Her,
She will keenly listen to their problems. The Holy Mother
would say, "Children, I need nothing from you except
your burden of sorrows. Mother is here to shoulder it."
She will sit there until everyone is received and consoled. Almost every day She finishes the darshan only
by two or three o'clock in the afternoon. Returning to
the room, the Mother will go through all the mail or
give instructions to the residents. She will be engaged
in giving necessary advice about the management of
the Ashram administration. Even while eating She will
be instructing someone or reading somebody's letter.
Oftentimes She will call a family or a person who came
too late for darshan. If it is a *Bhava Darshan* day then
She will again come at around five o'clock in the evening
to lead devotional singing. After the singing, the *Bhava
Darshan* will begin which might last until three or four
the next morning. Until then, the Holy Mother will be
seated in the temple receiving the devotees one by one
and listening to their problems, whether spiritual or
worldly. She not only listens to them but also solves
their problems by mere touch, look, or through a pure

sankalpa (resolve). The Holy Mother Amritanandamayi is a unique phenomenon even in this sacred land of India. Assuming the *Bhava* of *Adi Parashakti* (Divine Mother), the Primal Supreme Energy, She ceaselessly serves the Lord's Creation with Her every breath. In the spiritual history of India, She stands unparalleled in Her limitless manifestation of Grace and Compassion for erring humanity. May Her divine life serve as a guiding star for all those who aspire to realize Supreme Peace and the Bliss of Self-Realization.

FOOTNOTES

[1]Henceforth referred to as Kasturi, the colloquial form of her given name.

[2]Henceforth referred to as Subhagan.

[3]The lotus posture of hatha yoga.

[4]The *mudra* symbolizes the oneness of the individual self with the Supreme.

[5]The metaphorical representation of the cycle of birth, death and rebirth.

[6]In the general proximity of where the old *Bhava Darshan* Temple now stands.

[7]A name of Krishna.

[8]A superstitious belief of this area.

[9]The place where Sri Krishna spent His childhood, where even today countless numbers of His devotees stay.

[10]An advanced state of meditation when one's consciousness is completely uni fied with the Supreme Consciousness.

[11]A sacred red marking worn by Hindus.

[12]The cowherd boys of Vrindavan.

[13]Equivalent of a penny.

[14]A coastal city 35 kilometers south of Parayakadavu.

[15]It is said that the chataka bird will drink only raindrops that fall during the rains. It does not relish any other water. The idea is that both the peacock and the chataka feel happy at the sight of clouds but become miserable in the absence of rain. Likewise, waiting for God alone to make one happy seems to be in vain after a prolonged fruitless search and spiritual practice.

[16]A meal offered to God or the deity in a temple before being given to the devotees to eat.

[17]Every month the household of a man named Sri Narayanan from the next village would conduct the reading of this great epic which highlights the life and sportings of Lord Krishna.

[18]This little shrine is located near the gravel road on the way to the oceanside from the Ashram.

[19]In India, marriages are traditionally arranged by the parents after an astrologer consults the son's or daughter's horoscope.

[20]*Tulasi* is a variety of basil which is considered to be holy and sacred to Sri Krishna.

[21]Cape Comorin is the southern tip of India, two hundred kilometers to the south of Parayakadavu.

[22]After *Krishna Bhava* began, Sudhamani never had Her monthly period.

[23]Oh Lord! Oh Lord!

[24]This refers to the eternal spiritual truths stated in the Vedic Scriptures.

[25]A pure resolve.

[26]A town in Kerala well known for its fish markets.

[27]Devotional scriptures like *Narada Bhakti Sutras*.

[28]The Primal Supreme Energy, the Creatrix, the feminine counterpart of the masculine 'Shiva' or Pure Consciousness.

[29]Severe austerities.

[30]The bald eagle is called '*Garuda*' in India. *Garuda* is the vehicle of Lord Vishnu of whom Sri Krishna is an incarnation.

[31]Circumambulating a holy object while keeping it to one's right.

[32]The miscreants were still in operation and would stand along the roadside where the devotees would pass and make cutting remarks. Not only the villagers but also Sudhamani's own father and brother would indulge in this. They would even try to discourage the devotees from remaining until the end of the *Darshan*.

[33]A divine gesture associated with the Divine Mother.

[34]The waving of burning camphor before the Deity as a form of worship.

[35]Kali Mata.

[36]Referring to Her experience of the Divine Mother.

[37]A description of Kali Mata.

[38]A stringed instrument always seen held in the lap of Saraswati, the Goddess of Knowledge.

[39]It should be remembered that as far as Her family was concerned, the Holy Mother was possessed three nights a week by Krishna and Devi, and the rest of the time She was a crazy girl.

[40]Since She was young She had accepted only God as Her real Mother and Father and thus everybody else was Her stepmother and stepfather.

[41]The feminine aspect of the Cosmic Energy personified in the form of Devi.

[42]A spiritual aspirant who observes the vow of celibacy.

[43]Vallickavu is the village on the mainland just opposite Idamannel. The Holy Mother is sometimes called the 'Vallickavu Amma'.

[44]Grains of rice beaten into flakes resembling rolled oats.

[45]An ardent devotee of Lord Krishna whose story appears in the *Srimad Bhagavatam.*

[46]Consecrated offerings blessed by God.

[47]The waving of burning camphor before the Holy Mother seated in the temple as Devi.

[48]Sacred mantra consisting of the thousand Names of the Divine Mother.

[49]Situated 20 kilometers north of Vallickavu.

[50]Now known as Swamis Purnamritananda Puri, Amritatmananda Puri, Pranavamritananda Puri, Amritamayananda Puri, Ramakrishnananda Puri and Amritasvarupananda Puri after receiving traditional initiation into sannyasa from the Holy Mother.

[51]A dark brown seed which is known for its beneficial effects, both physical and spiritual.

[52]Now known as Swami Premananda.

[53]A detailed description can be found in Nealu's book, "On the Road to Freedom" by Neal Rosner, M.A. Center, U.S.A.

[54]This is a Supreme Court landmark ruling in India which rules in favor of the individual's right to freely choose his religion.

[55]"We do not see any grounds for releasing a notice to Mata Amritanandamayi, nor do we find anything defective in the judgment of the Kerala High Court in concluding the state of normalcy of the petitioner's son and offering him the right to pursue spiritual life in Her Ashram." (13th March, 1987)

GLOSSARY

AARATHI: Waving burning camphor before a deity, representing the offering of one's individuality to God

ADI PARASHAKTI: Primal Supreme Energy

AHIMSA: Non-violence in thought, speech and action

ALAPPAD PANCHAYAT: A group of villages

AMMA: Mother

AMSA AVATARA: Partial incarnation of God

ANANTASAYANA: Lord Vishnu reclining on the serpent Ananta (the infinite Time), representing the State of Transcendence of Time and Space

ATMAN: Self

AVATAR(A): Incarnation of God

AVESA AVATARA: God temporarily manifesting through someone

AYURVEDIC: Science of longevity founded by ancient Indian sages

BHAGAVAD GITA: The teachings of Lord Krishna to Arjuna at the beginning of the Mahabharata War. It is a practical guide for common man for every day life and is the essence of Vedic wisdom. *Bhagavad* means 'that of the Lord' and *Gita* means 'Song', particularly, an advice.

BHAGAVAT BHAVA: Divine Mood

BHAGAVATAM: The book about the Incarnations of Lord Vishnu, especially Krishna and His childhood antics. It upholds the supremacy of devotion.

BHAJAN(S): Devotional singing

BHAKTI SHASTRAS: Scriptures whose main stress is on the path of devotion to God

BHAKTI YOGA: Union with God through devotion

BHAVA: Mood, feeling, attitude

BHAVA DARSHAN: The occasion when Amma receives devotees in the exalted state of the Universal Mother.

BILVA TREE: Tree sacred to Lord Siva, the leaves of which are used in His worship

BRAHMACHARI(N): A celibate student under training of a Guru

BRAHMANA: Priestly caste

CHINMUDRA: Mystic sign of the hand indicating oneness with God

DARSHAN: Audience or vision of a holy person or deity

DEEPARADHANA: Waving lit oil lamps before a deity

DEVI BHAVA: Divine Mood or identity with the Goddess

DHARMA: Righteousness, in accordance with Divine Harmony

DHOTI: Cloth wrapped around the lower half of the body

GARUDA: Eagle, the mount of Lord Vishnu

GHEE: Clarified butter with the water content boiled out

GITA: Song, usually referring to Bhagavad Gita

GODDESS PARVATI: Divine Mother, Consort of Lord Shiva

GOPA(S): Cowherd boys, companions of Lord Krishna

GOPI(S): Cowherd girls, companions of Lord Krishna

GURU: Spiritual Master/Guide

HANUMAN: Incarnation of Lord Shiva in the form of a monkey, devoted to Lord Sri Rama

IDAMANNEL: Name of Mother's family house

ISVARA: The Lord

JAPA: Repetition of a mantra, prayer or God's Name

KALI: Goddess of destruction

KANJI: Thick rice soup

KARMA BHOGA: Enjoying the fruits of one's actions

KARMA YOGA: Union with God through desireless action

KARMA YOGIN: One who follows the path of Karma Yoga

KATHAKALI: Classical dance style of Kerala, India

KRISHNA: Priciple Incarnation of Lord Vishnu

KRISHNA BHAVA: Divine Mood of Krishna

KRISHNA LEELA: Lord Krishna's sporting amusements (lit. play)

KSHATRIYA: Warrior caste

KUCHELA: Poor childhood friend of Lord Krishna

KUNDALINI YOGA: Union with God through the raising of the life force to the top of the head through visualization of different centers in the spine

KUNJU: Child

MAHATMA: Great Soul

MALAYALAM: Mother's native language, language of Kerala

MANTRA: Sacred formula, the repetition of which can awaken one's spiritual energies and bring the desired results.

MANTRA DIKSHA: Initiation by a Guru into the repetition of a mantra

MANTRA JAPA: Repetition of a mantra

MAYA: Power of Universal Illusion that makes the world of manifestation seem to be real and the unmanifest Reality seem to be non-existent

MUDRA: A sign by hand indicating mystic spiritual truths.

NAIVEDYAM: Offering of food to a deity

NAMAH SHIVAYA: The Panchakshara Mantra (mantra consisting of five letters) meaning "Salutations to the Auspicious One (Shiva)

NIRVIKALPA SAMADHI: Absorption into the Formless Reality

OM: Mystic syllable representing the Supreme Reality

PADA PUJA: Worship of the Guru's feet

PADMASANA: Sitting lotus posture

PAISE: Indian currency, 100 paise to 1 rupee

PANCHAMRITAM: Food offering made to the deity consisting of honey, bananas, sugar and ghee

PARA BHAKTI: Supreme devotion

PARASARA: Ancient sage of Vedic times in India, father of Vyasa, codifier of the Vedas

PARASHAKTI: Supreme Energy

PARAYAKADAVU: Mother's village

PEETHAM: Seat or stool for sitting

PRADAKSHINA: Circumambulation

PRASADAM: Consecrated offering

PUJA(S): Ritual worship

PURNA AVATARA: Complete or full Incarnation of God

PURUSHA: A Being

RAJASIC: One of the three qualities of Primordial Nature, the quality of activity

RAMA: An Incarnation of Lord Vishnu, hero of the Ramayana

RAMAYANA: Ancient epic tale of Sri Rama's life

RUDRAKSHA: A holy bead sacred to Lord Siva

RUKMINI: Lord Krishna's wife, an Incarnation of Goddess Lakshmi

RUPEES: Indian currency

SACRED ASH: Ash blessed by a deity or saint, which can be used to alleviate physical and mental suffering

SADHAK: Spiritual aspirant

SADHANA: Spiritual practice

SAIPPUS: Malayalam word for "foreigners"

SAMADHI: State of absorption into God, the Self

SAMSKARA: Mental tendencies accumulated from past actions

SANKALPA: Creative, integral resolve manifesting as thought, feeling and action. The sankalpa of an ordinary person does not always bear corresponding fruit. The sankalpa of a sage, however, always bears the intended result.

SANNYAS: Stage of complete renunciation

SANNYASIN: A renunciate monk

SANSKRIT: Ancient language of India

SATGURU: Realized Spiritual Master

SATTVIC: One of the qualities of Primordial Nature, the quality of light, clarity and peace

S(H)IVA: God of destruction, Auspicious One, Consort of Goddess Parvati

SIDDHA VIDYA: Knowledge of the Perfect Ones, a system of spiritual science belonging to southern India

SITA: Consort of Sri Rama, heroine of the Ramayana

SRI LALITA SAHASRANAMA(M): Thousand Names of the Divine Mother

SRI VEDA VYASA: An Incarnation of Lord Vishnu, codifier of the Vedas, author of the Mahabharata, Puranas, and Brahma Sutras

SUBRAMANYA: Youngest son of Lord Siva, Commander-in-chief of the army of the gods

SUNDARAKANDA: Portion of the Ramayana about Hanuman

TAMASIC: One of the qualities of Primordial Nature, the quality of darkness, inertness, sleep

TAPAS: Literally "heat". The practice of spiritual austerities

TULASI: Basil plant, dear to Lord Vishnu

UPANISHADS: Concluding portion of the Vedas, containing the teachings of Self-Knowledge

UPASANA MURTHI: The form of a deity that one meditates on

VALLICKAVU: Village across the backwater canal from Mother's village

VASANAS: Latent tendencies of the mind, resulting from prior actions

VEDANTA VIDYALAYA: School for learning the Vedanta philosophy

VEDANTIC : Pertaining to Vedanta philosopy, the system of thought that proposes an underlying Unity to the diversity of creation

VEDANTIN: A believer or practitioner of Vedanta

VEDAS: The ancient revealed scriptures of the Hindus

VEDIC: Pertaining to the Vedas

VEENA: Ancient stringed instrument of India

VISHNU: Manifestation of the Supreme Being, Lord of Preservation

VRINDAVAN: Place where Lord Krishna grew up

YOGA: Science of Union with God

YOGI: One who follows the path of Yoga

YOGIC: Pertaining to Yoga

INDEX

tue   73–74, 101–102
punishes Sudha-
   mani   32, 34, 50–52
Dattan the leper   228–230
Devi Bhava. *See also* **Bhava**
   Darshan
advent of   143–144, 144
changes in Mother follow-
   ing   144–145
triggered by distraught devotee   143–144
devotion   109
shallow vs. true   51

E

experiences of devotees
Bhargavi Amma
   Krishna appears to   217–218
Bindu
   Mother appears to   219–221
Chandramati
   dead grandson revived   235–
   236
Dattan the leper   228–230
Dr. Gangadharan
   cured of neck pain   251–252
   sister cured of cancer   252–
   253
Dr. Srivastava   216
Francis Daniel
   false documents burned   228
   falsely accused of
   crimes   227
Kunjamma
   son's death transferred to
   dog   234–235
Kunju Raman
   nosebleeds cured   263
   shown place to medi-
   tate   261–262

Kuttappan Nair
   keeps vow of silence   231–
   232
Mother gives child through
   sankalpa   236–237
   Shakti Prasad I   237–240
   Shakti Prasad II   240–242
   Shakti Prasad III   243–244
   Shakti Prasad IV   244–246
Mr. Gopakumar
   cured of insomnia   253–
   254
   family reunited   255–256
Mr. Nair
   dances during Krishna
   Bhava   257
   told of father's death   260
Mr. Narayan Nambiar
   dreams of Mother twenty
   years earlier   266
   holds vibrating trident   268
Mrs. Kunjukutty Amma
   given vision of
   Mookambika   260–261
Neelambaran
   girl gives money to   226–
   227
Puvampuzha Swami
   Mother quotes Gita
   for   258–259
Radha Bai
   sent to Mother in
   dream   259–260
Ramamurti
   lost daughter returns   223–
   225
Ramankutty
   deaf & dumb daughter
   healed   221–222

OTHER BOOKS ABOUT AMMACHI

For My Children
(Mother's selected teachings)

Awaken Children, Volumes 1-7
(Mother's inspiring conversations with spiritual seekers)

Immortal Light
(Advice to Householders)

On the Road to Freedom
(A Westerner's twenty-five year spiritual journey in India)

Puja
(Instructions on how to perform ritualistic worship)

Available at your local bookstore or
can be ordered from:

M.A. CENTER
P.O. BOX 613
SAN RAMON, CA 94583
TEL: 510-537-9417

Ammachi's audio and video tapes also available from
M.A. Center.